Silenced Lives

The Sex Offender's Legacy

*"Thank you
from the bottom of my heart
to all of you whose kindness and
encouragement made the
writing and publishing
of this memoir possible."*

– Janet Mackie

A book like *Silenced Lives,...*

by veteran social worker Janet Mackie, is long overdue. Until now, the public has never had concrete proof that the silent-shame cycle of sexual abuse is responsible for churning out victims, offenders, and enablers generation after generation. Now there can be no doubt.

Many "experts" on sexual abuse deny that abuse causes abuse. Perhaps they want to reassure survivors that we are not in danger of becoming "monsters." And they are right that most survivors do not go on to abuse. Still, a disproportionate number of sex offenders were sexually abused as children. Mackie doesn't let this seeming paradox distract her from writing about the actual dynamics and facts of inherited abuse.

In *Silenced Lives*, Mackie puts a human face on sex offenders, survivors, and enablers by inviting us into her family's legacy of "hand-me-down" pain. Mackie was intimately violated by people who were violated by people who were violated by ... and so on. Mackie proves that one generation's abuse caused the next generation's abuse when she depicts idiosyncratic similarities of the abuse rituals that were handed down from one perpetrator to the next.

Silenced Lives shows sex offenders hiding away in shame—the very shame they act out during their crimes. If they dared seek help, no one would help them anyway since conventional wisdom is, "Once a sex offender, always a sex offender." They are considered monsters beyond redemption. Meanwhile, the survivors in *Silenced Lives* get the message that if they were abused, something must be wrong with them. They are told "We don't talk about such things." So, they don't get the help they need either. Those who suspect or know of abuse don't want to get tainted by the shame associated with it, so they remain silent. And the secret abuse continues.

Like Mackie, I was sexually abused as a child. Unlike Mackie, however, I chose to act out the secret shame by perpetrating a sex crime of my own. I don't blame what I did on what happened to me. I made a choice. However, if I had been able to read *Silenced Lives* before I let my life get totally out of control, I would have understood the cause of my rape fantasies. Both I, and the person I harmed, might have escaped the cycle.

Better late than never. That's not what you'll be saying about the ending of "*Silenced Lives*," though. Painful as the family legacy is, Mackie writes so well you'll want to keep reading even after "the end." And that's as it should be, because, as *Silenced Lives* makes clear, we are a long way from "the end" of the cycle of abuse.

– Paul Hanley,
author of *Roller Coaster to Hell and Back: A True Story of Sexual Abuse and New Hope.*

In the age of "#MeToo"...

Janet Mackie's Memoir, *Silenced Lives* - recounting generations of inter-family abuse - brought to mind the strictures I was raised with, even in a non-abusive family. They are "Don't talk; don't tell." and its corollary "What happens in the family stays in the family." Not only does it stay in the family, it isn't even mentioned or acknowledged. That pervasive culture of silence has been overwhelmingly effective for centuries, and tragically, it continues today: the story of *Silenced Lives* is a compelling illustration. It takes great courage to share a story like this with the world; I hope and believe such courage will be rewarded by bringing others out of that silence, and putting a focus on what can be done to prevent other lives from being likewise silenced.

– Terry Stein, M.S. Ed.

Silenced Lives, The Sex Offender's Legacy...

is a beautifully written, raw personal account of the transgenerational effects of sexual abuse. As a treatment professional of sex offenders as well as victims, I highly recommend this glimpse into the cycle of sexual abuse as an adjunct to scholarly literature on the subject for social workers, psychologists, teachers, law enforcement, clergy, medical professionals, healers, and anyone who wishes to prevent or treat trauma. Thank you, Janet Mackie, fc your courage in sharing your voice to make a difference for others.

– Dr. Nancy B. Irwin, PsyD, C.Ht.
Therapist/Clinical Hypnotist/
Speaker/Author

Praise for Janet Mackie's book...

Reading like a novel, this book shines a bright light deep into the da recesses of child sexual exploitation. It also starts to unravel the bet inter-generational aspects of this phenomenon. As a family court ji has witnessed first-hand hundreds of such cases, I submit that the shame and humiliation experienced by child victims are even mo dous than those experienced by the brave women of the #MeTo who are outing sexual exploitation by powerful men. Unfortur hard to produce a sea-change in public awareness, but if this ' wins wide readership, then the resulting outrage just might p tolerance policy our society needs to begin to put an end to behaviors by predatory men (and sometimes women) man' likely victims themselves.

– Charles M. McGee
Sr. District Judge; Second Judicial District Cc
State of Nevada, Washoe County

Silenced Lives

The Sex Offender's Legacy

By
Janet Mackie

Wind Harp Tree

ISBN-13: 9780988573703
ISBN-13: 978-0-9885737-0-3

Library of Congress
Control Number: 2018911755

First edition

Cover design,
photo work and formatting:
Keith Carlson

Cover background photo:
The family farmstead at Black Tower

Photo, page 330:
© Can Stock Photo / Dubova

Wind Harp Tree Publishing

P.O. Box 11272 Reno, NV 89510
windharptree.jm@gmail.com

On breaking the Silence:

In choosing to write *Silenced Lives, The Sex Offender's Legacy,* I sit Seder in honor of the bravery of all those, living and dead who have gone before. Those who, whatever their choices, for good or ill, did the best they were able given the legacy handed down to them in past generations.

I sit Seder in honor of all those who struggled, and all those who struggle still, each of us, everyday, still faced with making our own, very personal, choices between kindness and cruelty.

May we find solace for the cruelties we have inflicted and for the kindnesses we have failed to bestow. May breaking the silences binding all our lives, finding words, sharing our stories, result in greater understanding, and the healing of wounds. And may the choices each of us make today leave behind a better legacy for all tomorrow's children.

Take care,
Janet Mackie

Table of Contents

Part IV: Prince Charming Come at Last

Part V: Happily-Ever-After, Try, Try Again

Part VI: Petals on the Wind

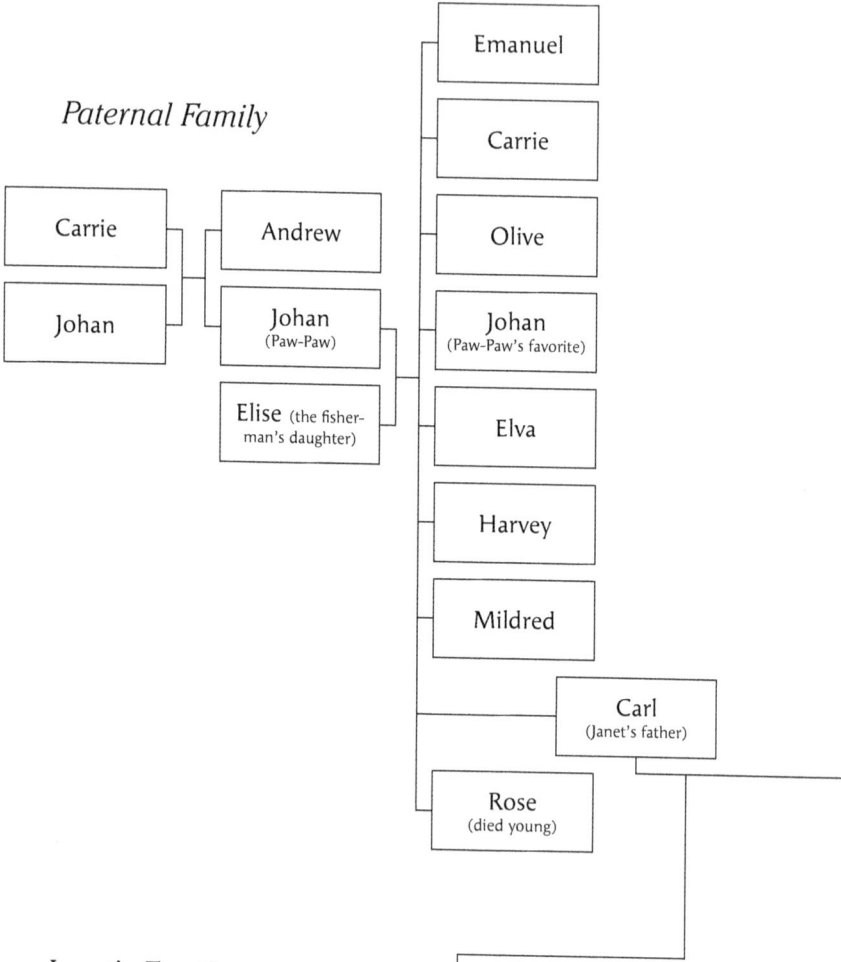

Paternal Family

- Carrie
- Johan
- Andrew
- Johan (Paw-Paw)
- Elise (the fisherman's daughter)
- Emanuel
- Carrie
- Olive
- Johan (Paw-Paw's favorite)
- Elva
- Harvey
- Mildred
- Carl (Janet's father)
- Rose (died young)

Janet's Family

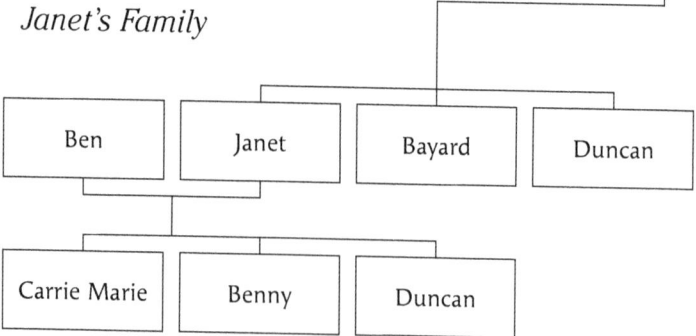

- Ben
- Janet
- Bayard
- Duncan
- Carrie Marie
- Benny
- Duncan

Maternal Family

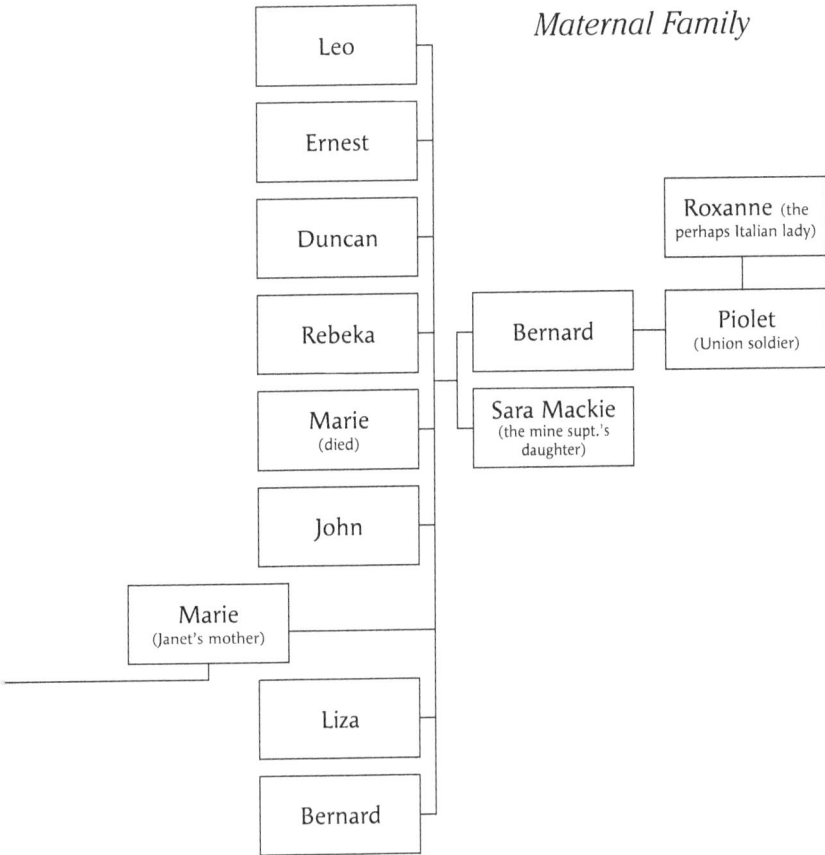

- Leo
- Ernest
- Duncan
- Rebeka
- Marie (died)
- John
- Marie (Janet's mother)
- Liza
- Bernard

Bernard — Sara Mackie (the mine supt.'s daughter)

Bernard — Piolet (Union soldier)

Roxanne (the perhaps Italian lady)

Names and places mentioned in *Silenced Lives* have been changed
to protect the privacy of family members.

A smiling little girl on a teeter-totter
who wondered even then "Why me? Why my family?

P<small>ART</small> I: T<small>HIS THE</small> B<small>EGINNING</small>

Chapter 1

My *father died one cold April day in 2011. He was ninety-six. He outlived my mother by nearly twenty years. In his will, he left me nothing. That was to be expected.* An old woman at his funeral made a point of telling me, "I loved that old man." My feelings were somewhat more complicated. I had known him longer.

His hands, folded in the coffin, were the same rough square hands I remembered, the same rough skin, the same ungentle fingers. I had half expected fists. Seeing his hands in the coffin forced me to remember untold tales, smothered secrets and his rough hands like vice grips pinning me down in the dark. They were secrets my brothers also suffered in remembering as they, like me, tried to forget the cruelties once visited upon us.

When my brother Buddy was perhaps four, and I was eight, on an evening when our mother was at work, he remembers our father shouting at me. Terrified of what was to come, Buddy ran and hid in the corner of our downstairs bedroom.

He soon realized he had not escaped, as our father dragged me, crying and resisting, into the same bedroom. Buddy forced himself further back in the corner until, from where he hid, he could just see our reflections in the mirror. He watched, terrified, as my father pinned me to the bed with his knee, hit me with one hand and sexually abused me with the other.

All the while, my father wept, telling me over and over that what he did was my fault. Because he said and then shouted—I was a slut. Because, he said, I had, once again, tempted him past all power of resistance. I had caused him, yet again, to do this sinful thing he did not want to do but, weeping, had done. Because, he said, I deserved a Good Spanking. I was a whore.

I knew there must be some mysterious, bad thing about me that attracted my father; some wicked thing that made my father cry and rage and do these things that hurt me— these things that were, he said, my fault.

I also knew that what my father did was our secret. Warned never to tell, I kept silent. I learned to pretend and then to forget. Thus I survived the unspeakable. Just as my father once learned to suffer in silence growing up, I too survived childhood.

Until the next time.

. . .

As the child at the center of my father's painful attentions, my memories are not the observations of a witness— not the pictures of a single event burned indelibly upon the retinas of my then-four-year-old brother observing a single situation. My memories come in flashes—fear, chaos, terror. Good Spankings, rape and rape repeated triggered again and again. With terror came unbearable anxiety that I might, once again, do that unthinkable something which attracted my father, which would force him, once again, to inflict yet another Good Spanking.

If the first law of childhood is survival, then the first rule of growing past the unspeakable is to drown memory beneath the dark waters of forgetting, wall off fear and trembling and in the ensuing silence allow life, somehow, to go on.

Triggered, wolf shadows return in dreams down silent halls. Memory shatters then splinters and splinters again. Terror, like shards of broken dreams, like obsidian tears, falls silently to disappear into a dead pool of forgetting.

Until next time.

On the day of my father's funeral, as I stood staring at those rough hands folded in his coffin, I remembered. I told myself, "Never mind. He's dead. It is finally, finally over."

But it wasn't.

. . .

The day after my father's funeral, I re-packed my single suitcase, ate breakfast, and bought gas, preparing to leave before a threatening cold front brought fresh snow and black ice.

Hurrying to avoid a treacherous return, I lifted my suitcase into the Camaro just as my cell phone rang. It was the old woman from the funeral—the one who'd said she loved my father, the one to whom my father had left my mother's house, the woman who now possessed all my mother's belongings.

"Glad I caught you."

"Yes?" I said.

"I've started clearing out the junk."

"Yes?"

"Well, there's an old cardboard box, moldy papers, bits and pieces, dusty letters, snapshots, old fashioned photos . . ." She drew a ragged breath as though she had just run up my mother's narrow basement stairs to phone me. "Come take a look. If you don't want the stuff, I'll throw it out with the rest. No use to me."

"Okay."

She was waiting in the driveway, surrounded by the leftovers of my parent's life, already preparing yard signs for her jumble sale.

I took the dusty, tattered Pandora's Box—my father's unintended legacy—and put it in the trunk next to my lone suitcase, anxious to arrive back home before dark.

"There." The old woman wiped dusty hands on flowered hips and stood back, waving, as I drove away.

"Goodbye. Goodbye."

• • •

Driving home, retracing lonely asphalt back roads, thoughts of Family followed me.

We appeared to be a very normal family. Respectable. Unremarkable. We adhered to all the correct beliefs. In the small town where I grew up, we were just another Happily-Ever-After family living Beaver Cleaver, Father Knows Best lives, attending church like the rest—a family sailing on above dark waters. Yet the specter of shaming, of shunning, hung forever in the air, silencing one and all in our small town.

"Don't tell" is the 1st Commandment in families like my own just as "Keep quiet or else," remains the 1st Commandment in much of America.

As a child, I knew to smile. Be nice. Make Mama happy. Obey Daddy. Never, never make Daddy cry.

Driving home, I asked myself, "What were the unexamined forces that led to an airless family structure that demanded we all endure? What forces required us to drown childhood beneath dark pools of forgetting? Learning to live in such a family is like learning to breathe under water. But we all did. We still do. But why?"

What had happened to my father, Carl? And to his father, Johan? How far back does terror go? How far forward might this secret legacy continue? If unbroken, how long might shame and toxic silence hold us all in thrall?

If I, too, keep the 1st Commandment, who might yet inherit cruelty? What child as near as tomorrow may yet suffer harm?

• • •

When I finally, finally reached home, I shoved the fragile cardboard box in a corner and fell into bed, exhausted.

Still sleepless at 3 a.m., I arose.

I began to sort through the Pandora's Box of scribbled letters and forgotten photos. I found sepia pictures of nameless young mothers, even their smiling babies now lost to living memory; their long-ago lives disappeared into nothingness. Were they too silenced by the hope of Happily-Ever-After, by promises destined to fail them just as they failed me?

I wondered.

In the dusty box, I discovered family trees arranged in lists, yellowing letters, and more photos. I wondered what my father thought about those nights when he, too, sat sorting through snapshots at 3 a.m., writing names on the backs of these same sepia photographs. I wondered if he reread the postcards he'd sent when he was courting my mother, back in a time when he might still have at least pretended to love her.

Perhaps Dad also read and then discarded the letters my brother Buddy, by then called Bayard, sent our mother from Seminary—letters Mama saved, reread and cherished; letters that kept her warm all those cold years after my father laid aside pretense.

Perhaps, instead, Dad read and reread letters from his mother, Elise, the Danish fisherman's daughter. Letters in which Elise addressed my father as her Dearly Beloved Son; letters written when she, too, must finally have given up hope of pleasing Johan, the husband she called Paw-Paw, long years when she, too, must have given up hope of discovering Happily-Ever-After in the new world.

But then, my father never dwelt much upon happiness. I suspect he spent those late nights nursing resentment and cataloging much-cherished grievances. Perhaps he dwelt upon the cruel legacy of his father, Johan.

I doubt my father understood or even much regretted his own cruelties after surviving such a childhood. But perhaps I am mistaken. For this is my father's story too; the tale of a boy-child derided, bullied and sexually assaulted by his father. "Treated like a girl," was my father's phrase. For Paw-Paw, too, was a cruel man who, as a youngster, was himself too well-schooled in the festering cruelties he handed on to later generations.

On my mother Marie's side, the Mackie side, of the yellowed pages, I found long-ago names and remembered Mama's mother Sara. I remembered Sara's romantic tales of the Perhaps Italian lady, who was grandmother to Bernard, the daring young man from Cripple Creek, who won the hand of Sara, the mine superintendent's pretty daughter. Sara was the grandmother who slipped me Butter mints, the grandmother whose kind presence saved me.

But then, wasn't it also Sara who said, "Don't think about it. Don't make yourself unhappy."

Until next time.

Sorting through the tattered box, I gradually remembered place names, half-told tales. I heard echoes of suicide and murder passed down. I recognized truth sunk beneath dark waters; drowned beneath a smiling surface; truth taken to the grave by now-lost women: Happily-Ever-After-Believers one and all.

"Don't tell."

A child, smiling through tears.

The best way to hand down cruelty's legacy is to deny language, counsel silence, avoid shame and seal secrets away in separate compartments, in musty old boxes. Generations pass yet the obsidian shards remain in the shape of whispered stories drawn up from the dead pool at 3 a.m.

Thus, one cold April morning, I opened a tattered box, dared begin the journey to understand my own silenced life, and gathered courage to see the hard truths that shaped my mother's and my daughter's lives and deaths, hard truths threatening to cycle down into generations of children as yet unborn if silence continues.

As I sat, sorting through the dusty box, I heard my grandmother Sara warn once again, "Don't think about it. Don't make yourself unhappy."

Mama's voice echoed in the cold room: "They will blame you."

Awake at 3 a.m., sitting, remembering, I shivered.

"Someone step on your grave?" The Wolf's voice.

A feral cat with ice-blue eyes, a cruel ghost from Paw Paw's past, looks on.

"Cat got your tongue?"

With trembling hands, I shut Pandora's Box.

Back in bed, a sudden a gust of wind rattles dark windows.

A twig snaps.

Shaken, I check and re-check locks. I test doors and windows. I brace against imagined stranger danger. Once again, I am that frightened child frozen in a little yellow bed, listening, dreading, watching Wolf Shadows move closer, ever closer down nocturnal halls in a house I well know no longer stands, in a life I hoped was long past.

Sometime toward morning, sleep arrived.

• • •

Daylight came at last. I showered and put on a suit. Dressed for work, I ventured forth a social worker—not a long-silenced daughter, not a sex offender's wife but a child protective services worker charged with investigating, writing court reports, and recommending protections for other children, other families.

Once at work, my life rights itself, becomes familiar.

As a social worker it is my duty to break the 1st Commandment. It is my job to tell. As a social worker, I delve beneath the surface. I hear frightened secrets as I never before dared hear my own; as I never before dared listen to my own children's stories until the day I returned from my father's funeral.

Now, somehow freed by my father's death, I dare reclaim the right to remember my own life, to know and tell tales of family. I dare to say #MeToo. I dare raise a mother's voice and voice my own, long-overdue, mea culpa.

Emboldened, I join with the Shahrazad of women, the multitudes passing on once silenced stories, claiming their right to tell near-lost truths, to be respected and listened to.

I join hands with the silenced women gone before who, in my childhood, still dared pass down whispered tales; tales told for the sake of that smiling little girl on a see-saw who, even then, wanted to puzzle-out, somehow, what had happened in her family. A little girl who wondered, even then, why me, why my brothers, why my father, why my family?

So, gather round.

Hear now my tale.

Learn how the Sex Offender's Legacy cast long shadows across four generations.

Listen now to this first silenced story of a young boy disappeared long, long ago; a boy-child, bullied and abused; a child who never lived to tell.

*Just a lively, always hungry young lad
disappeared right at suppertime.*

Chapter 2

Long ago, on a Nebraska farm, a sleek feral cat with a twitching ginger tail and ice-blue eyes moved silently through sweet mowed hay stacked high in the loft of a tall barn. Raiding bird's nests, the ginger cat paused only to play a deadly game with a tiny pink mouse. The cat's paw batted the tiny terrorized thing back and forth, back and forth, just to hear it squeak, just to see it run, just to smell its desperation, and revel in its helpless despair. Until, with one last swat of the ginger cat's paw, the tiny pink thing lay forever still.

Pausing to lick its ginger fur and purr, the feral cat heard desperate sounds from far below.

"Stop! Please stop! Please, please stop!"

Smothered sounds. Laughter.

"Now say, 'Pretty Please.'"

Smothered protests, sounds of struggle.

"Say it! Say Pretty Please!"

"No!

"Say it!"

"I'll tell Mama! I will!"

"Stop! Please Stop!"

A desperate voice full of tears, a young boy's voice cut suddenly short.

Ice blue eyes peering down through dusty shafts of light to the barn floor, the ginger cat watched two brothers, one large and one small, sprawled below.

"I'll tell! I'll tell!" a frightened voice cut off.

Unmoved and unmoving, the feral cat watched as the older boy played a familiar game, jeering, laughing, smothering, until the smaller boy lay silent, his desperate threats forever stilled.

The ginger cat stretched and purred himself asleep.

· · ·

"What's going on here?"

Awakened, the cat peered down.

"Johan, where's your brother?" The boy's father, a milk pail in each hand, glanced around.

Johan shrugged, turned both hands palms up, and dropped his eyes.

The father fell silent, considering.

"Well, no doubt he'll soon turn up. Milking won't wait."

Handing his older son both pails, he turned to go.

"Lively, now. Mama's near got supper ready."

Supper came and went, leaving behind a little boy's still-empty chair and untouched plate.

Just a lively, always hungry, young lad disappeared at supper time.

Later, in the shadowed barn, the ginger cat discovered a small boy's body hidden in the sweet-mowed hay.

Ice-blue eyes considered but moved on, seeking smaller prey.

By morning even the small body was no longer.

A mother's child disappeared.

A father's son, gone.

Days pass. Life moves on.

But inside the farmhouse, newly built out on the still-wild prairie, a mother grieved to see her missing child's still-waiting chair, her small son's still-empty place.

Morning becomes night; cloud shadows move across fresh planted land. Night becomes morning once again.

Summer passed and Christmas came.

A still-grieving mother looked across the festive table at her son, now a young man. His ice-blue eyes drop before hers.

"Cat got your tongue?"

The older boy shrugs, turns both hands palms up. Icy eyes slide away.

The young man's mother considered for yet another moment before reaching across the festive table to remove her son's plate still piled with goose and gravy, sauerkraut and sweet potatoes. She scraped her remaining son's plate into a pan and set the pan out on the back stoop. Still silent, hands on hips, she watched as the feral kittens of the ginger cat, growling and hissing, pushing and shoving, ate Christmas up.

Survival of the fittest.

So ends the first long-silenced tale, the smothered story of a child named Andrew, a lively child disappeared long ago.

• • •

Then one cold April morning, I opened the tattered Pandora's Box and discovered a sepia photograph of my great grandmother, Carrie, and standing behind her, her young son Andrew. Quiet and sober, the image of my own youngest grandson, Andrew looks back at me from across 100 years of silence. I turn the photo over. There, written in my father's hand, next to the name, Andrew, the single word: "Disappeared."

Seeing Andrew, I wondered, "Who, indeed, was Andrew's older brother, Johan, the grandfather I knew only as Paw-Paw?"

Why had I assumed it all began with me?

• • •

I was Paw-Paw's ever-curious granddaughter. One summer when I was about 10, our family visited Paw-Paw and Grandma Elise.

I asked, "Paw-Paw, Why did you come to America?"

"Because I would not fight in the Kaiser's army," he said.

Filled with the militant patriotism of 1950s America, I'd expected a red-blooded coming-to-America story like the ones taught in school.

But, here, my Paw-Paw said he was a Draft Dodger!

Already well warned to "never tell family business," ashamed of shame, I kept Paw-Paw's secret. I vowed to protect Paw-Paw the Draft Dodger, and, by extension, protect my family from the dangerous gossip, finger-pointing and loose talk targeting nonconformists in small-town America.

In my resolve to protect family, I guarded Paw-Paw's secret most of my adult life.

Months after my father's funeral, I told my youngest brother, Duncan, that I was thinking of writing a memoir. Duncan and I shared secrets and marveled at how siloed by fear and shame each of us once was, at how silenced and isolated all of us were still.

"Did you know Paw-Paw was a Draft Dodger?" I offered.

Duncan laughed and said it was the Danish defeat at the 2nd Battle of Schleswig in 1864 that, years later, led to Paw-Paw dodging 20 years conscription in the invading Prussian-German army.

Early on, Johan's parents apprenticed their young son to the Carpenter's Guild, the ancient system training Nordic carpenters and shipbuilders since Viking times. Through Guild Membership, Paw-Paw's family thought to ensure a prosperous future for themselves and their sons.

Apprenticed young to a cruel Master of the Guild who beat, bullied, and sexually brutalized each trainee in turn, Johan's apprenticeship became a test of will, played out gladiator style, within a cruel and malignant arena. In time, Johan graduated to bullying and dominating his own small crew of terrorized apprentices as he sought to clear a path toward someday claiming his place as Master of the Guild.

Fearing their son and heir's looming conscription into the Prussian army, his parents cut short Johan's ambition. Against his wishes, they bought Johan out of his apprenticeship and fled Denmark for America. Angry and resentful at the thwarting of ambition, Johan turned his vengeful attentions on his younger brother, Andrew, by now the darling, the beloved, of their mother.

Arrived in America, Johan's prosperous family, once denied land ownership in Prussian-occupied Denmark, purchased nearly 1,000 acres of farmland just outside of Lincoln, Nebraska. They settled among other like-minded, ambitious, correctly respectable farm families also come from afar to settle America's heartland. There Johan's family built a large house, raised a tall barn, and settled in to raise their sons, safe in America.

But then, in this respectable German-Lutheran family, prizing Nordic blood and male heirs above all else, the younger son, Andrew, disappeared.

"Disappeared" became the agreed-upon story, a tale told to neighbors, passed down through family. Theirs was a respectable narrative meant to smother questions, forget what the ginger cat saw, and protect their son Johan.

But, even so, a mother's heart remembers, ponders, bides time. Eventually even a mother's heart thirsts for revenge. Perhaps other farm families knew details the ginger cat forgot. Perhaps there was gossip, loose talk. Perhaps other German-Lutheran fathers held back their darling daughters, disapproved marriage to one such as Paw-Paw, with his cold blue eyes, ginger hair, and smothered past.

Then one day, into this cold silence, came Elise—small, blond, and lively, twenty-two and virginal, come half way around the world. A Danish fisherman's daughter, the silk ribbons of her little white prayer cap tied firmly beneath her chin, Elise came seeking to marry, have children, and live Happily-Ever-After, as romantic tradition and her religion decreed.

And marry she did.

Yet even a dream achieved, might carry within it the ever-ripening seeds of a cruel fate. And might not cruelty itself be Genesis to a dark legacy?

But who was Elise, this lively girl, lately come upon the scene?

*Going without, she saved enough to buy her only child a one way
ticket to what she hoped would be a better life.*

Chapter 3

A*s I sorted through the Pandora's Box my father left to me, I remembered the admiring tales Dad told about Elise, his much-loved mother.* In a way, the Danish defeat at Schleswig, and the subsequent Prussian-German occupation conspired to change Elise's fate more, even, than her father's death.

Elise's father was a fisherman. Kind, brave, and devout, a Good Provider, my father said. Like Nordic fishers before him, Elise's father took to the Northern Seas in frail fleets of open wooden boats. Like his father and his father's father, like all the village fishermen since Viking Times, Elise's father followed the great shoals of cod into the mists and frozen darkness of Arctic seas.

Early one morning, Elise, lying snug in her little bed tucked up beneath the eaves, heard a loud knock on the door below. The door squeaked open; Elise heard somber voices, heard her mother's stifled cry, and she knew.

The Arctic sea had claimed another.

Elise wept, prayed, and dressed. She tied the white ribbons of her prayer cap firmly beneath her chin. She made her way down steep wooden stairs to comfort and pray with her now widowed mother.

Once the somber fishermen left, their wives brought bread and salt cod taken from their own meager larders. Then they went away to feed their children and pray for their own husband's safe return.

As days passed, impoverished by their loss, Elise and her mother faced grief and growing hunger. Forced by circumstance, they went knocking on the back doors of

rich relatives, reminding them of shared blood and desperate necessity. It didn't help that Elise wore her prayer
cap, signaling to one and all her continuing obedience to a
"Resister" church, opposed both by the Prussian occupiers
and by Elise's rich German-Lutheran relatives.

Stigmatized, grudgingly offered servants' work in
a cold, disapproving house, Elise and her mother barely
kept body and soul together. But still Elise wore her prayer
cap; still she prayed for marriage and children, knowing
she had no dowry, no fortune to tempt a suitor. All the
young ethnic Danes who might have courted her were
gone. Forced into 20 years' service in the Kaiser's Army,
Danish boys returned old men, their lives spent, now more
German than Dane.

Faced with the seemingly impossible, Elise and her
mother slipped down to the docks when the fishing fleets
returned. They earned pennies mending nets for fishermen
who had been shipmates of Elise's lost father. Elise's mother
set aside every penny. Going without, she saved enough
to buy her only child a one-way ticket to a Happily-Ever-
After life, in an America full of daring young men, where
dowries weren't required.

Once arrived in New York, speaking no English and
still wearing her little white prayer cap, Elise bought a train
ticket to Lincoln, Nebraska. There, she expected to find a
community of like-minded, Danish-speaking Believers. At
least in America she thought, she would not be shunned
due to her religion.

Small, blond, and virginal, Elise braved adversity and
traveled halfway around the world to marry and have children. A devout Happily-Ever-After-Believer, Elise no doubt
imagined her husband would be as kind as her lost father.

Soon after arriving, Elise wed a silent man, five years
her senior, a man with ice blue eyes and ginger hair. She
wed a man whose German-Lutheran mother still grieved
for her disappeared young Andrew.

• • •

My father preferred to tell romantic tales of the fisherman's brave daughter. His stories omitted mention of draft dodgers and the Carpenter's Guild. His stories forgot what the ginger cat saw. My father's was a child's narrative, tales told to him by a mother who dearly loved her youngest son but was powerless to protect him from what was to come.

My father, Carl, was Elise's youngest son, and he loved her—still loved her so much that he wept as he backed our car down the driveway, leaving his mother behind after a visit to Black Tower, where my Dad grew up.

Across the intervening years, I can still picture us in my mind's eye.

"Goodbye! Goodbye!" All of us piled in the car, smiling, waving, as Dad backed down Paw-Paw's driveway leaving for home.

I can still see Elise standing, trapped behind the big front window of Paw Paw's house. A worn out, little old woman, Elise still wore a tattered white prayer cap. She wept as she waved goodbye—a broken-hearted woman, her face shiny with tears as her beloved son left and her long loneliness returned.

I saw my father's face shiny with unbidden tears, mirroring Elise's. He ducked his face into the crook of his elbow, wiping away his tears again and again as he slowly backed our blue station wagon down Paw-Paw's drive.

"Real men don't cry," Dad said, razzing, bullying, and demeaning my little brothers. "Just to get a rise," he said. Calling them "sissies," "pansies," "fraidy-cats," all because they cried. Because he said they "couldn't take a little kidding."

Dad taught his sons by cruel example, just as Paw-Paw once taught him—father to son, master to apprentice. Each young son, each young apprentice, vied for the master's withheld approval. Each Father's son, jealous to be his father's favorite, each hoping to rule someday, if not in Denmark, then in America.

But here was my Dad, crying, ducking his face into the crook of his arm.

Sitting in the back seat of our new station wagon, my little brothers sitting on either side, I knew with a child's sudden certainty that my father was afraid—afraid he would never see his mother again. Perhaps the child in him still longed for her protection, much as he had all his life.

But then, perhaps my father wept because even grown, he'd never dared protect his mother from Paw-Paw. Perhaps he'd been ashamed of round little Elise with her prayer cap and broken English? Had his desire to gain his father's cruel approval outweighed love? Had he, too, sided against his mother?

My son, Benny, told me that in old age, my father reluctantly admitted that Paw-Paw called Elise "Mule," laughing, while her sons stood by, while her sons joined in.

Right there at the feed store in front of everyone, Paw-Paw laughed and called Elise "Mule"—not even my mule, because a husband's ownership went without saying.

Just "Mule," he said.

Paw-Paw bought 100-pound sacks of grain and loaded them on his wife's back, while she obediently carried each one outside and down the dusty wooden steps in front of everybody. Elise loaded each feed sack into the old truck and returned for more while her four sons looked on.

"Mule," Paw-Paw called her. After years of marriage, after Elise had borne his children, Paw-Paw "joked" and called her Mule. Even after Elise and his children, proved up the Home Place, kept the homestead going out there in the endless, flat land at Black Tower where only the burning blue sky shields a woman and her children; Black Tower, where Paw-Paw's greed almost destroyed them all in the years to come.

. . .

Soon after Elise arrived in Nebraska, the two wed.
Johan's new little wife soon found herself shunned by her
German-Lutheran in-laws. Not because she failed in her
wife's duty to bear children. Elise bore Johan three children; Emmanuel, a son and heir, and daughters, Carrie and
Olive, all born in those first four years before the little family was shunned and sent away.

It was said the shunning came about because Elise
refused to convert to the family's German-Lutheran religion. At least that's the public story Johan's family put
about to neighbors. I suspect religion was but the respectable excuse for a still-grieving mother's sorrowful revenge.
Whatever the motive, Johan, and Elise were banished and
Elise blamed.

• • •

*The couple took their three small blond children and
set off in search of new lands.* At the last minute, a tiny
ginger kitten was tucked in for their children's amusement,
a cruel omen of things to come? The little family traveled
by rail car in search of a place to homestead where no one
knew their secrets, where no whispers, no loose talk, no
shunning would follow.

Paw-Paw and his little family set off in search of land,
first denied him as an ethnic Dane in occupied Denmark,
and then denied him a second time in Nebraska by a grieving Mother's revenge.

When their train stopped in Waurika, Oklahoma, in
1905, Waurika was no more than a raw frontier town, a
settlement straddling the line between Texas and the still-
wild Oklahoma Indian Territory.

Johan laid claim to a beautiful, treeless meadow where
the land lay fallow, ready to plow and plant requiring
apparently little effort.

But, come spring, the treeless meadow became a
lake. Elise caught fish to feed her growing family in the

swampland Paw-Paw laid claim to where the soggy ground drowned crops and bred mosquitoes, malaria, and fever.

Elise fell ill. Unable to nurse her fourth child—Paw-Paw's name-sake—Elise hired a black woman to wet nurse the baby while she recovered. When, in turn, the black woman fell ill, Elise, to Paw-Paw's glowering displeasure, wet-nursed the black child until his mother, too, recovered.

Johan may have dodged conscription in Denmark and fled to America, but he brought with him a Kaiser's pride in his Aryan purity. Paw-Paw lived in dread of Tainted Blood. Long possessed of a peasant's enduring suspicion, Paw-Paw eagerly imbibed Southern prejudice that said one drop of black blood forever defiled a man as indelibly black, no matter how white his skin.

In Paw-Paw's German-Lutheran family, inordinately proud of its whiteness, even imagined "pollution" must have counted against Elise as no small treason.

Failing in Waurika, Paw-Paw gave "Run out by chills and malaria" as his excuse. He pointed to Elise's illness as his reason for pulling up stakes and setting off in search of drier land to homestead. Excuses made, Paw-Paw paused only long enough for Elise to deliver a fifth child. They named the little blond girl Elva.

Afterward the family set off by wagon to claim land outside Black Tower, a raw frontier town located in the dry northeast corner of the New Mexico Territory.

Arrived at Black Tower, the stakes of his 160 acre homestead safely driven in, Johan revived his dream of someday possessing not only the 160 acres, but 1000 acres before denied him in Nebraska.

· · ·

They had only just dug their first sod shelter at Black Tower when a wildfire appeared across the far horizon. All day Elise watched as the fire blew up. Tall smoke and burning embers blackened the sky. Suddenly the wind shifted. The firestorm turned. It seemed ravenous flames would surely engulf the little family pinned down upon the endless prairie, surrounded by tinder-dry grasslands.

Bright, windblown embers began to fall upon the small blond children. My father said Elise's prayer had power to turn back death. In the face of flame and firestorm, Elise prayed, wrestled, bargained, with her God. All the while she and Johan made preparations to flee. They spread the sod strips lately cut to cover the roof of their dugout, over the precious canvas and lumber they'd brought all the way from Waurika. That done, Elise and Paw-Paw piled the frightened children into the buggy and raced for their lives.

No story says what Paw-Paw thought as he whipped the horses to outrun a fiery death. But thanks be to Elise's God or to Chance, the raging fire burnt itself out. Spared, the young family returned, unearthed their buried provisions, built a cramped little house and settled in to endure the years ahead.

Elise's little house was divided into a kitchen, a tiny sitting room where all the girls slept, and one dark little bedroom room filled to the edges with a rope bed for Elise and Paw-Paw and an ever-waiting cradle. A pull-down ladder in the tiny hall led to the loft where Elise's sons slept. Shivering in winter, sweltering in summer, crowded together, hissing and shoving, each boy sought to ape Paw-Paw's cruelty and thereby gain his forever-withheld approval.

Survival of the fittest.

• • •

With the house built, a windmill raised, and the corral fenced off Johan left Elise and his children on the farm and went to live in the comfort of Black Tower. "To earn cash money," Paw-Paw said. He took Carrie, the oldest daughter who might have been the most help to Elise, to live with him in town. With Carrie and later Olive installed as his little town wives, Johan forgot all but the pretense of loving Elise.

In 1908, Black Tower was the new railhead for the Atchison, Topeka, and Santa Fe Railroad. With the arrival of the railroad, cattle drives to Dodge City became a thing of the past. With the arrival of the AT&SF, homesteaders shipped their Keefer corn to market by railcar. The 20th century had begun.

In Black Tower, Johan hired out as a master carpenter. Skilled carpenters like Paw-Paw were paid a premium in raw boom towns. Johan bossed the crew that built Black Tower. With the cash money, Paw-Paw bought beans to feed Elsie's hungry children while he hoarded the rest to feed his hungry ambition to possess 1000 acres. All the while, Paw-Paw left Elise and her children to prove up the Home Place. Plowing and planting, Elise eventually secured Paw-Paw's original 160 acres.

All the while, Paw-Paw kept Carrie in town.

"To do for me," Paw-Paw said.

In my father's box, I found a sepia studio photo taken a bare five years after they all escaped the range fire. The studio photo shows Elise, Johan and the six children then born. Johan's favorite son, his namesake, sits relaxed upon Johan's knee. In this picture Johan's oldest son, Emmanuel stands to the left, his face and body telegraphing distress. Elise's angelic little blond daughters are garbed in pristine white dresses. Johan is a dark presence in their midst—a Wolf Shadow among lambs.

Over the next few years three more children, including my father were born. Elise almost died giving birth to her last child, Rose. Both mother and baby remained gravely ill for months. Hardly more than a baby himself, not yet graduated to long pants, not yet possessed of his first hair cut, my father pressed his small body against his mother's closed door, weeping, afraid Elise would die and abandon him.

It was a time of terror my father remembered even as an old man.

Chapter 4

I*t was a time of terror my father still remembered even as an old man—for Elise's prolonged confinement left my father unprotected from Paw-Paw and his brothers up in the sweltering loft at night.*

Johan did not move back during Elise's illness. Nor did he send Carrie, his little town wife, or his second daughter Olive, by now also doing for Paw-Paw in town, back home to help care for Elise and new-baby Rose. Instead, Elva, the fifth child, was taken out of school. At ten, deemed an expendable girl-child, Elva was judged old enough to cook, clean and watch over her mother, baby Rose and the children left out on the Home Place.

A second family photo bears witness. In this photo, taken not in a studio but out on the farm, Emmanuel, by now half grown, stands in the back. Carrie is missing, gone to California or enrolled in secretarial school, while Olive, Paw-Paw's other little town wife, stands behind Elise. Elva, taken out of school, stands next to her mother in the picture. Mildred stands to Paw-Paw's right. Johan, Paw-Paw's favorite is behind Paw-Paw. Harvey stands between Paw-Paw and Elise. My father, little more than a baby himself, sits on Paw-Paw's lap. He looks toward his mother, Elise, who holds baby Rose on her lap. For her part, Elise's face reflects despair.

Nights out on the Home Place, Elise and baby Rose slept in the stifling downstairs bedroom. Elva and Mildred shared a couch in the sitting room. At night all Paw-Paw's boys, big and small—including my father, perhaps

three—whiled away the long hot nights on pallets laid
down in the loft.

In the loft, they wrestled and fought. Paw-Paw's favorite son, Johan, bullied, and abused the others—calling
them "Sissy Boy!" when they resisted; saying "Pansy"
if they wept. Paw-Paw, it seems, joined in as desire took
him when he visited the Home Place. Just as Paw-Paw had
before joined in aping the master of the guild, life on the
Home Place now became survival of the fittest for all but
Paw-Paw's favorite.

One night, shortly after Rose's birth, Paw-Paw was
asleep next to Elise in the room below when the older boys
in the loft, led by Paw-Paw's favorite, ganged up and began
to bully, and abuse the younger.

Paw-Paw awakened and ordered, "Silence."

The commotion continued. Paw-Paw got out of bed
and climbed into the loft.

· · ·

*Once in the loft, Paw-Paw witnessed my father being
sexually abused by his brother Johan, Paw-Paw's favorite.*

Seeing his father, the little boy wept and screamed.
Desperate to tell, he trusted that this time, at least, Paw-
Paw would protect, would rescue him.

Instead, my father remembered, Paw-Paw joined in.

Paw-Paw placed rough hands over his son's mouth,
commanding, "Silence."

When the hysterical little boy who was my father persisted, begging for a father's protection, Paw-Paw's rough
hand tightened its grasp over the squirming child's mouth.

"Please, Daddy, please . . ."

Smothered sounds as Paw Paw's thumb and forefinger
pinched the weeping little boy's nostrils together, cut off
his breath.

"Please! I can't breathe. Please, stop!"

"Say, Pretty Please."

"Say it!"

Silenced, smothered, and gasping for breath, by then fearing death, the weeping child gave up hope, surrendered. The rest, smirking and jeering, took turns once Paw-Paw had his way.

Defeated—forced to beg, to say "Please," then "Pretty please" —the little boy who became my father turned a tear-streaked face into his pillow. He stuffed his own mouth with blankets. He silenced himself. Smothered and numb, he shuddered, and lay unresisting, obedient to Paw-Paw's demands.

That night, something vital died inside the little boy who became my father. Smothered into submission by Johan, "Treated like a girl," was Dad's phrase, my father's betrayal was visceral. All his life he was terrified of closeness. Instead, he craved the safety of emotional and physical domination. He sought power to be the one forever on top.

Perhaps only in the momentary thrill of risky sexual domination could my father overcome his childhood humiliations and reassure himself he was as much a man as Paw-Paw. If so, as Dad's children, as Paw-Paw's grandchildren, my brothers and I paid a terrible price. Had there been help for that weeping little boy up in the loft so many years ago, there might have been no need for me to wish for miracles later.

I well know that not every boy or girl molested by brothers, fathers, priests, or coaches chooses to become a tormentor themselves. But each one, tormented, smothered and silenced, violated and betrayed, must somehow find courage to endure, and then, somehow, allow closeness, discover empathy and thus refrain from acting out the sex offender's legacy.

Absent kindness in word and deed, cruelty too often begets cruelty.

...

*In spite of cruelty, torment, and hunger, in spite of
an ever-encroaching drought that led, eventually, to the
Dust Bowl and America's Great Depression, Elise and
her children struggled on.*

Every year Paw-Paw, living in town, with no experience of farming, consulted the Farmer's Almanac, then sent
strict instruction to Elise as to exactly when she should
plow and plant the dry land her efforts had so far proved
up. Even after years of canny farming, Elise awaited Paw-
Paw's instruction.

In 1949, Elise and Paw-Paw, by then praised as the
quintessential "American Pioneer Couple," were interviewed by a local reporter. Elise told the reporter that she
and the children always began plowing and planting on
Paw-Paw's appointed day.

"But," Elise said, "The ground was as hard as this
floor. I tried to plow, but the Keefer corn didn't get planted
until it rained."

It seemed the dirt itself, or maybe Elise's God, refused
to obey Paw-Paw. Perhaps, in spite of Paw-Paw's orders,
God dragged His feet, "forgot" to send life-giving rain at
Paw Paw's appointed time. Maybe God just got tired of
being told. If Elise was secretly glad for a divine excuse
to disobey Paw Paw's orders—I never heard. Except that
once, when Elise made reference to "ground as hard as
this floor" and dared laugh—before she cut careful eyes
toward Paw-Paw, watching to see what price the Pioneer's
wife might pay once the young reporter left.

Paw-Paw told that same reporter that he owned not
just the original 160 acres he pioneered but, by then, he
owned nearly 1000 hungry-earned acres of flat dry prairie out where none but God sheltered a woman and her
children from sun, fire, or fury. For years, Elise and her
children were all but abandoned out there on the Home
Place, where day after day Elise's children ate beans and
made do, while Paw-Paw, safe and well-fed in Black Tower

with Elise's daughters to do for him, held back cash to feed his hungry lust for land.

How could I have imagined such cruelty began with me?

. . .

Paw-Paw raised his sons in his image. None escaped unscathed. Emanuel—the oldest, but never Paw-Paw's favorite, smothered literally and figuratively by his brother Johan—left home as soon as he was able. Harvey escaped to Texas in his early teens. A male survivor, like my own brothers, he struggled all his adult life in the afterglow of his cruel childhood.

I've heard there was a grandson, a cousin of my generation, left too long with Paw-Paw. It is said that child grew up to follow in Paw Paw's footsteps and then "disappeared"—perhaps into prison. Perhaps his name is one of the 900,000+ names listed on America's ever-burgeoning Sex Offender Registries. Who knows?

For his part, my father claimed they never again used him "like a girl" because he soon learned to outrun and outwit his brothers.

"I gave as good as I got," Dad said. Tit for tat, cruelty for cruelty. But maybe that was only after Dad's friendly little puppy bled to death.

Dad told my son Benny that when he was about five, he owned a friendly little puppy—a warm, squirming, adoring little thing. Something all his own to pet, play with and protect out there on the farm where toys were nonexistent, and children's clothing, threadbare hand-me-downs, belonged to no one child for long.

One day, as Paw-Paw sawed and hammered, repairing the chicken coop, intent upon getting back to Black Tower before dark, Dad's bright little puppy wiggled out of my father's lap and crept too close, wagging his friendly tail; his bright eyes watching Paw-Paw saw and hammer.

Paw-Paw bent down. The puppy's tail struck Paw-Paw across the face. Without a word, Paw-Paw picked up an axe and chopped off the puppy's tail. The whimpering, beseeching the little thing crept back into Dad's lap and bled to death in my father's arms. Dad wept as his brothers danced around laughing at his tears, jeering, calling out "Sissy!" "Pansy," aping Paw-Paw, hoping for his approval.

As for Dad's puppy? Dad claimed courage to retaliate for his puppy's death. One day, when his brother Johan was using the outhouse, Dad threw a board studded with sharp nails over the top of the outhouse door.

The heavy board struck Paw-Paw's favorite and wedged the door shut just long enough for Dad to run to the house. Once Johan managed to pull up his pants and pry the door open, he came barging into the kitchen, looking to retaliate—but Elise intervened, "Go back outside. Can't you see Carl's helping me here?"

It was Dad's turn to smirk and gloat. His the victory, for a little while at least.

I don't know if at that moment my father switched from being a tormented child to one who felt the joyous frisson of a tormentor as he joined the others in gang raping, abusing, and taunting Harvey. Years after young Andrew's disappearance, my father, too, "disappeared." Lost, then somehow reborn conflicted, a predator, a trickster, he was a little boy traumatized, offered no help, his manhood remade in the cruel image of Paw-Paw.

With time, my father's telling and retelling of his Puppy Story became a trickster's tale, told strategically in order to engender sympathy, loyalty, and understanding in the tender hearted. Dad used his tales to soften hearts, enthrall listeners, to justify and thereby absolve himself of his own legacy of cruelty passed down. A man who smiled at the world, behind closed doors my Dad, too, showed us all a Wolf's face.

But still, all my life something in me did feel sorry for my father. I blamed myself. I too wished I could soothe and somehow earn approval. Enthralled, I would have done anything to make up to him for the pain he suffered out there on the Home Place as a boy-child used like a girl.

Afterwards labeled "Pansy," "Sissy-Boy," his abusers said his manhood was rendered suspect by the very abuse they heaped upon him. They said his abuse was his fault. They told him that he, too, just naturally attracted the abuse visited upon him and, in an exercise in circular homophobic reasoning, they claimed that the very fact that they had abused him proved he was a "Pansy," a "Pervert," a "Sissy-Boy," biased words branding him as innately unworthy of a 'real' manhood like their own.

As a girl-child, "treated like a girl," molested and abused, forced to submit and forget, Good Spankings showed girls "treated like girls" their woman's place in a Paw-Paw world. My father told me I, too, had attracted cruelty. I'd "asked for it." Like his abusers, in blaming me, he absolved himself of blame. Handed down, the legacy of shame, blame and bullying twists and silences all our lives unless we change the cruel words we use and thereby, change the way we think and act.

My mother and grandmothers carefully taught me to take a woman's place, to aspire to be a submissive "nice"wife. "Don't think about it" was their formula for happiness, as if it were not the commission of the crime, but thinking of "it," which was the root-cause of a woman's unhappiness. Dis-remembering, smiling through, was their formula to avoid recognizing even the shadow of crimes committed.

"Just don't think about 'it.' Don't make yourself unhappy," made twisted sense when the unspoken corollary was, "In any case, there is nothing to be done about it. He will call you a liar. You will be shamed and blamed. Scapegoated and cast out."

And of course they were right.

"Pitchforks and burning torches?" Well, maybe, but it's the indelible labels and the fear of being skinned alive by their words that silences us, one and all.

But time passes. Courage has its own rewards.

So at 3 a.m. that cold April morning, after my father's funeral, I began to think about the unhappy, silenced things that went on for years out there on the Home Place, unnamed and unacknowledged cruelties that did not begin with me but echoed, echo still, down through my life and the lives of my children and grandchildren.

Memories flew unbidden from Pandora's Box and with them came guilt, regret, and shame. But with them also came a resolve to continue connecting the dots. For if the unspeakable didn't begin with me, how might I hope to prevent the future if I, too, chose to leave the genesis of cruelty and powerlessness unexamined; if I, too, used the old language of the mob to prevent thinking about the future? If I, too, agreed to go silent to my grave?

• • •

Perhaps someone in Black Tower dared to think about Paw-Paw and his little town wife. There were whispers, loose talk, speculation about the crimes committed in Paw-Paw's house. After all, Carrie was growing up, still Paw Paw's little town wife, while Paw Paw's wife, humiliated, called Mule, was left virtually abandoned out on the Home Place.

When teenage Carrie suddenly gained weight in all the wrong places, Paw-Paw's solution was to send his little town wife by train to California to a mother-and-baby home. Carrie returned slimmer, sadder and childless. Afterwards Paw-Paw built a separate little house for Carrie and Olive, nextdoor to his house in town. That done, eventually Paw-Paw moved Elise, my father, and the rest into Black Tower to live with him, thus, effectively silencing the gossips.

Paw-Paw, the Pioneer, told the reporter he moved his family to town because Elise failed to make crop several dry years in a row. And it is true the ground was hard as a floor as the rains failed and the Dust Bowl encroached. It's true that Elise had long watched her fields swirl away to form walls of dust blocking out the sun. But absent loose talk and knowing looks, there's no telling how long Paw-Paw's arrangement might have continued.

Once moved into town, Elva, taken out of school when Rose was born, was finally allowed to graduate with my father's class. Rose, always delicate, married young, gave birth to two little girls but died when her little girls were mere babies themselves. Growing up, I fear, Rose's little girls also spent too much time alone with Paw-Paw in his backyard shop in Black Tower.

After her mystery trip to California, Paw-Paw sent Carrie to secretarial school and then married her to a rich old man. The Aunt Carrie I remember was a cranky old woman forever waving and "shoo-shooing" me away from her prized knickknacks. She always said she'd never wanted children anyway.

Dad's sister Olive, Elise's second daughter, also taken to town as a child to do for Paw-Paw, spent her adult life in the company of too-generous old men with lecherous eyes, men she said were just friends, old men my Dad said chased him around as a teenager.

Paw-Paw's boys hired out on combining crews or worked on the railroad. Dad hated that the combine crews bunked together on the road. After graduation, Dad read law and clerked for an attorney in Black Tower, but he couldn't earn money enough to finish reading law and pass the bar.

Dad tried. He hired out cleaning houses, doing woman's work with his sisters for nineteen cents an hour. Dad ignored the by now familiar jeers of Paw-Paw and his brothers but he was eventually starved out. Defeated in his hope of becoming an attorney, Dad joined the combine crews, forced once again to bunk with the hated tormentors of his childhood.

Meanwhile, Paw Paw's nearly 1,000 acres swirled away across the prairie.

The Great Depression wore on.

In spite of everything, Elise's children persisted.

They had to.

Then, in Pandora's Box, I found an amazing picture of my father taken in 1939. It's the picture of a smiling, blond young man, leaning back against the first car he ever owned. At the time, Dad was a Steel Foreman for Brown Brothers Construction in Kansas City. No longer forced to bunk with the hated combine crew, Dad finally had a city job earning a Man's Salary.

A year or so later the smiling young man in the picture met my mother. Both were passengers on the Santa Fe Super Chief. Dad was riding back from steel work in Kansas City. Mama was returning to her woman's job as personal secretary to the head of Bell Telephone Co. in Oklahoma City.

"We just hit it off," Mama said.

"We fell in love, just like in the storybooks," she told me.

I'm sure the persona Mama fell in love with was that of the charming young man projecting such hopeful pride, smiling, leaning back against his first car, happy to have a Man's Job at last.

Dad told her his Puppy Story. Mama's tender heart broke.

Enthralled, as time passed, she became as wedded to mothering the five-year-old as she was in love with the man the five-year-old had become.

Of course they "just hit it off." Of course she "just fell in love."

Then, the man she met on the train, invited her to visit his family in Black Tower.

Here was Prince Charming, come at last, to make her romantic dreams come true before the clock said she was too old to fulfill a "woman's destiny," and have children, before she was forever labeled "old maid," and cast aside.

Of course they "just clicked."

Mama, like Elise, like my Grandma Sara, was a Happily-Ever-After-Believer. She believed a nice woman's one true destiny was marriage and children, no matter what happiness or sorrow followed after.

But then, hadn't Mama already waited faithfully, long, fruitless years for Jimmy, her childhood sweetheart, to return?

Sweethearts, their's was a silent declaration,
a promise ring for the future.

Chapter 5

There is an old snapshot of Mama and Jimmy, Mama's childhood sweetheart, taken long ago and treasured for years. Mama is nearly ten, and Jimmy is probably twelve. Sweethearts, theirs was a silent declaration, a promise ring for the future. Children playing house together, the two pushed Mama's youngest brother, Bernie, my grandmother Sara's last child, in a baby carriage down a shady sidewalk in that long ago perfect summer. Mama and Jimmy growing up in Oklahoma City before the leaves fell, before the Great Depression changed everything for Mama and her Jimmy.

In the 1930s, older now and unemployed, Jimmy was still hoping to keep his promise and marry his childhood sweetheart—but to be a husband, a young man had to have a job, must prove himself a Good Provider.

Jimmy searched for work in Oklahoma City but was greeted only with soup lines and discouragement. Desperate, Jimmy joined thousands of other men riding the rails, following rumors of work to far off places.

Jimmy left promising, "I'll write. Once I have a job, I'll send for you. We'll marry, build a house and have children."

Instead, Jimmy disappeared "riding the rails" with thousands of other men hunting for work during the Great Depression. Mama, Jimmy's mother, and his sister watched and waited. Winter became spring, the months turned into years.

For a nice woman—a loyal, loving, romantic woman like Mama—Jimmy's disappearance was both humiliating and heartbreaking. She wanted marriage, a husband, and children. By then, she was thirty. Still, faithful, she waited—then she met a handsome stranger on a train trip. He invited her to visit his family in Black Tower.

"We fell in love," she said years later.

A nice woman, well-schooled by her mother, Mama sought male advice from her boss at Southwestern Bell as to whether she should accept Dad's invitation.

Ignoring Mama's reservations, her boss encouraged the visit.

"It's only a visit," he said, laughing. "Nothing ventured, nothing gained." He too believed "a woman's place" was marriage and family.

Still, Mama hesitated.

Then one morning, the mailman delivered a postcard.

Treasured all these years in Pandora's Box, I discovered the postcard tucked next to that smiling picture of my father leaning back against his first car. On the front sits a puppy with large, soulful eyes. On the back, written in my father's hand, "I feel lonesome as this Pup."

What could be less threatening, more in need of a woman's loving kindness, than an abandoned puppy?

But then, fate arrives silently: a butterfly's wing, a ginger cat's tale, a Puppy Story. Two strangers meet on a long lonesome train ride; love's romantic beginning before the clock stopped, before time ran out.

Brushing aside her reservations, Mama bought a ticket to Black Tower.

After all, she told herself, hadn't her own mother, Sara, fallen in love at first sight, and married a stranger at seventeen? Here was Mama, nearly twice the age Sara was when she wed. Here was Mama, an aging "office girl," a near-old maid, still loyal, still waiting and watching for the uncertain return of a disappeared sweetheart.

• • •

In my mother's family, romantic stories abound. My darling grandmother Sara, my mother's mother, told stories of falling in love at seventeen with Bernard, a stranger, the son—or the grandson, or maybe even the great grandson—of the Perhaps Italian Lady, another of Sara's romantic falling-in-love stories my mother grew up hearing.

Sara and Bernard did marry, and according to Sara, despite their disparity in station—Bernard a coal miner, Sara, the daughter of the mine's superintendent—the two lived Happily-Ever-After in spite of sorrow.

Sara said, "It was love at first sight."

Still, perhaps there was more left unsaid, even in Sara's love story.

. . .

Bernard first noticed slender young Sara walking home from school in the company of her sisters. Laughing, the sisters spoke in anticipation of skating parties, of gliding across the thin ice on the arm of a handsome young stranger once the ponds froze. Smitten at first sight but smeared with coal dust, just up from his shift in the mines, Bernard followed the laughing girls. He watched as the sisters entered the front door of the mine superintendent's fine house.

Undaunted, Bernard thought, surely the ice skates I saw yesterday in the cobbler's window would fit her dainty feet? He went back to his miner's lodging, polished his brown skates, pawned his father's gold pocket watch, and bought ice skates for young Sara. After that, Bernard saved every penny in anticipation of the first hard freeze, the first skating parties. He hoped against hope to arrange a chance meeting on the ice.

That winter, Sara and Bernard did indeed, meet by chance on the ice.

Sara said, "We just hit it off."

Bernard gave Sara a pair of ice skates. The two skated all winter long with a party of her friends. Sara gliding across thin ice on the arm of her handsome young man, Sara twirling and smiling at the daring young man Sara said she fell in love with at first sight.

Bernard soon asked the mine superintendent for his daughter's hand in marriage. Eventually, all was arranged. Their engagement pictures show a handsome, dark-haired man and a graceful seventeen-year-old girl, one of a family of stylish girls from a prosperous, straight-laced family lately come to America from Scotland.

In spite of social disparity, the mine superintendent gave Sara's hand in marriage. But perhaps her father consented, not only because the two had fallen in love, but because of a more compelling, little-mentioned, connection between the two families.

For, while Sara and Bernard's marriage was indeed a love match, Bernard's family, like the Mackies themselves, were assimilated Jews. In a well-hidden past, the Mackies had spelled their name Mackiowitz.

The Mackies emigrated from Eastern Europe and its pogroms when Scotland first allowed the entry of Jews needed to manage Scottish tin and then coal mines. Once in Scotland, the Mackies anglicized their name and assimilated, glad to escape the organized massacres, the pogroms, common in the east. Escaped, the Mackiowitz became staunch Presbyterians in the centuries before America beckoned.

Bernard, on the other hand, was the descendant of the Perhaps Italian Lady.

Sara whispered a love story about a Jewish woman named Roxanne on Bernard's side of the family. Roxanne, she said, eloped with a priest and came to Philadelphia before the American Revolution. Sara retooled the tale of Roxanne, the Perhaps Italian Lady, in order to make what she referred to as Bernard's mixed bag Jewish heritage respectably romantic. Who knows what Sara left out in the telling?

For centuries, a perfect veneer was the seamless shield handed down generation to generation by women in our family, a shield intended to protect family from targeting and worse, indelibly stamped by older fears of a family fleeing pogroms. While Sara was a very well brought up respectable girl, kind and in love with Bernard, Sara was further steeped in the prejudices and romanticism of Edwardian times.

When I caught sight of the striking young woman with tight black curls and fuzzy hair, a woman with remarkable light eyes pictured in the sepia photograph, I recognized Roxanne as Sara's Perhaps Italian Lady. When I drew Roxanne's picture from Dad's tattered box, I looked into her eyes and I knew. I had only seen such eyes in black women carrying a lot of light blood.

Paw-Paw would instantly have judged, "Tainted blood."

Roxanne's eyes were the eyes of a North African Sephardic Jewess whose family came to the new world by way of Italy, mere centuries after Iberian Jews fled to North African shores to escape Spain's fearful Catholic Inquisition. I recognized Roxanne as one of the obscured Jewish women, a perhaps one-drop woman, descended from Bernard's side of Mama's family.

But, of course, Sara's family, too, had their share of dangerous secrets, retooled and retold to ensure protection. Mackie women hid their stories. Memory of fear hidden deep, taught succeeding generations the necessity of hiding even rearranged secrets beneath a protective veneer of respectability. And for good reason. Prejudice against Jews, like prejudice against blacks, was, then as now, dangerously entrenched in the Eurocentric psyche of America's white, Protestant forefathers.

When recounting her courtship, Sara only remembered how clean, how fastidious her dark haired Bernard was. She said Bernard was "noticing," attentive and kind toward her even during the most difficult times of their long marriage. Although my mother sometimes referred to Bernard as "high-tempered," Mama never actually said her father was "a drinker." That went too far. That infringed upon Men's Business.

Sara, a well off mine superintendent's daughter, had far more options available to her than Elise. For Elise, it was religious belief and Paw-Paw's cruelties that stifled thought, smothered speech. For Sara, it was her insistence upon Happily-Ever-After, and the preservation of family at all costs which prevented Sara from dwelling upon Men's Business.

"Just don't think about it," Sara said. But then, it was also my darling Sara who told me the story of the Perhaps Italian Lady, carefully keeping family history alive into the next generation.

But then the Mackies hid dangerous secrets all their own.

Chapter 6

*Once Bernard and Sara married, their children came in
quick succession. The first, born in 1895, was called Leo,
after Bernard's father Piolet.*

When Leo was still a smiling baby in bright curls, not
yet graduated into long pants, he fell backward into a
washtub of boiling water. Rescued too late, Leo could not
be comforted. His skin peeled away. Infection gathered.
Gradually, Sara's once shining little son fell deathly silent.
Leo died slowly as a grieving Sara watched, helpless.

Sara accused herself during Leo's lingering, pain-filled
days.

But then aren't all women taught as an act of faith that
mother-love is the magic that automatically protects? If
loved enough, the children of nice wives, good mothers,
won't die from war or suicide or scalding, won't die of
misadventure or influenza or ovarian cancer. Won't suffer sexual abuse at their fathers' hands. If only we love
enough, they will be safe in spite of everything. Isn't that
why women guard family secrets, keep on trying, hoping,
praying? Isn't that why women "just don't think about it?"

Sara's second son, Ernest, was born in 1897. Duncan,
their third son, was born in 1899. Following Duncan's
birth, Sara's first daughter, Rebeka, was born in 1902. Then
a daughter, Marie, was born in 1904. Marie, the baby girl
who, Sara said, died "before she hardly drew breath."

The same year Sara's little girl died, Sara and Bernard
lived through the Bonanza Race Wars. Prejudice against
blacks and Jews ran rampant, mirroring the pogroms of

Eastern Europe. Only the thinnest veneer and their white skin shielded the young family from what was to come.

· · ·

In 1904, Barnard was one of 500 white miners digging coal in a mine that Sara's father superintended for the Central Coal and Coke Company in Arkansas. Conditions down in the Bonanza mines were fit for neither man nor beast. When it seemed that labor unrest might cause work stoppages and curtail the owner's income, management leased chain gangs of black men sentenced to jails all over the South and brought them in to dig coal in place of white miners like Bernard.

The new legal slavery was stark testimony to the continuing failure of reconstruction in post-civil war America where the Ku Klux Klan organized race hatred pitting black and white miners against each other to the enduring benefit of the owners of Central Coal and Coke and canny superintendents like Sara's father.

On the night of April 27, 1904, 200 Klansmen met and posted their demand that the approximately forty "Negrah" prisoners leased by Central Coal and Coke leave Bonanza or be "forcibly removed." Night Riders brought burning torches and hanging ropes. By morning, all the blacks in Bonanza were indeed "removed." Black men were slaughtered outright, many chased down and summarily hung in the woods as they tried to outrun the Ku Klux Klan.

By early May 1904, newspapers reported the Bonanza Race War was at an end. Newspapers proclaimed Bonanza was safely under Jim Crow Law, transformed into a "sundown" town. On pain of death no one with 'tainted blood' roamed Bonanza's whites-only streets after sundown. Business as usual. "Now," they said, "white women are safe."

Bernard's father, Piolet, fought on the Union side to free the slaves in Lincoln's Civil War yet who knows what part Bernard played in the unrest? But with a lynch mob rampant in Bonanza, had it been known they were a family of Jews, assimilated or not, there would have been real reason to fear night riders.

For in Bonanza, as all over Northern Europe, Aryan blood pride stoked rampant prejudice. The ever-present threat of violent reprisal lay coiled just beneath the smiling veneer of respectable white society. But if there were loose talk and hate speech, intimations of Jewish blood, might not vigilantes strike even the children of a mine superintendents' daughter?

. . .

After the Bonanza Race War, Bernard quit Central Coal and Coke. He never again mined coal or worked for Sara's father. In making this decision, Bernard cut off all possibility of money and quick advancement he might otherwise have enjoyed. In following her husband, Sara, too, broke with family, but not with romantic tradition. A good wife, Sara followed Bernard away from Central Coal and Coke, forsaking all others like Ruth of old.

In 1906—the same year that Elise farmed the lake in Waurika, Oklahoma and presented Paw-Paw with his forever-favored son, Johan—Sara and Bernard's young family arrived in Oklahoma, just in time for Bernard to stake his claim to land in the waning days of the Oklahoma Land Rush.

On the appointed day, eager white men lined up by the thousands racing to claim Indian lands in the soon-to-be-State of Oklahoma.

Bernard too, "rushed." He staked a claim. Unlike Paw-Paw, Bernard was not land hungry; he didn't hoard money or lust to own even 160 acres. Instead, he traded his unimproved claim for several acres in Oklahoma City. There, after ten years of marriage, Bernard built Sara a home of her own.

The family barely settled in before a son, John, was
born. As the story goes, Bernard heard John's first cry just
as he "nailed the final shingle onto the peaked roof" of
Sara's house at #2211 Pawnee. Not long after, in 1909,
my mother drew breath. Sara named Mama Marie after
that first little Marie, the baby who died. Liza was born in
1914. In 1916, Sara, by then forty, delivered her last child,
a son. She named him Bernard after his father. The well-
loved little boy was called Bernie by the whole family.

· · ·

When he worked on Studebakers, Sara's husband
Bernard swore and threw tools across the back yard.
When Mama was little, she lost her temper, threw her doll,
and spouted the same swear words she'd learned from
Bernard. Mama said she still remembered Sara's spanking
all those years later. Sara raised "nice little girls" safely cut
to pattern. Sara said, "Nice little girls don't talk like that."
Nice women with nice manners fit safely into nice neighborhoods. The children of nice women are safe.

Once, when Mama was about ten, she told Sara about
the broken whiskey bottles she'd discovered behind the
wardrobe in her Brother John's room, a sort of secret club-
house where John and her sweetheart Jimmy passed afternoons together.

"Men's Business," Sara scolded.

All nice girls knew to steer clear of Men's Business.
Not-nice girls knew all about that sort of thing. Not-nice
girls got bad reputations, were bad—and bad girls, Sara
said, never, never marry Prince Charming.

"Mind your P's and Q's."

"Act like a lady."

"But…"

Sara sighed, "At least, try!"

My grandmother did her best to impart the lessons of
the Happily-Ever-After Believer to me. But I was often too,
too angry and nice girls must never show anger. On her

summer visits, even my darling Grandma Sara sometimes resorted to willow switch spankings that turned my legs to fire.

"It's for your own good," Sara said reminding a recalcitrant little girl to "Be nice!" "Behave!" "Be quiet."

Grandma Sara's willow switch was intended to turn me into an obedient wife who minded her P's and Q's, steered safely clear of Men's Business, and never, ever nagged Prince Charming into having to reteach a wife forgotten childhood lessons.

"No one in our family ever divorced," Sara said, an ancient dictum which, I now realize, was passed down mother to daughter back then as necessary to preserve and maintain a husband's protection and a family's survival in an often violent world.

"Pray about it," said Elise, retying the ribbons of her little white prayer cap. But then the power of prayer was the only power left Elise by her "unthoughtful" husband.

"Don't think about it," Mama said. "Don't make yourself unhappy."

But still, I often found myself unaccountably angry.

"Snarky," Sara called it.

"You are just like your father," Mama said.

"Am not!"

Safer to back-talk Mama, or even to displease Grandma Sara, than risk telling stories of Wolf-shadows coming down the hall in the dead of night. Wolf-shadows waiting, waiting, in gathering darkness.

· · ·

In 1918, when Sara's much-loved youngest son, Bernie, was barely two, Sara's oldest son Ernest enlisted in the US Army and went off to fight in the First World War.

"The War to End all Wars," the recruiting posters promised.

My mother remembered sitting with Grandma Sara on the front porch at #2211 Pawnee in the early morning cool, while Sara waited for the newspaper to arrive. Mama remembered watching Sara run a trembling finger down each new day's list of war dead, afraid this time she would find her son's name among the dead. Sara waited every day, my mother said, until, at long last, Ernest returned home safe from mustard gas, barbed wire, and bullets—finally safe from death in the trenches on the Western Front.

While Sara waited on the front porch, in the bedroom behind them Sara's son Duncan, barely eighteen, died in his bed from the Spanish Flu. The Spanish Flu killed more people than Wilson's War to End All Wars but no newspaper dared publish the death toll from Spanish Flue. President Wilson ordered the mounting civilian deaths kept secret "for the sake of the war effort."

A distraught Sara smiled in public for her children's sake. In secret, Sara wept.

• • •

The Roaring Twenties roared on in spite of the end of WWI. The women's vote, gained in the 1920's, was supposed to civilize the political process, end drunkenness and protect children from their father's cruelty.

After WWI, Soldiers returned to a different world. In the risky years leading up to the Great Depression and on toward the Second World War, labor unrest continued. Bosses got richer. Henry Ford's assembly lines required mind-numbing repetition and denied work to skilled workmen like Sara's Bernard. The Man from Cripple Creek, Sara's Good Provider who had once blasted and dug his way through mountains of coal, who rushed for land and built a home for Sara, was made redundant. No one valued a middle aged man adept at building things from scratch.

No owner willingly paid a living wage to white or black, no matter how divided.

• • •

Mama said she never realized how poor her family was because, on cold nights, when Sara spread coats over her children's beds to keep them warm, she told her children to pray for other little children down the street. Because, Sara said, "they aren't lucky enough to have coats to keep them warm at night." When Sara's family ran out of food, Sara sifted grain bought to feed their cow and cooked porridge for her children to spoon up with the cow's milk.

"We managed," Mama said. "It'll hold us over" was a phrase I heard whenever we too "ran short" in my childhood.

Sara said, "Marry a Good Provider," as she taught me to carefully scrape the last bit of goodness out of every mixing bowl. "Waste not, want not," Sara said as she wiped the last bit of margarine off the wrapper and onto my waiting slice of bread. It was a sentiment Elise also would have appreciated, as she stretched beans to feed her brood. To describe a woman as "saving" was high praise indeed.

My father remembered his poverty with bitterness. He so hated the memory of eating beans as a child that, even when he was a very well-off old man, he shouted at the cooks at the Senior Center if they dared ladle pinto beans onto his plate. While mama's family thought of poverty as "running short"—a temporary thing to be temporarily endured—my father, denied both food and safety in childhood, forever experienced himself as impoverished at the core of his being. Like a bucket with a hole in the bottom, he took and took but never felt himself full.

No matter the harms done, the person Dad felt most sorry for was himself. Everyone should overlook and forgive. No son or daughter Dad "treated like a girl" could claim to have been as cruelly harmed as he had once been as a child.

My father was perpetually jealous of Mama's love for my brother Bayard. Perhaps Paw-Paw was forever resentful of Elise's love for the adult son, Elise's letters, always addressed as "My Dearly Beloved Carl." Perhaps the same cruel resentment led to Andrew's "disappearance" out there in the barn in Nebraska?

In any case, as an adult, for whatever reason, my father may have "prayed about it" but he never chose to restrain himself or find ways to grow past his bad childhood. Again and again, he acted upon base impulse, blamed others and moved on.

But then, had he reached out and asked for help before or even after he acted, what help would have been available? Would abiding prejudice and more cruelty have been the only result? "Once a sex offender, always a sex offender" is a dictum too often used to elect politicians, empower lynch mobs and justify registries. Full of sound and fury, calls for ever more draconian punishment often impede successful intervention.

. . .

Jealousy and resentment handed down, father to son. Cruelty justified. Given such perpetual resentment in the man she loved, what nice wife or loving mother could have hoped to love enough to satisfy?

Mama said that when her "high-tempered" father forgot himself and swore at the dinner table, Sara always said, "Why, Bernard!" in shocked tones, as though she had never before heard her husband swear.

Just so, my mother always said, "Why, Carl!" in probably the same shocked tones when my father hit her, as though each blow were the first. So well trained were nice women at "forgetting" that each time may, indeed, have felt like a fresh wound opened.

I don't know if Bernard ever hit Sara; I doubt it.

But well-trained, nice little girls learn never to inquire. Nice women know to forgive and forget. They try harder, resolve to love better, pray more, and keep their family safely together.

"A good wife is the last to know."

Saying, "Sorry," keeping family together, is the wife's duty.

Perhaps leaving a little money in trust for his great-grandson's college tuition was my father's way of saying, "Sorry." If so, I'm grateful. If it was Dad's way of achieving his college ambitions through them, I'm still grateful he offered his great grandsons chances denied him by Paw-Paw.

Sara and Bernard, poor as they often were, managed to eke out enough to send Ernest, Bernie, John, Liza, and my mother to college at a time when attending even one year of college ensured a cherished child's future. Even though Paw-Paw starved out my father, he chose to send Carrie, his favorite little town wife, to secretarial school once she returned childless from California. But then maybe Paw-Paw intended to ensure not Carrie's future but her continuing silence?

Between two wars, Ernest married and had two daughters. Mama and Jimmy fell in love. And Sara's oldest daughter, Rebeka, met and soon married a "daring young flyboy." Charley was a WWI pilot lately returned from strafing and bombing Germans. Sara told me romantic tales of Rebeka, Sara's perfect example of a marriage for me to emulate, should my own Prince Charming ever arrive.

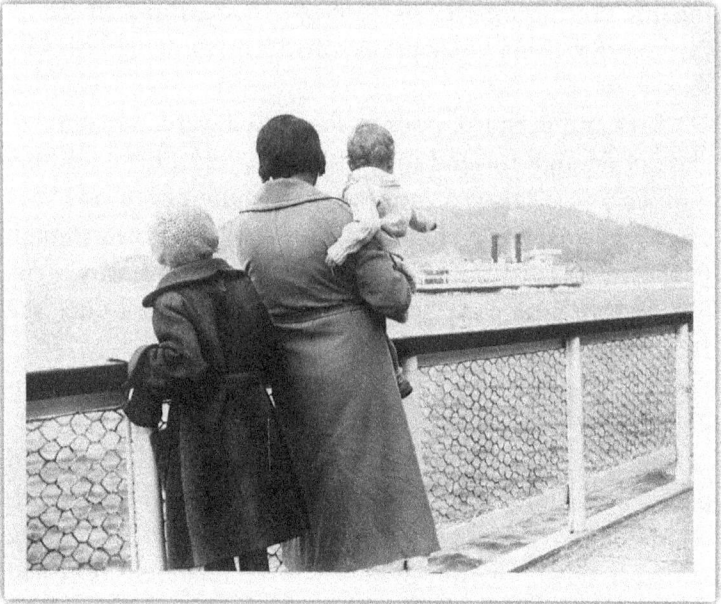

Rebeka says to tell you not to worry. Things are going to be alright.

PART II: THESE THE LOVE STORIES,
THESE THE UNFORTUNATE CONNECTIONS

Chapter 7

As *Sara's story goes, Rebeka loved Charley and Charley loved Rebeka. According to Sara, Rebeka was everything a nice wife ought to be.* For his part, Rebeka's Charley was a brave, handsome Prince Charming, one of the intrepid WWI fliers who later invented air mail, and started air freight. Adventurous dare devils like Rebeka's Charley explored the wild blue yonder between two wars while their adoring wives asked no questions, made no demands.

Even when ill, such wives brushed aside their pain to loyally await their husbands' return from tending to Men's Business out in the big world. Rebeka was Charley's perfect wife, the ideal Sara hoped we all would grow up and follow.

Just as Elise followed Paw-Paw to Black Tower, just as Sara followed Bernard away from Bonanza, Rebeka followed her Charley from airfield to airfield. A good wife, Rebeka tended his children, cooked, cleaned, kept house, and waited faithfully for her Charley's return.

According to Sara, when Charley came home from his adventures, Rebeka never complained, never mentioned illness. Never said how lonely the waiting had been. She never said she was afraid to sleep alone in their wide bed all those long nights when her Charlie was off flying.

While there is no question Rebeka loved Charley, and no doubt Charley loved Rebeka, I wonder if sometimes even Rebeka suspected her Charley might love the wild blue sky just a little more? But as the perfect wife, Rebeka watched and waited for her hero's return. Yet even the

perfect wife worried when her Charley's plane was overdue, must have searched the empty sky, but bit her tongue
when her hero finally returned?

Still, it wasn't Charley's fate, but Rebeka's, that led
to the most grief. Rebeka's fate led to profound changes,
changes which reverberated down into my life as well.

...

*In 1921, Mama said she traveled to Tulsa to keep a
pregnant Rebeka company while Charley was off flying.*
While there, Mama made friends with a neighbor girl.

The two girls played hide and seek from closet to closet
in the girl's house. Hanging there in the back of the parents' closet, my mother discovered the imperial robes of
a Ku Klux Klan Wizard, complete with peaked hood and
vacant eyeholes.

What might have happened had Mama told her friend
Sara's whispered story of the "Perhaps Italian Lady" whose
Jewish blood also ran in Mama's veins? What if the KKK
Wizard had learned of the perhaps-one-drop story?

Luckily, already well-schooled in the necessity of protecting family, at twelve Mama knew the virtue of silence.

For in 1921 virulent prejudice once again ignited mob
violence, this time in Tulsa. Rebeka's Charley was flying air
mail cross country out of Tulsa's Curtis Southwest Airport.
During the Tulsa Race Riots of 1921, pilots employed
by Curtis Southwest were leased to the city of Tulsa.
Charley, already experienced in the bombing and strafing
of Germans during WWI, was one of the pilots hired by
the city of Tulsa to strafe and fire bomb prosperous Blacks
during the terrible days of Tulsa's Greenwood Race Wars.

Just as in the Bonanza Race War, white newspapers
referred to the "unrest," in Tulsa as "race hatred." Few
dared call it Aryan Blood Pride. No one dared imagine
pogrom. Few admitted that poor whites, already pushed
to the bottom of the ladder, would not countenance blacks
to prosper, perhaps move up past them.

In America's splintered under classes none dared say that black lives did matter. The roles of Blacks, Jews, Mexicans, Indians, and well-brought-up white women were fixed in place. "Biblical," preachers said. Should "those people" try to rise above their station, "get uppity," of course violent consequences righteously followed.

According to Whites, the openly prosperous Black residents of Greenwood "got above themselves." To teach Blacks their place, Tulsa's White leadership hired experienced pilots like Charley, unleashed the lynch mob and put uppity Blacks back in their place. As in Bonanza, rightful order was restored. Death reigned.

"They asked for it."

For white Americans born of respectable parentage, espousing correct beliefs and Aryan blood, all was, once again, set right with the world. Afterward, Americans conveniently forgot Tulsa, just as they had quickly forgotten Bonanza.

As the Mackie women well knew, best to attract little notice. "Don't make yourself unhappy. Don't think about it." Whether political or personal, remembering history, like telling the story of The Perhaps Italian Lady, like speaking up, like connecting the social "dots" that support the continuing legacy of sexual assault, breaking the silence is, indeed, "asking for it."

A family's safety all too often depends upon teaching silence from the beginning.

· · ·

Soon after Rebeka's Charley strafed and firebombed Greenwood, Charley quit flying for Curtis Southwest. He found work managing Grand Central Charter Services in Glendale, California. Rebeka loyally followed her Charley halfway across America, taking her two daughters with her.

I found a picture, snapped in 1933 and sent back from California to Sara in Oklahoma City. In that photo,

Rebeka is standing with her first little girl and holding her second baby, leaning against the rail of the Oakland Ferry in that long ago time, before the Golden Gate Bridge spanned California's San Francisco Bay.

In California, Rebeka and her daughters waited while Charley and the other pilots hired by Grand Central flew out over the snow-covered Sierras. Grand Central pilots measured the height of Mount Shasta and mapped Death Valley from the air, completing the first perilous aerial survey of California. Until then, no one had glimpsed the Golden State.

Most of Rebeka's letters, found in the dusty little Pandora's Box my father left me, are brave and funny. Rebeka, Sara's well-brought-up daughter, was, indeed a good wife. Still, alone and far from home, I wonder if Rebeka ever got over her fear of sleeping alone in Charley's wide bed—got over worrying about her Charley out mapping California?

But Charley was not the one Rebeka's family should have worried over. Following the whif of loneliness in Rebeka's letters home, come letters foreshadowing illness. Then a letter, written by Charley one Sunday night in Oakland and sent back to Rebeka's family at #2211 Pawnee:

"Dear Folks. Just left Rebeka, she is getting along as well as can be expected for an operation like hers. She has two special nurses, day and night. They do everything they can to make her easy, but she suffers a lot at that. She will pass the critical point by Tuesday, and from there it will be easy going.

"It is too bad because this could have been done 18 months ago. Had she said something, it would have been a very simple matter then.

"Rebeka says to tell you things are going to be all right, not to worry. "

Charley's letter goes on, "Outside of living on sand-wiches and baked beans, the little girls and I are getting along fine. Will sign off now and write more later."

"Love to all C."

Then, on October 8, 1935, another letter arrived also written in Charlie's hand:

"Mrs. M, the longest month has passed. Just a month ago, Rebeka left us, and it seems like an eternity since she left. If I could just reconcile myself to the fact that she's gone, it might be easier, but I still feel like it's a bad dream. I try not to be morbid, but it is no use. I miss her more than words can tell.

"Liza has sure been wonderful. [Liza, mom's younger sister went by train out to California to help Rebeka after her operation and to cook for Charley] I will be in your debt forever for all the kindness and goodness you people have shown me and mine.

"Tell Marie, [my mother stayed behind at #2211 Pawnee, still awaiting Jimmy's return, working for Bell Telephone and sending money to California.] Tell Marie, to thank Dr. Royer [the Mackie family's Presbyterian minister] for writing such a nice letter. I will answer it later this week. Right now I cannot look at life as he does and might say something I would be sorry for.

"We went down to Olivera St. and had two copies of Rebeka's picture made.

"Well, such is life. The girls are waiting. We are going to the airport and mail this, so I will sign off. Please answer real soon. Love, C. and the family. P.S. Liza is a swell cook. Somebody was kidding about her not being able to cook."

• • •

In early 1936, Sara, Bernard and their twenty-year-old son, Bernie, left Oklahoma to join Rebeka's sister Liza in California. Rebeka's family had come to care for her now-motherless daughters. My mother sent her paychecks to Sara and Bernard to help them care for her nieces.

Although heartbroken and lonely without his perfect Rebeka, Charley soon found a new wife to ease his grief. She was Rebeka's perfect replacement. Unfortunately, Charley's new beloved focused only on her Charley. She had no interest in mothering Rebeka's two little daughters, although perhaps had they been sons Charley might have insisted.

Charley willingly handed over day-to-day care of his daughters to Rebeka's family, however Charley retained legal custody and required that his daughters live close by. Thus Liza, Bernie, Sara and Bernard's temporary visit to California became permanent.

In 1939, Charley signed a contract to map the Argentine Andes, much as he had once mapped California. His mission? To fly through the forbidding, and as yet unexplored, Andes to discover and map air mail routes through the distant heart of Argentina's jagged ice-bound peaks.

But one day Charley's little plane ran short of fuel, sputtered, and fell out of the icy blue sky into the darkness of some frozen crevasse.

Just as Rebeka had waited and prayed for Charley's safe return all those years before, they waited and waited at the airport, straining for some distant sound, some glint off Charley's wing tip, signaling his return, but to no avail.

Charley, it seemed, had dared Fate once too often.

"Such is life," Charley said.

They died as they lived; Rebeka, forever the nice wife, Charley, forever Rebeka's intrepid hero, Prince Charming still flying somewhere out there in the blue beyond.

• • •

Hearing Sara's story, I wanted to imagine Charley found his faithful Rebeka waiting out there somewhere in the wild blue, somewhere above the sun set, somewhere in those mountain passes. His "Home," his Rebeka, still waiting for her Charlie out there in the great beyond.

Hearing Sara's story, I yearned for Happily-Ever-After; I too imagined that if I was nice, if I was loyal, if I just didn't think about it, I might escape home and create a perfect marriage like Rebeka's own.

Sara's story told me, "Nice girls keep quiet. Perfect wives don't make a fuss."

So I tried harder; didn't make a fuss; blamed myself. I waited. Prince Charming would be my escape to Happily-Ever-After. Sadly, I never realized in Sara's Happily-Ever-After, Rebeka wasn't the hero of her own story.

My mother, too, was a Happily-Ever-After-Believer.

She worked and sent her paychecks to California. Left alone at #2211 Pawnee when the rest of her family went to California to raise Rebeka's children, Mama waited for her Jimmy's return. But Jimmy, too, disappeared, never to return. Mama waited and hoped, shamed when her friends at work whispered she was abandoned.

Still, Mama waited.

The silent rooms of #2211 Pawnee must have echoed with the voices of family, the lost laughter of childhood, Jimmy's promises made but not kept, her own family gone to California, never to return. Like Rebeka extolled as the perfect wife, Mama might have gone on waiting—except that, as fate would have it, she met a charming stranger who enthralled her with his puppy stories on a lonesome train ride back from a visit to California. Mama hesitated. But then came the stranger's invitation, to visit—just visit—Black Tower. The stranger's invitation promised one last lucky chance to live Happily-Ever-After.

One last chance, she thought, before time ran out and hope died.

*The newlyweds honeymooned a few days in Paw-Paw's little house.
Then my mother returned alone to Oklahoma City.*

Chapter 8

Fate feeds upon isolation, a sister's loss, a lonesome train ride, a puppy tale. In spite of reservations, Mama, like legions of romantic women before and after her, set off on the only respectable quest allowed nice women.

She went in quest of a husband and children and a home of her own. She went in quest of Sara's Happily-Ever-After, where "try harder" and a good woman's love is a magic talisman with the power to protect children and set even a bad marriage right.

After all, as Sara said, "No woman in our family ever divorced."

According to the announcement posted in the Black Tower news, Elise's pastor performed their marriage ceremony on October 8, 1941. There had been no time to inform, much less invite Mama's scattered family. Announcements came later.

Once arrived, overcome by charm or perhaps by rude insistence, there was no turning back once Prince Charming had his way.

"He swept me off my feet," Mama always said. It was "love at first sight."

How could she say or think otherwise? How could she not have acquiesced?

Raised to expect kindness, prepared to find romance, waiting so long alone at #2211 Pawnee, how could a nice woman not have feared Prince Charming might pass her by?

...

*They wed in Elise's shabby little front room in Black
Tower in the same house where Paw-Paw once brought
Carrie to do for him.*

There, Paw-Paw had built the only fuse box into a wall
above his bed. Every night until he died, Paw-Paw reached
up and flipped the breaker dividing day from night, decree-
ing bedtime for everyone. But Elise, alone in the dark half-
bedroom assigned to her in 1926, stubbornly read her
Bible by candlelight in spite of Paw-Paw.

Paw-Paw's house spoke volumes if you had ears to hear
or eyes to see. I don't know how soon after the wedding
my mother realized that all of Elise's living room furniture
was nailed to the floor. Even the rocking chair was nailed
in place with leather straps arranged just so, no doubt to
facilitate Paw Paw's nocturnal comings and goings.

When I was a child, hooked screen doors and moved
furniture led to endless arguments in our house. Furniture
secretly moved from its appointed place becomes the early
warning system of powerless children.

But what happy bride, swept her off her feet by Prince
Charming, is prepared to contemplate such things? What
Happily-Ever-After-Believer thinks a Wolf sleeps with an
electrical panel above his bed and, God-like, divides Day
from Night in the same little house where she vowed to
love, honor and obey, for richer or poorer, till death do
part."

I'm not certain just when Mama realized the consequences of her decision to visit, and then marry, the man
Elise forever referred to as her "Dearly Beloved Son."

But marry they did.

· · ·

*The newlyweds honeymooned a few days in Paw-
Paw's's little house, then my mother returned alone*
to Oklahoma City to quit her job and empty out #2211
Pawnee, the only home she had ever known.

She packed Sara's things, all hastily left behind when Sara left for Rebeka's funeral but stayed to care for Rebeka's little girls.

It was painful, lonely work.

Just when Mama could bear no more, Jimmy's mother came to help. A mother still waiting for her lost son's return, Jimmy's mother sorted and packed all Sara's precious bits. It was her final gift to the girl who had waited so long for Jimmy's return—a wedding gift to the now-married woman who, had things been different, might have been her daughter-in-law.

From any friend, it would have been a selfless act. From a woman who died still waiting for her only son's return, a woman who might have hoped to be a grandmother to Mama's children, the selfless act was love itself.

Survival in dark days depends upon such acts of kindness.

. . .

Three letters, each addressed to #2211 Pawnee, arrived in quick succession. The first, found in Pandora's Box and dated October 30, 1941, was written by my father's sister Mildred, anxious to reassure the new bride that even though my father showed no emotion when he put Mama on the train, their parting had, indeed, affected my father. In her letter, Mildred wrote.

"When Carl got back from the train I saw it was getting him pretty badly and I said, 'It is a pretty hard bump in the road to let her go, isn't it, Carl?' He couldn't speak, just went into your room and stayed for a while.

"When he came out, he had been crying. He said, 'Guess I really am more of a Pansy than I thought. But, anyway, I kept my chin up 'til the train left!'

"I said that I hoped he hadn't seemed thoughtless toward you. He loves you so much. Paw-Paw is thoughtless of mother, and I can see we all take after him in that way."

Reading Mildred's letter now, I shake my head. To describe Paw-Paw's cruelties as merely "thoughtless" is much like imagining that the euphemistic term "inappropriate touching" adequately describes incest, rape, or the sexual assault of either boys or girls.

Even my father's euphemism "used like a girl" hardly describes the fear male survivors experience when assaulted and bullied, derided and silenced by homophobic threats that tell them just the act of weeping, the experience of being sexually overpowered, reveals homosexuality or has power to change male sexual orientation itself.

Pain trapped in euphemism is effectively silenced. Thus my father, in tears, tells his sister, "Guess I really am more of a Pansy than I thought." For her part, Mildred only dares describe Paw-Paw as "thoughtless."

• • •

Mildred's letter goes on: "Always remember, Marie, we all love you. Even Paw-Paw remarked how he liked you. And that is pretty unusual for him."

It seems that although Paw-Paw did quite uncharacteristically approve of his son's dark-haired bride, Elise had reservations. She judged her beloved son's new bride to be too citified, too inexperienced, to be much help on a farm. Elise pointed out to her daughters that their sister-in-law was "too thin," her hips "too narrow" to bear the numerous healthy children required for farm work.

Conversely, Elise suspected Mama was too experienced in other ways. At 31 and four years older than Elise's cherished son, Elise suspected that Mama had secretly used her wiles to trap her inexperienced youngest son into marriage.

As for my father, he didn't mind being caught between two women jealous for his attention. He well knew how to play both ends against the middle to his advantage.

Following Mildred's letter, there came a gently chiding letter from Sara, still in California:

"I just received your letter. Couldn't say I was surprised. Your letters led me to think you liked him plenty but to give a daughter as fine as you to someone I don't know is what I once did already with Rebeka. Although I do feel everyone should decide for themselves.

"If he is as good and kind as the Danish people I know . . . There was never a kinder husband than Mr. Hansen. He was always so thoughtful of his wife. Kindness is what counts. I read your letter aloud to Dad. He thinks as I do."

Sara's letter goes on:

"We want you to have a home and be happy. You can be happy any place if you are with a husband you love. Of course, we wish you all the happiness. I think, to be contented and happy, a home of your own is the place to find it."

Despite the storied kindness of one father-in-law and the "un-thoughtfulness" of the other, both families unanimously agreed: marriage was indeed forever, no matter what un-thoughtfulness marriage might entail.

· · ·

In his new bride's absence, my father got busy. He sent a telegram quitting his job in the Kansas City steel mills. He put all Mama's savings down on a farm adjacent to Paw-Paw's now near 1,000 acres. In Mama's absence, Dad moved in, arranged the furniture to please himself, purchased cattle and shipped them out to his farm—all, he said, as a surprise for Mama upon her return.

With Dad's purchase of the farm, the couple was instantly deep in debt. "Land poor," they said back then. Mama's savings spent, there was no money to pay the mortgage, none to buy cattle feed, none left to buy food for themselves.

Like Paw-Paw before him, my father decided to work on the railroad to earn cash money. Dad's paycheck would keep the farm afloat.

On December 7, barely two months after my parents wed, the Japanese bombed Pearl Harbor, Congress declared war. Millions signed up for the draft. Neither "railroader" nor "steel mill worker" would have prevented Dad being called up. But my father could now list his occupation as farmer, his status as married.

In his youth, Paw-Paw's family emigrated to avoid conscription in the Prussian army. Elise's Resister Religion still opposed military service except as conscientious objectors.

While Elise never sent any son to war, Sara's sons, Bernie and Ernest, volunteered. Ernest served twice, first in WWI and again as an Army Postal Inspector in the Far East during WWII. Bernie, Sara's youngest, was a captain in the Signal Corps.

With a war on and her farmer-husband away working on the railroad, my city mother, much like her sister Rebeka, was left isolated and alone for weeks on end. Mama had no car, no telephone, and no money. Mama knew no one except her disapproving in-laws. Hers was an isolation calculated to make a new wife grateful for even an unthoughtful husband's return. More grateful especially because such small attentions were rare.

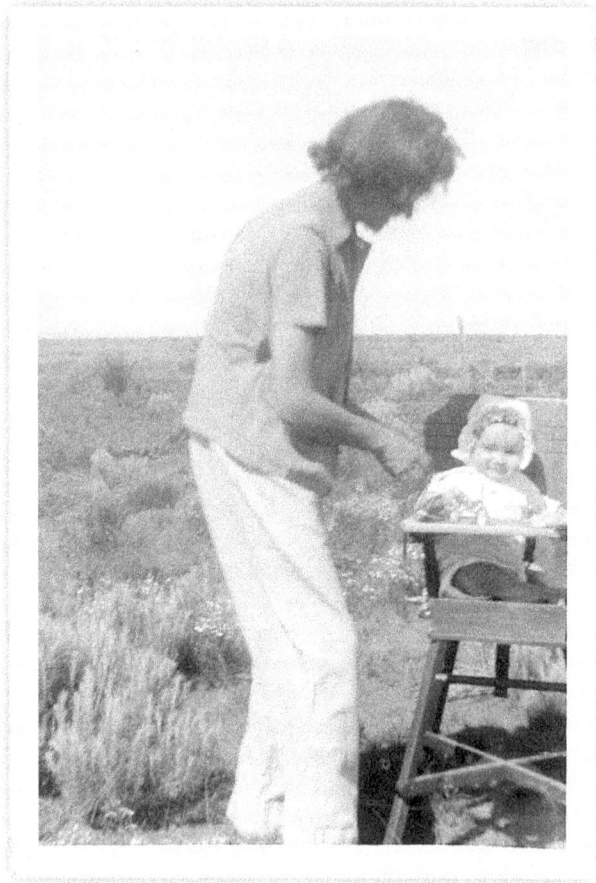

The body remembers long before there are words
or age or courage to speak aloud of such things.

Chapter 9

Born two years later, in 1943, I was their first child—a stubborn, forever- uppity, little girl born, my mother said, with a blaze of black hair sticking out in every direction. Mama always said I looked like a Perhaps Italian baby. Soon all the black hair fell out to be replaced by short, nearly invisible blond hair.

Mama said from a distance I looked bald as an egg. She kept me in baby bonnets long after other children sported curls; not a propitious start for someone expected to grow up and someday become an nice wife with long golden curls.

As on many farms, our barn was built strong and tight, home to rats and mice and feral cats. The construction of the farmhouse itself seemed an afterthought. There were no closets, no real kitchen counters. There weren't even window screens to keep the billion biting horse flies outside.

As a toddler, I remember a well-worn expanse of linoleum covering every floor. My mother's Cherrywood settee sat lonely and abandoned in the echoing shadows of what seemed to me to be a cavernous front room.

In the absence of a playmate, I invented Egypt—an imaginary friend gleaned, I suppose, from Bible stories Mama read to me. Stubborn Egypt and I conspired in whispers. We were Israelites forever planning our escape to a Promised Land free of ogres.

Behind our house, across a vast expanse of burning sand, stood a one-hole outhouse. I lived in perpetual fear of falling in. Egypt flatly refused to pee out there. Convinced I saw rattlesnakes and pharaohs' eyes peering back at me from the smelly black depths, I insisted I'd use the potty-chair in the safety of my bedroom, thank you very much.

Mama protested. She said the potty-chair was smelly too.

But how could Mama expect me to run out across a stretch of burning sand to the ogre's castle? Or even gather courage to first sidle past the black cook stove standing guard just inside the back door? Mama didn't understand that with its one leg propped up on bricks, the tall stove loomed, teetered, and threatened attack.

Mama rolled her eyes. "Just silly, you have way too much imagination."

On the other hand, I loved the cast iron water pump fastened to the end of the kitchen sink. At my urging, Mama pushed the pump's black handle down, and down, and down again until finally, I heard cool water gurgling up from below. Then, to my delight, well water splashed from the mouth of the pump into my waiting glass. Straightaway, I poured the water down the drain and held up my waiting glass again and again.

Finally, tired of pumping, Mama said, "No."

Once refused, I wailed, stuck out my bottom lip, drew myself up and pouted. "Never! Ever!" No nap time for me. Stubborn Egypt agreed.

. . .

My mother had once been an efficient secretary to an important manager at Southwestern Bell Telephone Company. Now, she found her life consumed by farm chores, little girl temper tantrums, and eternal wifely waiting. Cooped up. Isolated. Married. She was reduced to watching out of windows for her husband's return. Like the ever-waiting Rebeka, my mother was left too much alone.

Loneliness, anxiety, uncertainty, such conditions engender in a stay-at-home wife an ever-increasing dependence. They ensure forgiveness.

Isolation welcomes even unthoughtful husbands whenever they choose to return.

⋅ ⋅ ⋅

Once in a while, we visited Paw-Paw's little house in Black Tower.

Ignoring warnings, I tried to tug the little nailed-down rocking chair from its appointed place. I told Mama that my new little imaginary friend, the Little Green Fairy, wanted to rock over by the window too.

"But why can't we rock next to the window?" I wailed.

A sudden electric silence telegraphed, "Be careful. Paw-Paw's looking."

"Never mind." My mother rolled her eyes. "Hush!"

Gradually all the startled aunties relaxed, went back to fixing Paw-Paw's supper.

Careful voices resumed quiet conversations.

Paw-Paw turned back to his newspaper.

Occasionally, while Mama, Egypt, the Little Green Fairy and I all waited impatiently for Daddy's return, the postman dropped a letter from Sara in our mail box out by the road. Once, I remember, Sara's letter included one precious war-time stick of Juicy Fruit gum just for me. Instead, I decided to save it as a present to please my Daddy when he came home.

To keep the stick of gum away from greedy imaginary friends like Egypt and the Little Green Fairy, I handed it over to Mama for safe keeping. I waited and waited with Mama all day in that empty house. I remember the sick, tight knot that gradually grew and grew until both my stomach and my heart ached. Where was Daddy?

The slow tuck, tuck, tuck of the metal wind-up clock echoed in the silent rooms.

That day, Mama taught me how to play Solitaire—a game she called Patience. We played at a table drawn up in front of the window that looked out on the long, empty dirt road that I knew ran on and on past forever, the road that promised to bring my Daddy home.

But I was just a little kid. I kept going back and back, begging Mama for "just one more teensy-weensy little piece" off the end of the stick of Juicy Fruit, until, when Daddy finally arrived home, long after dark, only the teeniest sliver of Juicy Fruit remained.

. . .

Someone once asked me, "When does memory of incest begin?"

Who knows? No matter, the body remembers before there are words or age or courage to speak aloud of such things.

In those early days it began with grooming. Once Dad finally returned home, instead of spending time with his lonely wife, he bathed me then brushed my sparse hair up, Kewpie Doll style.

Mama objected. She said I looked ridiculous.

Young as I was, I knew I did, but I was desperate for Daddy's undivided attention. I wanted so much to please him. I sided with him against Mama.

If that wasn't the beginning of the "inappropriate touching" it certainly was Dad's entering wedge, and the beginning of a toxic estrangement between Mama and me.

He was a husband paying rapt attention to a small daughter, ignoring a wife who waited, watched, and hoped for her husband's love. He played Mama and me off against each other, much as he played Elise and my mother's jealousy to his advantage. Just as much later, Dad, forever afraid of genuine closeness, played the old woman at his funeral, the one who wept and said, "I loved that old man," against the rest of us.

All those years, my mother's aching isolation went unremarked, as though isolation were simply a wife's lot. How dare any nice, well-brought-up woman imagine she was jealous of her small daughter? But isolated and lonely, what nice wife, denied any real life of her own, wouldn't be jealous of her husband's attention?

Mama probably told herself Mildred was right. Dad was far too Manly to show feeling openly.

"Real Men don't cry," they said.

Still say.

Mama followed Sara's advice: "Don't make yourself unhappy."

A good wife, Mama, kept herself busy out there on the farm. Forbidden to "think about it," day after day, Mama did her chores, just as Elise had—and like Elise, like Rebeka too, Mama waited.

She learned to be grateful for small mercies.

• • •

The war brought rationing and long waiting lists. Dad's name was on the list to buy a new car. Mama already had one small child and, at 35, she was dangerously pregnant yet again. There was no phone on the farm, and with no car, she had no reliable way to get to the hospital once contractions began. Dad gave the agency Paw-Paw's phone number to alert them once the car arrived.

Months later the dealer called Paw-Paw. The dealer said Mom and Dad must come quickly and pay cash. If not, he'd sell their car to the next people on his list.

Paw-Paw said, "My son's wife doesn't need a car."

By the time Dad learned of Paw-Paw's refusal, it was too late.

My mother's second baby was also a girl, a baby with curly red hair. This baby girl, like Sara's, died "before she hardly drew breath."

Dad told the family doctor to write his old girlfriend's name, Seri Delores, on the baby's birth certificate. Much later, when I pressed Mama about the baby's name, she went silent. Then she sighed and said, "He said he only ever liked her name."

Who knows? But even at such a remove, this retelling of my father's unthoughtful shaming still shames and embarrasses me. Even now I want to think my father would have been kinder, not so like Paw-Paw.

Soon after Mama's new little girl was born, the doctor wrote the name Seri Delores on that tiny girl-baby's death certificate.

All this before she "hardly drew breath."

I longed for a sister but Mama said my baby girl, "went away to Heaven." The Little Green Fairy refused to believe death was death. I held to the stubborn belief that, if I behaved, if I were good enough, that Stupid Old Stork might relent and fly my little red-headed baby sister back to me.

· · ·

My grieving mother was perhaps too ill to dwell upon humiliation. Mama had developed a visible goiter during this second pregnancy. Soon after my new baby sister went away to heaven, Mama took me and we went away to California to consult a specialist. Sara paid for both the train tickets, and Mama's goiter operation.

It was Christmas, Sara's family came together and Bernie, home on leave from Officer Candidate School, took pictures of me. One photo of me shows a smiling little girl, caught in the act of pulling a fragile decoration off Sara's glittering tree. Another photo shows me holding a Christmas noise-maker.

After Mama's operation, we two returned to Black Tower by train. Wartime trains were full of eager young men on their way to war. They were required to leave on schedule. Arriving a few minutes late, Mama ran to catch her train.

As she drew close, Mama managed to hand me up to the conductor, who then reached out to pull Mama up too. Just then the train lurched forward, picking up speed. Two

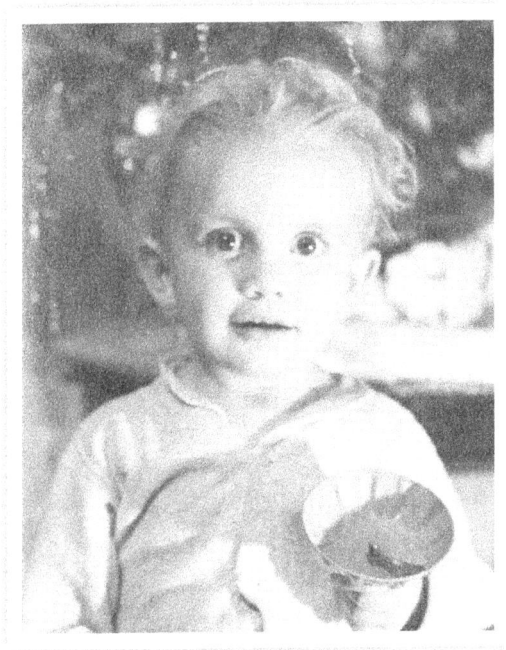

Why did I ever imagine it all began with me?

young soldiers stepped up and between them, they managed to lift Mama onboard.

For years, Mama had terrifying dreams of "losing" me. She dreamed of hands taking me away, just as hands had taken her other baby girl away.

When Mama's train finally arrived in Black Tower, my father wasn't at the station. She waited and waited. Finally, she left her suitcase behind, and carried me across town to Paw-Paw's house, where we waited until Dad finally came.

Days later, Dad broke the news: the check from the sale of #2211 Pawnee arrived while Mama was in California, and just as when Paw-Paw used his unquestioned male authority to deny Mama a car, Dad cashed Mama's check, then promptly spent all the money. He didn't pay off their farm loan or pay down their mounting debts.

Dad spent the money on "good times," driving around impressing the guys, partying with friends. Maybe he even bought a present for his old girlfriend. Who knows? Back then, "boys will be boys" was a saying that covered a multitude of sins.

It may have been the first, but it certainly wasn't the last time my parents fought bitter battles over disappeared money.

Once, after a violent argument, I asked my mother, "When was the very first time Dad hit you?" I wanted, hoped, to hear of an idyllic time before the violence began—an imaginary Happily-Ever-After time, before the hurting began. Perhaps there was a romantic time when my father at least pretended to love her?

Mama looked at me but didn't speak.

I asked again.

Finally, she said, "The first time he hit me, you were in your highchair outside the kitchen door on the farm at Black Tower."

Then she began to weep. Silently, steadily. Forever, it seemed.

In Pandora's Box, I found a picture of me, a bald baby in a ruffled bonnet sitting in a highchair just outside the kitchen where that tall three-legged cook stove waited to ambush little girls. Mama is wearing her city-girl slacks.

Stretching away behind me in my high chair are lonely fields. Always the endless, empty land, the waiting, the long silences and the forever-unthoughtful Wolf cycling toward Black Tower.

• • •

Years later, when my brother told Liza, my mother's sister, about Dad's violence, Liza said she never heard about the squandered check, never knew of the violence, the isolation, that drove my mother to her knees.

For Mama to have told the truth about her marriage, even to her sister Liza, meant humiliating herself.

Well-schooled by Sara's romantic stories, my mother knew in her bones that a good wife deserved a good husband. If a husband wasn't good to his wife, it only meant his wife wasn't good-enough. She plainly hadn't tried hard enough. She had failed to love her husband into loving her back. It was her fault.

"What did you do to cause your husband to hit you?" was the first question even a sympathetic Sara might have asked.

"Turn the other cheek" the church advised from every pulpit.

"A good wife would have known better."

"You made your bed."

"No one in our family ever divorced."

"Don't make yourself unhappy. Don't think about it."

. . .

As Mama's daughter, I, too, knew in my bones, that if I had only been a better little girl, a child who had not somehow enticed my father, not caused him to weep, then my father would not have had to give me all those Good Spankings. And, like my mother, I too knew, since it was my fault, I dare not tell anyone. Shamed already, I could not face any more blame than I'd already piled on myself.

It was all too, too, confusing. Even the warnings were vaguely worded so as not to give away The Secret that Secrets existed. Often, I didn't know exactly which poisonous secret bit, in particular, I must never, ever reveal. I didn't know exactly which radioactive bit I must guard with my life, lest my family suffer grievous harm in the telling. For that harm, too, would be my fault.

My brothers, too, say they were forever fearful something might slip out, break the silence, and, like a bolt from the blue, zap safety away. If we weren't very, very careful, some Secret thing, accidentally revealed, might leave us orphaned and starving, shivering children without parents.

All because we discovered vocabulary and courage enough to break the silence, to describe what went on behind the closed doors of family.

• • •

When I was a kid, they called crazy people fruit-cakes; my Dad did anyway. I had Technicolor visions of being so stuffed with shards of glass, with unspeakable secrets that, like a fruitcake, my insides were full of dark little bits, not of preserved fruit, but shards of splintered memory, implanted like shrapnel, pushing out from deep inside.

I feared I might open my mouth intending only to insert a fresh stick of Juicy Fruit gum. Instead, I imagined, secrets would pour out. Shards of glass disguised as raisins, pecans, and candied cherries would spew forth, forming a surreal, Salvador Dali–like fountain of disguised and unruly Secrets: Dangerous Secrets suddenly spewing forth in the middle of a Thanksgiving dinner, complete with frowning adults all gathered round, fingers inserted in deaf ears, la-la-la-ing away.

I was afraid. Perhaps over breakfast, while every sane amnesiac in the family silently spooned up dull oatmeal, I might start spouting like a little blue whale, trapped and swimming round and round in Sara's China Blue sugar bowl. All my unspeakable secrets would escape to drop down like spring rain upon spun sugar waves right there at the breakfast table.

But what, I wondered, what if no one around that table even took notice of the toxic bits I'd held so long inside of me? What if all the grown-ups just went on spooning up their dull oatmeal? What if I told the secrets burning like live coals inside of me and not one person was brave enough to listen? What if I insisted that they pay attention, but they all just stopped eating dull oatmeal, stuck their fingers in their ears, and began la-la-la-ing away their own pain?

Sara said, "Just don't think about it."

Until the next time I somehow did that terrible thing that made my Daddy cry?

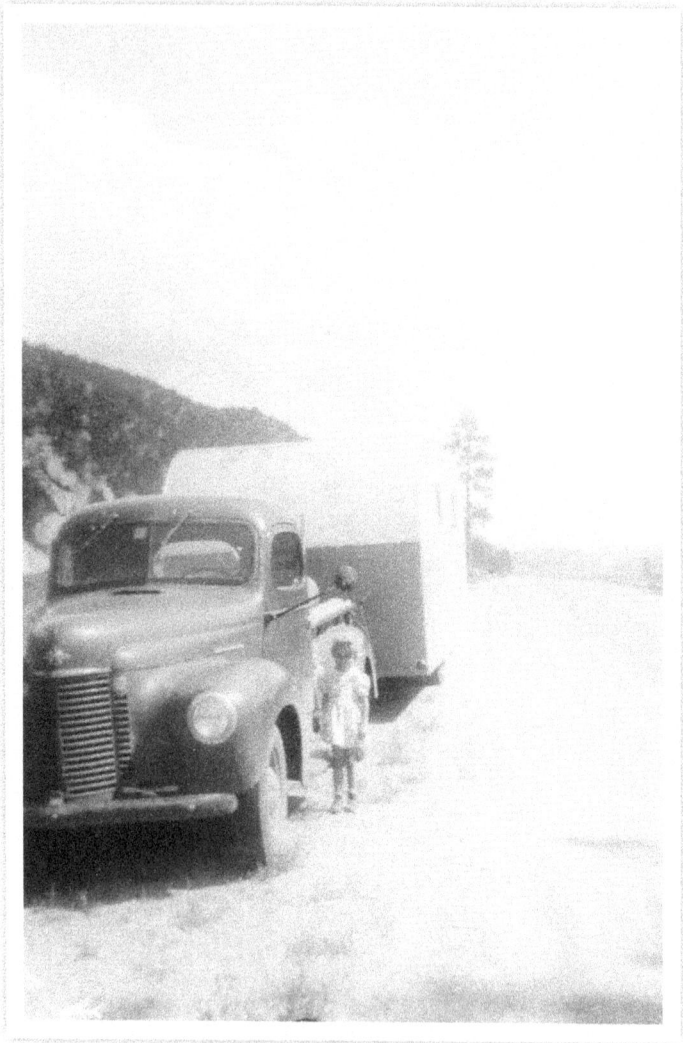

When Buddy caught pneumonia and nearly died,
we stopped awhile in Topanos

Chapter 10

Oh, my mother did try to tell her father, Bernard. She needed his help to escape.

Sometime after we returned to Black Tower after Mama's operation, Bernard traveled back to Oklahoma. Now 63, he intended to work and send money back to provide for Sara and Liza, still raising Rebeka's little girls. On his way to Oklahoma, Bernard stopped off at Black Tower to see my mother and to meet my father for the first time.

When Bernard stepped off the train, Mama asked her father for help, maybe she even showed him her bruises. She had to have Bernard's help, without her family's help a woman couldn't escape. Mama was ill again, and pregnant for the third time. Knowing Dad, she may also have needed Bernard to step in and provide physical protection once Dad realized she was leaving.

Mama asked Bernard to take us with him. Once arrived in Oklahoma City, Mama planned to stay with friends, have her baby, and make a new life. Failing that, Mama would go by train to California and deliver her baby. Sara could care for us just as she was caring for Rebeka's girls. There was war work. Rosie the Riveter was on every poster.

Mama said, "I'll do anything, anything. I worked before. I can work again. We won't be a burden. I promise."

Bernard said, "No."

Just, "No."

Bernard's "No" nailed Mama in just as surely as when she said "I do" in Elise's shabby living room where even the little rocking chair was nailed to the floor.

"No woman in our family ever divorced," Sara said.

Perhaps Bernard agreed with Sara.

Perhaps he believed that survival of the family was, in the long run, more important than the sacrifice of any one family member's personal happiness?

Perhaps he could not bear to hear his daughter's pain.

In any case, visit over, Bernard boarded the train for Oklahoma City where, at 63, he worked and sent money back to Sara and the little girls still in California.

Mere months later, word came that Sara's Daring Young Man from Cripple Creek, the young man who fell in love with Sara at first sight, the father Mama said hugged her and told her he loved her bushels and bushels, was dead of a heart attack, his death at 63 also a sacrifice to family?

• • •

My mother's last letter to me, ended saying she loved me bushels and bushels, reminding me once again that when she was a little girl, Bernard always hugged her and said, "I love you bushels and bushels." Until her death, Mama went on praising her father, calling him the Handsome Young Man from Cripple Creek who went down in the mines when he was seven, and grew up to marry Sara, the mine superintendent's pretty daughter.

No doubt Bernard did love his daughter bushels and bushels. But in what must have been the most heart-wrenching decision of Mama's life, Bernard's love failed her. Bernard sided against the daughter he loved and for a tradition that favored abusive husbands and religious beliefs. He abandoned Mama to her fate.

 Life went on as before.

Soon after Bernard died, my brother, Bayard, was born. We called him Buddy after Mama's brother Bernie. I know Mama loved Buddy bushels and bushels.

• • •

The milk cows my father bought with mom's savings contracted bags disease. The herd had to be put down. The bank foreclosed. The sheriff brought eviction papers. Shortly after that, an auctioneer sold the farm to the highest bidder.

Paw-Paw, hoarding money, always greedy for land, refused to lend Dad money to pay the bank and help save the farm. Instead, Paw-Paw bid at the auction and got Dad's farm for pennies on the dollar. Dad's farm lay adjacent to the Home Place. Paw-Paw joined the two and handed management of both over to his favorite son, Johan.

Even after the sale, left-over debt pursued my parents.

The bank sent a demand letter for the balance still owing.

Evicted, they soldiered on.

My ever-resourceful father built a one-room silver trailer, small enough to pull behind his pickup and moved us all in. With that, my mother, my father, my new baby brother Buddy, along with me, Egypt and the Uppity Little Green Fairy, began our years-long trek as Dad followed construction jobs northward.

We stopped at farm labor camps or sharecropped on rented farms. Somehow my father always expected that new land, new prospects; a fresh start waited over the next horizon. He never gave up trying but his goal was always the same. Dad was forever looking to prove himself, hoping to finally, finally prove himself man enough to gain Paw-Paw's grudging approval.

For that ambition, we paid a fearful price.

• • •

When Buddy caught pneumonia and nearly died, we stopped a while in Toponos, Colorado. Sara sent us money to buy Buddy's medicine. Then, when it seemed Buddy would surely die, Sara left Rebeka's little girls with Liza and came herself to help Mama until Bayard recovered.

One Sunday, perhaps to thank God for Bayard's miraculous survival, all of us went to a little Pentecostal church set out in fields of alfalfa. Moved by the Spirit, the worshipers fell on the floor, writhed, shouted and prayed in tongues. Frightened by the very un-Presbyterian commotion, I screamed and cried —raising an unholy fuss.

Dad took me to the pickup and gave me a Good Spanking. And all the while I could hear the congregation 'Thank-You-Jesus-ing" inside the church. The experience left me with unfortunate connections to God-the-Father. I imagined him an old man like Paw-Paw who punished little girls who broke the silence or dared reveal secrets.

• • •

Eventually, still trekking northward, our family reached Cedaredge, Colorado. There we left the tiny one room silver trailer behind and moved into a rented farmhouse perched high on the side of a Colorado mountain.

Sara came again when our family moved out of the little silver trailer and into the farmhouse. By then I had graduated from little girl to "Big Sister." Buddy called me Sissy now. My apprenticeship had begun. My job was to take care of Buddy and, in the process, learn how to become a nice wife and good mother.

Sara and Mama proceeded to snip off the uppity bits of me that didn't fit the approved nice-girl, good-mother pattern intended to rein-in big sisters and rambunctious, often angry, little girls, like me and turn us into "little mothers."

"Train up a child in the way they should go and when they are old…"

It all felt like so much Chinese foot binding.

At six I did want to pattern myself after Mama and Sara. I loved Sara's romantic stories about Rebeka. I did want to live Happily-Ever-After. It was just that when they said, "Act like a lady!" well, the Uppity Little Green Fairy rebelled.

"Heck Fire! All the time?"

They said I was too big to act-up. No Little Green Fairy stomping, wailing and refusing for you. Mama even invented a game called 52-card pick-up. She said, "Young lady, no more throwing all the cards across the room when you loose at Patience."

But what to do with all my anger?

Well, at least, Green Fairy whispered, "You get to boss Bayard around."

"Be nice, now." Mama said.

"No hitting," Sara said. "No pinching. And, remember, smile."

"Now, that's my good girl."

But I frowned. I chafed. I saw drawbacks aplenty. Heck, 'Nice' little girls couldn't even say "heck." No bad words! No Men's Business? Heck Fire!

And "No saying 'Heck Fire' either young lady."

No more loud honking noises when I blow my nose?

No?

Nice is no fun!

According to Sara, nice little girls always wore clean underpants.

Because?

"What if a little girl got run over and had to go to the hospital? What if they blamed your Mama because you weren't clean down there?"

"Don't make me ashamed of you!" Mama said.

"Set an example!" Sara said. "You are Big Sister now."

I added clean underpants to my list. Never embarrass Mama. Be good. Never tell. Protect family. Stay out of Men's Business.

"Heck Fire!" is that all?

"A Lady does not lose her temper!"

Heck Fire! Why was it okay for Bayard to throw himself on the floor, yell bloody murder and bang his stupid head? Boys got to whine. Boys got to shout, "No!" Boys got to bang their heads and kick their feet. Boys got away with stuff.

But, No! Big Girls can't do that—"be nice." "Act like a lady!"

"Now, don't make me give you a good spanking."

But Bayard? "High-tempered. So like his grandpa," Sara and Mama agreed when Bayard had a fit, threw himself down on the floor, kicked his feet, and banged his stupid head black and blue.

Sara and Mama worried, asked each other, "What set Buddy off?"

I shrugged, "He's just a boy. After all, Boys are Boys. Boys act up, don't they?"

Mama said, "Shame on you. Big sisters don't sit around laughing and pointing. Find him a toy. Help him up."

It seemed, Bayard, too, was often somehow inexplicably angry.

Apparently, little girls were supposed to be the natural born helpers. And if they weren't naturally "full of sugar and spice and everything nice," like my story books said? Little girls just had to try harder.

Suitably chastened, I tried harder. I put on clean underpants and set about learning to be nice, fall in love, and marry a Good Provider as Sara's stories instructed. I'd marry. I'd escape. Safely ensconced in a home of my own, I'd be free. I'd create my own Happily-Ever-After family. Better-than this.

When I'm all grown up, I told myself, no nailed down furniture, no Big Bad Wolves, no scary Secrets. No Good Spankings. No smothering tricks. No aching silence.

Not in my house.

So I set about remembering to be good. I picked up after Buddy. I stopped throwing cards around. I watched as Sara baked bread and made her peach pies. I learned to measure a teaspoon of salt in the palm of my hand, just like Sara. I tried. I really did try. And when I was good, very, very good, Sara let me lick the spoon when she made jam. But when I was bad?

Well, sometimes all that "Nice" just wore me out. So I was horrid. Like the little girl with the curl in the middle of her forehead, I flounced around. I shouted "No!" at our cat. I pinched Bayard until he threw a fit and banged his stupid head.

The Little Green Fairy and I laughed and pointed.

Of course, I denied everything, but Mama got out the long willow switch, kept behind the kitchen door just for such an occasion.

"For your own good," Sara said.

I did want to be nice. I didn't want Sara's willow switch to turn my legs to fire. It was just that sometimes I forgot. I found myself angry, angry, angry: Men's Business, a nice woman's Bound-Duty; Big-Girl lessons; Being Big-Sissy; Keeping all those Secrets safely sorted in secret compartments.

Shouting "No!" was indeed a dangerous rebellion.

"Needs a Good Spanking," Daddy said.

"I'll be good. I promise. Please? Pretty please?"

When I was good, Mama praised me. Sara took me aside and slipped little melt–in-your-mouth Butter mint candies into my hand. "For my good girl," Sara said.

"Butter mints just for me?"

If I was good, but what if I forgot? What if I really was all horrid inside? Tempted my father? What if my underpants got sticky stuff in the crotch?

No more Butter mints?

Ever?

"Pretty please?"

. . .

So I learned to be nice—not exactly good, but nice enough to get by. I even began to feel happy up there on that little farm high up in the mountains. There are pictures of me holding my baby doll in front of a barbed wire fence piled high with wild pink roses. There are pictures of me holding Buddy's hand on the front porch of that farmhouse. There's even a picture of me on a teeter-totter, smiling into the camera.

That summer, I watched the bluebirds make nests up in our porch rafters. The mama and daddy flew back and forth. They were a blur, taking worms to their naked little forever-open-mouthed babies while I rode my blue tricycle around in circles, fascinated. Eventually, the babies grew pin feathers, then the little bluebirds of my first happiness flew, too soon, away—then, worst of all, Sara took the train back to California. She left me already wishing for her return.

And, as for Mama?

In Cedar Edge, unlucky death caught up with Mama once again

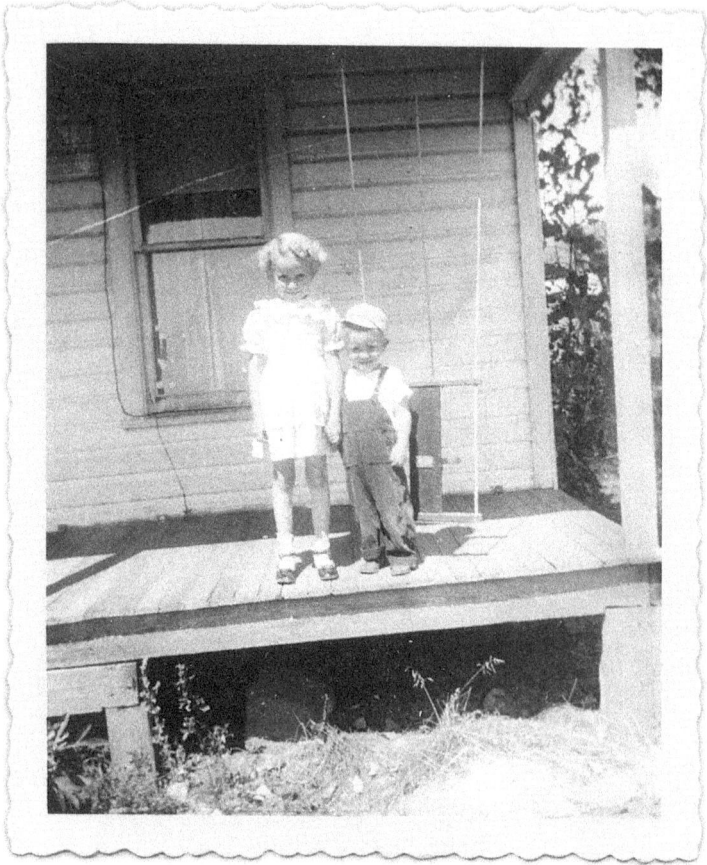

*In my mind's eye I can still see Mama, reaching up,
answering the phone.*

Chapter 11

Up there on the farm, we had an old-fashioned wooden box phone with a wind-up handle that hung on the living room wall next to the front door. In my mind's eye, I can still see Mama, reaching up, answering the phone.

Mama said, "Hello."

She held the earpiece and listened. Then she dropped the phone. The earpiece swung back and forth, back and forth. The scratchy voice continued, but Mama wasn't listening.

Unlucky death had found us.

Bent forward, Mama leaned her shoulder against the wall, both arms wrapped around herself as though for protection from the tinny sounds still pouring out from the earpiece onto the living room floor. The scratchy voice said, "Marie. Marie. Are you there?"

Mama backed away. Made dry mewing sounds. Shed no tears.

I knew what Mama did when Daddy hit her. But this was different. I held my breath. Mama put out one hand, steadied herself. She felt her way blindly off toward her bedroom. Mama shut the door, shut herself away in darkness.

Eventually, the scratchy voice inside the telephone stopped speaking. The receiver stopped swinging and hung straight down from its cord. I was afraid Mama would die. I called to her, but Mama didn't answer, wouldn't open the door. I pushed against the door, but I couldn't get in.

Mama's brother Bernie was dead.

. . .

The story of my Uncle Bernie's suicide waited sixty years for the telling, because Sara was so shamed by the circumstances surrounding Bernie's death. The blurring of boundaries in a Paw-Paw World is a dangerous rebellion even today.

But then, wasn't it Sara who sent Bernie back to Oklahoma City to live with Mama that last year before Pearl Harbor?

"For keeping bad company," Sara said.

In retrospect, an ominous judgment.

But in the end, perhaps it was Sara's rejection Bernie dreaded most of all.

. . .

Years later, Mama told my brother Bayard, she had her suspicions when Bernie was sent back to Oklahoma, but she said nothing. Mama, too, was too well trained in respectability to inquire. Anyway, even to broach suspicion was to insult, to make a forbidden intrusion into Men's Business.

Besides, what words would Mama have used had she tried to ask outright? What words were nice women permitted to know?

For truth, you must read the letters I found saved all these years in Pandora's Box. For truth, listen closely. Hear echoes of love and a beloved son's sacrifice.

Bernie was a much-loved youngest son, the favorite of his parents, of my mother, and especially of his sister Liza. Bernie's second-grade class picture reveals a serious, tow-headed little boy in a sailor suit gazing not into the camera with all the rest of his classmates but off to the side, at something more interesting to a bright seven-year-old.

But, perhaps, like my brother Bayard, like my son Ben, Bernie knew even then.

. . .

Sara sent her son back to live with Mama at #2211 Pawnee because, it seems, he had been hanging out in

San Francisco keeping bad company and learning pho-
tography from the likes of Maynard Dixon.

Once arrived in Oklahoma, Mama found Bernie a
job at Bell Telephone where she worked. On February 2,
1941, ten months before Pearl Harbor, Bernie enlisted in
the Oklahoma National Guard.

Army records indicate Bernie was a lineman and ser-
viceman for telegraph, telephone, and power. "College: 1
Year," the records said. Bernie's was the perfect skill set
for assignment to the Signal Corps. Signal Corpsmen were
attached to Headquarters units on the battlefield. During
the heat of battle, Signal Corpsmen drove their Jeeps in
ahead of advancing army units, stringing telephone lines
so generals and colonels could pass orders to enlisted men
fighting in forward positions.

After Pearl Harbor, they transferred Bernie's National
Guard unit to the regular Army Air Force. Bernie was
issued a new service number and sent to Signal Corps
Officer Candidate School. Bernie soon emerged a 2nd Lt. in
the 501 Signal Air Wing (SAW) assigned to Headquarters.

When Bernie enlisted, the US Army wasn't interested
in Jewishness, nor did they ask questions about sexual orientation. England was in a fight for her life. The United
States Army wanted men willing to carry M1 Carbines,
give and follow orders—men brave enough to fight to the
death at Bastogne if need be.

Field promotions came based upon intelligence, leadership, and valor in combat. Starting as a private, promoted
to 2nd Lt., Bernie's unit invaded on D-Day. Bernie earned
campaign participation credit for Normandy, Northern
France, Rhineland, Ardennes-Alsace, and Central Europe.
By war's end, he held the field rank of captain in the 501
Signal Air Brigade. For his bravery, France awarded Bernie
the Croix de Guerre.

Tucked in Pandora's dusty box, I found a picture of my
Uncle Bernie, by then promoted to field captain, standing

with two other soldiers. Between them, the three grinning men hold up a captured German flag emblazoned with a huge swastika. Behind them, across the Rohr River, is German soil.

In April, 1945, US Army units liberated the Dachau concentration camp. General Eisenhower ordered Signal Corpsmen from the 501 SAW to photograph and document what they found. Bernie said the stench of death heralded the existence of Dachau long before his soldiers saw the stacks of putrefying Jewish corpses, before they heard the huge swarms of black horse flies, or witnessed the starved and brutalized prisoners begging for water.

On General Eisenhower's orders, Signal Corpsmen took photographs of Nazi death camps. And, Bernie, now a Captain, put his talent for photography to good use photographing the survivors of Hitler's final solution. Later, Signal Corps photos provided hard evidence to convict Nazi leaders in the Nuremberg Trials. Even now Signal Corps photographs put the lie to modern day Holocaust deniers.

Photographing the piles of still-smoking corpses and the walking dead left already battle-hardened men like Bernie wrestling with fresh horrors.

Bernie himself must have been heartsick with the realization that had not the Mackiowitz left Eastern Europe, changed their name to Mackie then immigrated to America, they too might well have been one of the scarecrows begging for water behind barbed wire. Bernie also realized he might well have been rounded up and murdered during Hitler's fearful 'final solution,' not simply because Jewish blood ran in his veins, but for yet another damning reason.

In 1941, the same year Sara sent Bernie back to Oklahoma "for keeping bad company," Hitler decreed homosexuality to be "as dangerous and infectious as the plague." In Hitler's Germany, as in Paw-Paw's America, homosexuality was a criminal offense. In the United

States, those labeled Pervert, Sissy-Boy, Pedophile, faced lynch mobs and imprisonment as much for what they were assumed to be, as for any attraction they may or may not have acted upon. The dangerous labels, once applied, presumed to define such men as indelibly evil.

After all, the first sex offender registry was invented in California in the late 1930s to satisfy rampant homophobia motivated by the same irrational fears, the same quest for toxic Paw-Paw-Manhood as in Hitler's Germany. Like Paw-Paw's fear of tainted blood, gender equality remains a homophobe's, a bully's, a bigot's worst nightmare. Like America's "one drop" fears, in Nazi Germany, Jewish or not, Hitler pronounced all Gay men "infectious as the plague." Hitler ordered homosexuals hunted down and exterminated to protect the eternal purity of his Thousand Year Reich.

Whether in Bonanza, Greenwood, or listed on California's "Sex Offender" registry, "divide and conquer" worked to turn diverse groups against one another while fear of being singled out, denied social citizenship, even murdered, kept the members of each group safely down. While the Signal Corps took pictures documenting the holocaust, back in California, Maynard Dixon took his camera and photographed Japanese American families forced to live in internment camps. To this day, in America, fear of being labeled "undesirable," targeted as "illegal" and "detained" continues to destroy human beings and balloon detention centers and registries.

So much for "keeping bad company."

· · ·

After the war, my Uncle Bernie returned to an America engaged in McCarthy-style witch hunts—this time focused on Communists, spies, traitors, Sissy-Boys and Perverts. Pervert morphed into an all-purpose label used by officials and bullies like Paw-Paw to dominate, degrade, forever discredit, or even kill all those seen as potential rivals. It was paranoia gone mad, much the same as when Tulsa strafed and fire-bombed Greenwood's too-prosperous blacks in 1921. Or today, when America builds walls against "Mexican Rapists" and puts little kids in cages at the border to protect the rest of us.

But in 1945, politicians and victorious American generals, fresh from defeating Hitler's Nazis, came home infected by the same Aryan blood pride, the same over-weening fear of "infection" as Hitler. Driven by prejudice, paranoia and McCarthy-era politics, the American mili-tary began its own savage purge of "undesirables."

Under newly minted Army regulations, any person so much as accused anonymously of "homosexual tenden-cies" was first interrogated by a military agent from The Office of Special Investigations (OSI). The accused were then summarily ordered by the military to a psychiatric hospital for "evaluation" where they were automatically labeled "dangerous sexual psychopath."

It was a pro forma process intended to summarily brand the accused as "unfit for service." Tame psychiatrists simply replaced openly homophobic labels like "Pansy," "Sissy-boy" and "Pervert" with more respectable sound-ing labels which conflated all the old prejudices but which were, in reality, no more "scientific" than the old scato-logical language long used by Paw-Paw's to demean and discredit.

Yet, when added to the DSM1 of the time, the "scien-tific" labels proved exceptionally dangerous. The DSM1 diagnosis rubber stamped what the generals and the gen-eral public already thought they knew: those accused were forever-dangerous-sickos and sickos were, by definition, unfit for military duty no matter their heroism in actual combat.

JAG officers or military investigators confronted the accused "Pervert" with proposed Article 125 sodomy charges. Interrogators offered the accused only one option:

sign a statement accepting the lasting public humiliation and disgrace of an undesirable (Blue) discharge in hopes of escaping conviction by general court martial and long imprisonment at Fort Leavenworth, Kansas.

Should an officer refuse to resign his commission in disgrace, the accused was then ordered to report to a mental hospital for psychiatric evaluation. Once targeted, denigrated and labeled a dangerous degenerate, the man faced summary court martial and imprisonment before being cashiered.

Both options had but a single intent: to "scientifically" label and forever destroy both the military career and the civilian future of every person so much as accused of being a "Pervert."

Personally and politically, it was an unfortunate time for Bernie. He had decided to stay in the Army and apply for training to become an attorney. But simply by winning a case when he was an acting Trial Judge Advocate, Bernie made a dangerous enemy. Opposing counsel was a spiteful colonel in the Judge Advocate General's Department

Bernie, a mere captain, dared believe that even soldiers charged with sodomy under Article 125 of the Uniform Code of Military Justice should be considered innocent unless and until proven guilty. Accordingly, Bernie mounted a defense and won.

Later, screeners investigating my Uncle Bernie's application for university training interviewed the Colonel. Still smarting from his loss, the Colonel accused Bernie of "homosexual tendencies." The Colonel's accusation immediately put a stop to Bernie's hope of becoming a lawyer and began his purge from the military.

Bernie refused to sign a Blue discharge. He was then ordered to report to an Army base in Iowa just across the river from Mount Pleasant, an infamous psychiatric hospital designated for persons scientifically labeled Dangerous Sexual Psychopaths. Much like civil commitment facilities

today, Mount Pleasant was the facility where tame psychiatrists routinely evaluated then rubber stamped as dangerous sexual psychopaths those the Army intended to discharge as undesirables, beyond hope, forever congenitally
unfit.

Once arrived in Iowa, after refusing to sign the Blue
discharge, Bernie drove into his garage, closed the door,
piped carbon monoxide into his car and, just to make
death doubly certain, Bernie shot himself as well.

The death notice makes no mention of the circumstances that drove Bernie to commit suicide. But the same
commanding officer who recommended my uncle Bernie
to the Air Judge Advocate's Office in Washington, DC for
university training, secretly sent his wife to visit Sara and
Liza.

The Lieutenant Colonel's wife told them the true circumstances leading up to Bernie's death. Except for whispered conversations later, Sara, Mama, and Aunt Liza took
the truth to their graves, so intent were they upon protecting Bernie, Sara, and all the respectable Mackie family
from scandal.

But, if truth be finally told after sixty silent years,
Bernie's suicide was in itself a sacrifice to family and to
honor, an attempt to deflect certain shame away from Sara,
the mother he loved and intended never to shame.

For Sara, like most people at the time, believed it was
a mother's fault if her son was homosexual. The Bible said
Homosexuals were bad. Gossips said such mothers had
raised a "mamma's boy." In a Man's World, especially in
a Paw-Paw World, breaking the silence, crossing borders,
blurring boundaries, is a dangerous business. "Sissy-boy,"
"Pansy," "Pervert" are the indelible labels some would
argue still apply even in the case of a brave man awarded
the Croix de Guerre by France.

Homosexuality as a perversion has been removed
from the DSM1, sodomy is no longer an offense. The "Sex

Offender Registry" has moved on, still applying many of
the same indelible "scientific" labels to the next group considered so dangerous as to be without hope of redemption.
Such scientific "labels" still cause unwarranted shame, self
doubt and often lead to suicide, prison or the registry just
as in my Uncle Bernie's day. As far as "recovery" from
homosexuality, "conversion therapy" is still recommended
by some evangelical practitioners who claim they are able
to change sexual orientation and thus save a respectable
family's reputation.

As for Bernie? Soon after his death the government
began sending Sara monthly checks, death benefits ensured
when Bernie refused a dishonorable discharge and chose
suicide instead. Sara's benefits were, indeed, bitterly earned

• • •

*Hearing the tragic news of Bernie's suicide, so soon
after hearing her father's "No," was, for Mama, the turning of yet another lock.* Mama may well have hoped that
her brother Bernie, once returned from war, would help her
escape her violent marriage even after her father Bernard
said, "No."

With Bernie's death, Mama may have considered asking her brother John, Jimmy's friend, for help—but John
was, by then, himself lost in alcoholism.

With Bernie gone, Mama had only one male family
member left who might agree to rescue her. Ernest, Mama's
oldest brother, was lately returned from WWII and living
with his wife and children in Oklahoma City. Ernest might
well have agreed to help Mama escape the locked confines of Sara's romanticized Happily-Ever-After, but before
Mama could ask, news of yet another unlucky Death came
to our little farm perched up on a Colorado mountainside.

For truth listen closely, hear echos of a beloved son's sacrifice to family

Chapter 12

After Uncle Bernie's death, it felt like the sun forgot to shine at our house. For a long time, I pushed aside the reality of how unhappy Mama was, how unhappy I was, isolated on a farm up there on the side of a mountain in Colorado, even before another fateful phone call brought news of murder.

We tried hard to smile.

"Don't cry," Mama said.

"Think happy things," Sara said.

So I tried. I knew if I were only a better child, my parents would be happy—at least, as happy as they pretended to be during Sara's summer visits. I told myself that if I just did the magical, comforting things my Grandma Sara did when she visited, then, when she left us, maybe the Little Green Fairy and I could magically stretch happiness until Sara's return.

Mama tried to smile, but with her brother and father both dead in quick succession, she was left more vulnerable than ever. She was nearing forty and there was yet another baby on the way. This time, I vowed, the baby wasn't going to be just another boy allowed to throw himself on the floor and bang his head black and blue.

I said, "Mama, this time, bring back my little red-headed baby girl."

Like all "nice" females bent upon Happily-Ever-After, I believed in magic.

I tried to stretch happiness.

I tried to remember what life was like when Grandma Sara was there. Tried to remember long summer days when she made gooseberry jam on top of the same wood stove that heated our bath water, summer days when Sara took her juicy peach pies out of the oven and set them in the window above the kitchen sink to wait for Daddy.

"The way to a man's heart is through his stomach," Sara said.

Sara's pies were magic.

My father claimed Sara made her pies just for him. Daddy loved food. We all did. Eating grandma's pie was the one time when we could all be happy. In our house, food came closest to love. I was safe when Sara made her pies.

Up in the mountains, Mama and Sara heated pans of water on top of the wood cook stove and my brother and I took baths in a big round galvanized tub set out on the kitchen floor. We splashed around laughing while Sara and Mama tried to wash us, clean our ears, and keep soap out of our eyes. Those were, indeed, happy times.

· · ·

Later, the magic innocence of bath time wore off. When we moved to Idaho, when both Mama and Sara weren't there, Dad took over bathing my brothers. Dad was just inventing new versions of Paw-Paw's smothering games to try out on his own sons. He held their heads underwater. They cried and struggled to breathe. Dad, like Paw-Paw, got his kicks out of smothering kids within an inch of their lives and laughing. Looking back, it's lucky that my brothers weren't disappeared too, like my father's uncle, Andrew.

· · ·

In Cedaredge, after our happy baths, Mama read aloud to us. I'm not sure when I learned to recognize the words for myself. She once found me hidden behind the kitchen door, engrossed in Alice in Wonderland.

"Can you read that?" she asked.

"I can think what it says," I told her.

Mama, Sara and Elise read their Bibles religiously, for comfort. I memorized the storybooks Mama read to me, then I turned the pages and retold the tales to Buddy who snuggled up and listened.

We all became lifelong readers. Maybe we just became lifelong escapees. All escape velocity required was a book and a little imagination and we flew away to Somewhere Else—Over the Rainbow, down Alice's rabbit hole. The Little Green Fairy and Bayard and I flew to anywhere we had the innocence and wit to imagine.

I hid with Brer Rabbit, drank magical potions with Alice, and disappeared with the smile on the face of the Cheshire Cat. I could even outsmart the Big Bad Wolf who smiled after he ate up Grandma. Together Egypt and I parted the Red Sea. We fled to the Promised Land. There, hidden in the bulrushes, I imagined a Happily-Ever-After where I'd be safe from wolf shadows and ice blue eyes peering into my dreams in the dark of night.

And then, then, I discovered school! First grade made me smile. My little yellow school bus even smiled as I climbed aboard.

And when we all arrived and trooped off my little yellow school bus?

Well, school was the most magical escape of all.

I can still see my first sunlit classroom, the shafts of light alive with motes of magic dust streaming down, not invisible at all. I loved the big, old-fashioned, echoing room with its high ceilings, tall windows, and polished wooden floors. I loved the smell of musty books and disinfectant. I loved my patient, no-nonsense teacher, so like Sara.

Once, lost in imagination, I tromped across the back of the class, my brown school shoes sending loud echoes into studious silence.

"Exactly what do you think you are doing, young lady?"

"Walking in my Daddy's big farm boots."

"Well, young lady, take off your daddy's boots and go sit down. You can't wear those farm boots in here."

"Yes, ma'am." Daddy's boots disappeared in an instant. I tiptoed back to my seat and took up other Green Fairy dreams escaping into yet another hidden life.

What a teacher. I loved her—and thanks to her, I learned to love learning. School was an interesting, orderly place. There, no one ever said, "Don't think about it." I never had to try to not know. In fact, I was supposed to know—required to discover answers, connect hidden dots, figure things out, add two and two, set problems right. School was a place where little girls like me got A's for knowing, for speaking up.

"Good job!"

Butter mints all round!

What freedom. My report card shows A's in Arithmetic, Phonics, and Initiative (self-help), and (probably well-earned) D's in Use of Time, Perseverance, and Courtesy. I was, apparently, bright, flighty, stubborn, loud and bossy. I spoke up first; then I raised my hand. Freedom pushed its way up through every tiny crack in the cement sidewalks surrounding my first school.

Maybe my first-grade teacher freed me for later, when, as a social worker in the world beyond home, I was free to investigate, find answers, and tell, once I escaped to Grown-up.

But not back then. Certainly not in that little farmhouse up on the side of the mountain. There, Home meant trapped; like an ant in honey. Like trying to breathe underwater. Like saying "Yes" when I meant "NO!" Like smothering all those secrets. Like waiting, waiting, waiting at the window for Sara to come back so I could remember baby bluebirds, peach pies, and happiness again.

· · ·

I discovered other escapes just outside my back door. Inside, Mama reminded, "Be nice." Even my darling Sara said, "Nice girls tip-toe. They take naps. They do not make rude noises on purpose just to wake up Little Brother"

My apprenticeship into the magical world of ever-so-nice women continued on the side of a Colorado mountain. I knew I was not ideal. I didn't have small feet. No Prince Charming would ever pick a girl who deserved Good Spankings.

In the meantime, Not-So-Nice little girls stood with their nose in the corner.

Misery, temper tantrums and tears.

"Don't cry or I'll give you something to cry for."

Sometimes, standing there, nose to corner, I scolded my own self, "Be Good!"

The Little Green Fairy stuck her tongue out at me.

She grinched. She got snarky. She refused to stifle herself.

"Okay, no Butter mints for you! Ever!" I warned the Little Green Fairy.

The Little Green Fairy kicked the wall. She just would not listen. "Yech!" She hated "Nice" almost as much as she hated Paw-Paw's cherry cough drops all covered with pocket lint.

• • •

On the other hand, the Little Green Fairy loved escaping to Outside almost as much as she loved School.

Outside there was sharp mountain air and the clean smell of tilled soil. I remember the smelly, slippery, icky mud that filled the corral out in front of the barn. I remember the joy of escaping to watch a newborn calf plop itself out of its mother and down onto a sweet bed of mown hay.

I remember the calf's rough, warm tongue when she tried to suck on the three fingers I held out to her. I imagined Brer Rabbit hid with me in the prickly, pink wild rose bushes climbing the mailbox by the dirt road where I hid and waited for freedom and my smiling yellow school bus to come round the last curve and stop at our drive.

• • •

Outside, my job was to collect the warm brown eggs from under those beady-eyed chickens in our weathered hen house. I would lift the handle, then push open the rickety chicken-wire door. I'd go in clutching my egg basket. First I had to tempt those nasty, pecking, cluck-clucking hens off their nests. Luckily the Little Green Fairy knew those beady-eyed hens were suckers for grain.

One day, I lifted the lid of the grain barrel only to discover a fuzzy little pink mouse running round and round, trapped and helpless inside. I looked down at him. The mouse looked up at me, squeaked, then ran faster and still faster. I hesitated. What if the mouse bit me? What if it ran right up my arm and ran round and round inside my clothes? I shivered. I felt as scared as that scared little pink mouse.

Even the Little Green Fairy hesitated.

I knew Mama screamed whenever she saw a mouse. Nice women were supposed to scream. The Sunday Comics showed women screaming at the sight of a mouse. People thought that was funny.

This was my first up-close-and-personal encounter. Just a terrified me and a scared little mouse, arguing over a barrel of grain in the chicken coop.

But what to do?

After feeding the chickens, I brought my basket of brown eggs to the house and told Mama about my argument with the little mouse down in our grain barrel.

"But what did you do?" she asked.

"Why, I killed him of course. I wasn't going to let that mouse eat up all our chicken feed."

• • •

Looking back on it now, killing that mouse and not giving in was probably my decision not to be a nice woman like Mama. Maybe my refusal to let on how scared I was, was just the Green Fairy's rebellion against a father who laughed and dangled still-twitching little mice in Mama's face. Just to scare her. Just to make her scream. Nice women were supposed to scream.

Nice women had a lot more than mice to be scared about.

I hated it. Hated giving in. Dad loved scaring the stuffing out of everyone. He called it "teasing," "tricking." Afterward, he shrugged and dismissed us—"Just getting a rise out of you." Dad loved it when we jerked back. He stifled his laughter until, pushed beyond reason, we protested, screamed, tried to run, began to cry, couldn't breathe. Once fear took over, Dad's pent-up laughter burst forth. Derision followed.

Once Dad found your fear, he picked the scab again and again. It was like pressing into the soft spot on a baby's head. Like dangling a live mouse in Mama's face when she was busy washing dishes. Always ambushed, always when least expected.

Living in dread, we learned to expect the unexpected.

Afterward, he laughed. "Your Mama just has no sense of humor," he said.

Killing the fuzzy pink mouse proclaimed I wasn't scared. Said I refused to be a "cry baby." I didn't want to learn Nice.

"Stop your crying!" Dad said. "Or I'll give you something to cry for." Well, nobody in their right mind would ask for a Good Spanking, would they?

So, if I smiled and acted unafraid, kept my head down and watched out, Dad would just have to get his laughs scaring Mama or some other too-nice person.

Fooled you.

No Butter mints for me?

Sara said "just don't think about it," so mostly I just tried to forget.

But then, in that awful frozen winter of 1949, unlucky death came up our road and discovered Mama once again.

Ernest survived two world wars. He came home to his wife and two daughters, Roxanne and Hannah. He took off his uniform and resumed work as a civilian US Postal Inspector.

Chapter 13

A*s though Bernard's heart attack and Bernie's death had not been enough to bring my mother to her knees, once again the phone rang, once again Mama answered.*
Her brother Ernest was dead, murdered that awful day in January—dead, a scant year after Bernie's suicide.

But Ernest's murder was not a silenced story, not a hidden tale that waited 60 years in shamed silence. Every newspaper reported that Ernest was a war hero struck down—a son, a father and a husband. Any family might be proud. This time, not fear of shame and blame but grief and pain hindered this tale's telling and retelling.

• • •

Ernest survived two world wars. He came home to his wife and two daughters, Roxanne and Hannah. He took off his uniform and resumed work as a civilian US Postal Inspector. Then in January, Ernest was shot in the back of the head by Don Joseph—a man who'd nursed a grudge against him since 1944 when both men were serving in Southeast Asia as America prepared for an assault on the Japanese mainland.

By unlucky happenstance, Joseph's family also came from Oklahoma City. When two $20 postal money orders, sent to him in Southeast Asia by his family, were stolen, it was my Uncle Ernest, then a US Army Postal Inspector, who had Joseph swear out a complaint and sign an affidavit setting out the particulars. Thanks to Ernest's efforts, Joseph's $20 money orders were recovered and the thief prosecuted even in the middle of war.

But Joseph, now returned from the war, wasn't satisfied. He demanded that Ernest return both his complaint and his sworn affidavit. His mother's fundamentalist religion forbade swearing "in court." Since his sworn affidavit was part of a permanent court record, Joseph's request was denied. Unhinged by paranoia, obsessed by his mother's rabid fear that for swearing in court her son was destined to burn in hell, Joseph solved the problem.

Joseph committed murder. He walked up behind Ernest in the main post office one Wednesday and shot Ernest in the back of the head with a .22-caliber pistol.

Ernest never recovered consciousness.

Spared the death penalty thanks to his well-connected family, Joseph spent the rest of his life in prison, dangerous, self-righteous, and forever delusional; presumably enjoying visits with the equally delusional mother who goaded him into committing murder to save himself from hell.

. . .

Mama couldn't travel from Cedaredge to Oklahoma for Ernest's funeral. She was pregnant—this time with Duncan–and in 1949 terrible blizzards, so intense that they froze cows in the fields, rendered the highways between our farmhouse and Ernest's funeral impassable.

Mother's girlhood friend Leone, Jimmy's still-waiting sister, attended Ernest's funeral and wrote Mama a letter.

Leone's letter tucked away with all the rest in Pandora's dusty little box tells details of Ernest's funeral. In it Leone refers to a long list of family and friends Mama left behind with marriage. Just reading their names must have made Mama feel lonelier, more isolated than ever up there on the frozen mountainside.

With her father and two brothers dead, there was no man left in Mama's family to say "Yes" instead of "No" had she once again tried to escape my father.

With each death, hope died.

All that winter, none dared travel. We barely hung on. Left alone on our little farm, we watched snowdrifts pile up and up. Even my little yellow school bus couldn't get up our hill. The wood cook stove smoked. We were cold, and it was dark. My mother was sick. She threw up every morning.

Still, Mama said she looked forward to meeting her new baby scheduled to arrive in the spring.

• • •

But this time, I told Mama, this time that stupid Stork had better bring back my lost baby sister, the one Mama said "went away" that day out on the farm in the sand hills surrounding Black Tower.

All that waiting, hoping, expecting just got to me. I tried to be nice if only to avoid more Good Spankings. I tried— but that dark winter, Mama's sadness and all that watching and waiting for the Stork to do the right thing, well, it just wore me out. The cold and the dark nearly got us all.

I forgot to remember happiness.

Finally, ice water dripped off the eves, snow drifts melted, and spring arrived.

My brother, Duncan, was born on June 1st.

The Green Fairy smiled and dubbed him June-Bug.

Predictably, when I heard the baby's name was Duncan, I threw a fit.

"Not a boy!" I wailed. I grinched. I kicked the wall, crossed my arms, and pouted. God had promised! Didn't He say, "Ask, and it shall be given?"

Well, hadn't I asked? And nicely too?

Steeped in the magic of prayer, I went back and told God He just better fix His mistake. "Exchange the babies," I ordered.

I talked the problem over with my friend, Egypt. Together we decided if I just put this boy baby out in the bulrushes somewhere, God would have a chance to rectify things. I'd surely return to find my little red-headed girl baby magically snuggled down in June-Bug's basket.

But alas, even these well-laid plans proved to be in vain. The only suitable bulrushes I could find were in pictures hung high up on the Sunday school wall. Egypt said those just wouldn't do.

In spite of her sorrows, Grandma Sara returned in June to care for us all.

"Just until your Mama gets back on her feet," Sara said.

After so much loss, Sara cooed and cuddled, rocked and sang to Duncan. Mama was clearly overjoyed with our new little boy. The whole family was. When the baby reached out his chubby arms and smiled that smile, even the Little Green Fairy's hard heart melted.

"Okay. No bulrushes for you! So much for magic." Outnumbered, I gave in. I told Mama, "June-Bug can stay."

Still, I vowed never, ever to forgive God or that Stupid Stork for mixing up my babies in the first place. But by then, even I knew that death was final, at least at our house.

• • •

As he always did when Sara visited, my father turned on his not inconsiderable charm. Sara was an official "outsider." He buttered her up. He called her "Mrs. Mackie." Dad smiled and held Sara's chair. Good Spankings stopped. Soon after Uncle Bernie's death, Sara started sending Dad money from Bernie's survivor's benefits check.

"To help out," she said.

My father was happy to accept.

With Sara back, life felt safe again, normal somehow. Whatever normal amounted to at our house.

Unless you've lived in such a household, it may seem hard to believe that my father could sustain a public persona so different toward outsiders like Sara, only to revert to ferocious, Paw-Paw-like violence when no outsider was present. Dad knew which side his bread was buttered on. No matter how out of control his actions might seem to be in private, I realized even then that my father turned charm on and cruelty off to suite himself.

Accompanied by my imaginary friend, Egypt, I vowed to escape both the charm and the cruelty. "Let my people go" was my favorite Bible story. The Uppity Little Green Fairy snorted, remembering unfortunate connections made in a Colorado alfalfa field.

Recently, I came across an old income tax form filled out when we lived up there on that unhappy little Colorado farm. My father declared $45 of income from selling milk, some money earned from eggs and hay, and not much else. We all worked hard, pulled weeds, hoed the garden, picked berries, collected eggs, but it was a loosing battle. Sara's money pulled us through.

Like Paw-Paw, my father applied for outside work. On his post office application, Dad used my mother's murdered brother Ernest as a reference.

• • •

Then Dad got wind of still unclaimed homestead land in Idaho but Mama argued for a move to California. She wanted a house in a respectable neighborhood near Sara, Liza, and family. For Dad to have a post office job and a steady paycheck, would put the icing on Mama's cake. We packed up and went on the road again, not West to California and Mama's family but North to isolation and parts unknown.

Egypt was left behind somewhere during that move—maybe he stayed with my favorite teacher in the school where shafts of light shed magic dust upon a library full of as yet un-deciphered words. Or maybe, in the chaos, Egypt escaped underground, sank beneath in the growing darkness created by my determination to "not think about it." Whatever happened, Egypt disappeared. By the time we got to Idaho, the Uppity Little Green Fairy and I found ourselves all alone with the Big Bad Wolf.

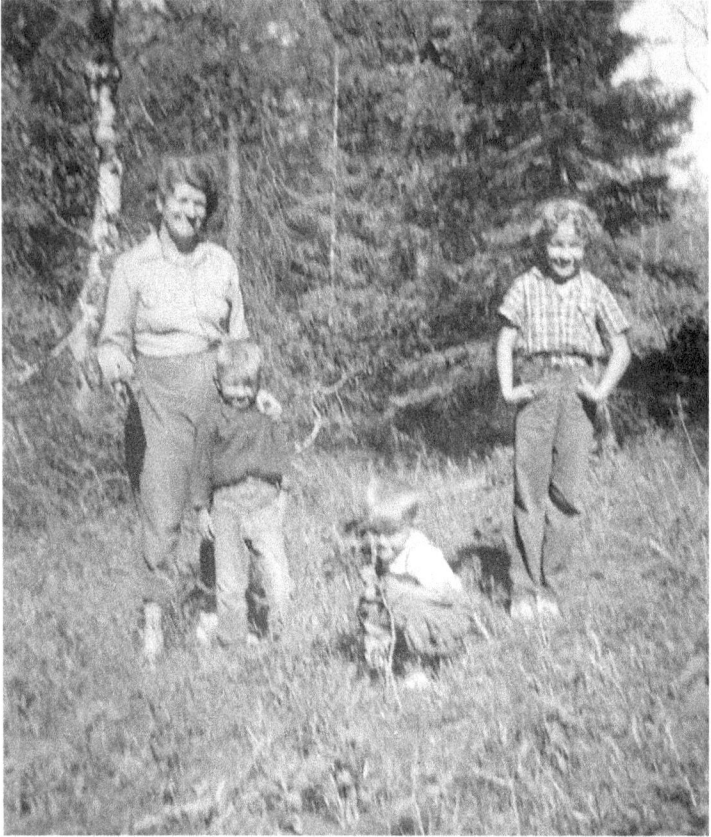

Arrived in Idaho, with money willed to Mama by her brother,
Dad bought a house near the bowling alley.

PART III: THIS THE HOUSE,
THIS THE LITTLE YELLOW BED

Chapter 14

Arrived in Idaho, Dad found all the arable land had been claimed long ago. Still, I am struck by my father's abiding ambition to somehow possess enough to impress even Paw-Paw, to prove he was, at last, Paw-Paw's equal.

Dad said we pulled up stakes "for Marie's health." He said, "The wife couldn't take the altitude" in Colorado. Just so, Paw-Paw said "for Mama's health" when he left Waurika in 1906. Both unthoughtful men used their wives as excuse for moving on. But then in a Paw-Paw world, no matter how tenuous a man's status in the outside world, once home he was master.

In Idaho, Dad went to work for the Department of Agriculture. The department was experimenting with processing potatoes into cattle feed. The processed potatoes were dyed purple to show they were "unfit for human consumption." My father brought the purple potatoes home, and we ate them anyway. Even Duncan, little as he was at the time, still remembers eating platefuls of "pink" potatoes.

Rescue came by way of money from an insurance policy Mama received following Ernest's murder. If Ernest hoped the policy might help Mama escape, he was wrong. Using Ernest's money, Dad bought us a house in downtown Jerome, on the same street as the bowling alley. Dad bought washers and dryers and set them up in the front room. We lived in the back. Mama divided her time between taking care of us and running the laundromat.

Later, Mama told me "Dad always found a job for me." She laughed. "Even before he found a job himself, he set me to work." But then, weren't a man's wife and children meant to be useful?

Meanwhile, Dad took more tests and waited to get hired on at the post office.

I finished second grade in Jerome. Duncan learned to walk in those rooms behind the laundromat. Rushing around, bent forward, forever curious, June-Bug over-balanced. I tried to watch out for him, but still he fell over so often that his forehead was bruised and purple. Finally June-Bug figured out how to arrive standing up.

My job as Big Sister was to keep my Little Brothers safe. I got them dressed, gave them breakfast. I tried to make sure Duncan didn't fall, and Buddy didn't burn his feet on the hot floor-furnace grate.

The Little Green Fairy rolled her eyes. "What do you expect? They're boys!"

Sara didn't come at all that first lonesome year in Jerome. Mornings were all right; I just didn't think about "it." But I dreaded bedtime. Tried to stay awake.

• • •

This is the house, this the bedroom, this is the narrow yellow bed I recall when, in splintered nightmares I see silent shadows coming down the hall, see cat's eyes and a Wolf's smile.

I remember swooning into smothered darkness when all else became unbearable.

But how prevent? For who might I have told all those years ago? What words did I know? Who would have believed a too imaginative little girl? How could I have said that a man with rough, square hands, with rough, ungentle fingers stole into my room at night—the same father who smiled at me across the breakfast table the very next morning, smiled the Wolf's smile and waited for me to smile back?

How could I have told them that when my father's hands passed me the sugar bowl at breakfast, I saw the same rough square hands, the same ungentle fingers seen the night before, but now those hands held out Sara's delicate blue sugar bowl, complete with spun sugar waves and an imaginary little blue whale spouting and swimming round and round?

When I saw his hands, I knew, just like Little Red Riding Hood knew, that the Wolf lived in our house. I wondered, did the Big Bad Wolf swallow up my father every night, just like he ate up Little Red's grandmother? If so, who, then, was this person smiling the Wolf-smile at me from across the breakfast table?

Spanked for saying, "Damn." Scolded when I said, "Heck Fire!" I most certainly did not know words to say what happened in dead of night. Even to say "Pee-Pee" was bad. "Nice" little girls say, "Wetty," Mama told me. Well-brought-up women merely pointed "down there." Bereft of the vocabulary, how can any "nice" child describe what the Wolf enjoys late at night? And older, how dare any "nice" woman break the silence?

Dad laughed at my confusion, laughed at me across the breakfast table every morning, the Wolf, "just getting a rise" out of me.

Yet, had I had words to tell, had I tried to save someone, might it have been wiser to intervene, to save the little boy whose puppy died in his arms long before I was born? And if I had thought to send the police out to the Home Place before these cycling tales began? Would they, would we even today, understand enough to intervene and save the little boy wolfed down long ago by Paw-Paw?

• • •

Even had I known words to tell, would not the police back then have chided me, thought me a too-imaginative little girl afraid of an imaginary Big Bad Wolf lurking somewhere in her darkened house at night? Lacking magic, I am still somehow afraid of tiny whales, and blue sugar bowls and things that go bump in the night.

Each morning, when the Wolf smiled at me from behind my father's eyes, I said, "Please." The Wolf smothered a laugh, I dropped my gaze, and my Daddy said, "Say pretty please, Sissy. Say, Pretty Please, pass the sugar."

Ever so nicely, I obeyed. And as I passed Sara's sugar bowl back across the breakfast table, Wolf hands reached out.

Life was confusing. And still, the splintered dreams return again. Still, I rise to check the locks at night. Still, I freeze at the sight of shadows moving across my wall.

Sometimes the ginger cat with shining eyes comes on silent feet to sit beside that little yellow bed. Watching, watching my little bluebirds of happiness fly away. A feral cat, barn-bred, still watches in deadly silence as a fuzzy little mouse runs round and round, trapped down inside a grain barrel, in a hen house perched on the side of a Colorado mountain. And the dreams? They are fierce eyes piercing the night. As alive as the Wolf-smile behind my father's eyes, as real as his rough hands reaching across the breakfast table. As real as those rough hands folded in his coffin.

Better to stay awake in the little yellow bed, better to read by purloined flashlight. Better to escape into imagination.

But what to do when Daddy says, "Shut off the light. Go to sleep."

What to do?

Afterward, I only remember swooning, disappearing in a pool of darkness. I don't remember being smothered by my father like Paw-Paw smothered his sons. By then I too had learned to stifle myself. Like all the other children, molested, incested, and silenced, I learned to breathe underwater, to breathe in a black pool of forgetting. Helpless, I learned to stuff my mind with blankets just like the silenced little five-year-old out there on the Home Place.

It was all my fault.

"Bad dreams for bad girls."
"No Butter mints for you!"
Never? Never ever? Never finally, finally over?
. . .

After school, the Green Fairy and I took the long way home. We chose deserted side streets; I looked up into tall tunnels of brilliant golden trees. I dragged my feet through a carpet of burnished autumn leaves. We drifted along the sidewalk until I turned that final corner. At the bowling alley, I paused to peer into the slotted windows. But, inevitably, home arrived.

When we lived behind the laundromat, my father took penicillin to cure some secret ailment, a nameless illness he vaguely referred to in his letters to Grandma Elise. When Dad took penicillin, his whole body swelled up with hives. Dad's secret malady had to wait for the invention of something else—something called Tetracycline.

My mother pronounced the crusty yellow discharge in my pink panties, a "yeast infection" and said I should be more careful, wipe better "down there," be careful to wear clean underpants. She dosed me with my father's penicillin. On me, the miracle worked just fine. I didn't swell up like Daddy. In fact, on me, the miracle of penicillin worked just fine quite a few times.

I never thought much about it. But then, I was lucky, since for a girl, the risks of eventual infertility increase with every episode of infection. And of course I always wore clean underpants, just in case I got run over and taken to the hospital and they blamed Mama.

Back then little girls were carefully warned, just as I was warned, to use the paper toilet seat protectors found in public restrooms to avoid catching some unspeakable something. Doctors had known full well from the beginning of the 20th century that non-contact sexual transmission was impossible.

But some practitioners refused to believe that little children who never went about unguarded could possibly be catching "it" from the fathers and grandfathers granted unquestioned power expressly for the purpose of protecting and guarding the vulnerable children entrusted to their care.

Those doctors chose not to imagine. They didn't ask. Didn't think about it. Doctors didn't believe little girls with bad dreams and crusty underpants. Instead, as today, they warned of Stranger Danger and cast blame on mothers and "unsanitary" toilet seats. Thanks to those doctors, today there are paper toilet seat dispensers in every public bathroom. Yet, although paper seat covers protect porcelain toilets, vulnerable children still go unprotected.

· · ·

Sometime after we moved to Jerome, my father received a letter from his mother, Elise, still waiting and hoping in Black Tower. Elise's letter, saved all these years in Pandora's Box, begins:

"Dear Beloved Carl and family, Sorry to hear of your sickness, or having been sick. I am really sorry to know you are moving so far away. Had been looking for you for some time every day but I as well quit now, but I am sure you know I will ever miss you all but the Lord's Protecting Care be ever with you. I pray God's richest blessing on you and yours where ever you go. You know I love you more than showing can tell even if you will rather be elsewhere than here."

After sharing more news of family sickness and weather, Elise's letter ends with, "Much Love, Paw-Paw and Mother and kiss the babies for me. Paw-Paw is tinkering around the shop now."

I can see Paw-Paw out tinkering in his shop, the shop where every visiting child was taken to look behind the secret doors and see Paw-Paw's Wolf-smile.

I am struck by how long Elise, left alone and long ignored there in that little house with nailed-down furniture, with Paw-Paw forever in charge of night and day, must have waited, hoped, and longed for her Beloved Son's return to Black Tower.

I am struck that Dad told Elise he'd been ill. How long must she have worried and watched for him out her window? How often must she have prayed? How corrosive, how haunted was the love between a mother and a son, forever powerless to protect one another?

And for his part, my father cherished Elise's letter, folded and refolded, read and reread for years. Elise's letter telling her Beloved Son that she loved him "more than showing can tell." Saved, read, and reread, comforted long after Elise was dead and my father was, himself, an old, old man. Just a mother's love letter tucked down between memories, long-treasured in a dusty old cardboard box.

Seeing the picture years later, Duncan said he could suddenly feel the searing pain of Paw-Paw's grip on his little boy hand.

Chapter 15

When the Korean War began, the military reactivated a little Army air base seventy-some miles distant. Dad decided to move the laundry there, thinking to prosper from the war boom.

Once there, Dad bought an old, gray, two-story house with a huge old maple tree in the front yard. Its gnarled roots pushed up our concrete sidewalk. Its branches shaded the whole house.

While my parents worked, I took first Bayard and then Duncan and registered each in turn, in first grade. Duncan tells me I taught him how to read before he started first grade. I don't remember. Perhaps we were escaping to somewhere far off together. After school we had a babysitter, but that babysitter taught me bad words—words so bad Mama said she'd never even heard Bernard say them.

Then a different babysitter regaled us with her sexual adventures. Mama fired them all. After that I was considered old enough to take care of Bayard and Duncan before and after school, and on Saturdays as well.

Mama said she knew I would never let anybody else hurt my brothers, but she said sometimes she was afraid I might kill them both myself.

The Green Fairy rolled her eyes.

Much to everyone's relief, school let out, summer arrived, and my Darling Sara stepped off the train. Sara come again to care for us while Mama ran the laundry and Dad worked at the grocery store, still waiting to be hired at the post office.

With Sara there, safety, kindness and order magically transformed our lives. In the cool of summer mornings, Sara baked pies, and we cleaned house. After lunch, we enjoyed a bath then took our naps.

When we woke up, Sara changed from her cotton house dress and apron into a nice dress. We kids put on fresh clothes. Then we all walked a few blocks to the park, ate little sandwiches, and rolled like puppies in cool green grass under summer trees.

In those days, before swamp coolers or television, summer seemed to last forever. I thought summer must be a little like heaven. Like life would be when I grew up, married Prince Charming, and had a home and family of my own: Happily-Ever-After all the time.

Grandma brought a single suitcase when she stepped down from the train. Inside she had small presents for everyone. Sara caught my mother up on family matters. She brought pictures of my cousins and bragged about how wonderful and well-behaved they were. Sara said they were perfect examples. I was jealous until Mama said that when Sara returned to California, she bragged about us.

Later, Sara took me aside, whispered what a good girl I was, slipped Butter mints into my hand and warned me not to tell my brothers.

"It's just our secret," she would whisper.

Then she did the same with each of my brothers.

I loved Butter mints, endless summer, and my Darling Sara.

Best of all, when she came, Sara shared my bedroom. I was safe. No nocturnal visits. No Good Spankings. No Wolf-shadows. Luxury indeed.

Sometime every fall, Sara packed her suitcase and prepared to winter in the California sunshine with Liza and her children.

One fall, Dad decided to take Sara with him to mind the little boys on a trip to Black Tower. From Black Tower,

Sara would take the train back to California. Dad left Mom and me to run the laundry. Well, really, Mama.

In Pandora's Box, there's a picture taken during that visit to Black Tower. Elise and Paw-Paw, Sara, Buddy, and Duncan stand all in a row in front of Paw-Paw's little house. Elise is to the left, toothless and sadly aged, but smiling, happy to have her Beloved Son home at last.

My father, the picture taker, is off camera. Bayard is backed up into Sara's protective skirts. Maybe Paw-Paw had already taken Buddy to visit his shop. Next to Sara in the photo, an unsmiling Paw-Paw grips June-Bug's hand. Duncan, stubborn and stoic, pulls a little apart from Paw-Paw and the rest.

Seeing the picture years later, Duncan said he suddenly felt once again the searing pain of Paw-Paw's grip on his little-boy hand. As the pain came flooding back across the intervening fifty years, Duncan remembered that Paw-Paw said nothing as he relentlessly squeezed Duncan's small hand tighter and tighter. The photo freezes pain in time: it both reveals and conceals abuse cycling down through generations of family.

Had Duncan cried out—"put up a fuss," grown-up's called it—then all the adults would have sided with Paw-Paw. The bad-little-boy who acted up would have gotten a spanking, been told, "Boys don't cry," and teased if he failed to stifle his little boy tears.

After that Duncan remembers he stood apart with his hands tucked behind his back. Duncan knew never to hold hands with Paw-Paw again.

As for me, I knew never to get up on Paw-Paw's lap, no matter the enticement.

"Come here, Sissy," he called during one visit. He held his hand out.

I froze.

"Come, take Paw-Paw's candy."

"Well," I thought, "What if Paw-Paw has Butter mints?"

So, greedy me, I took one step closer. I craned my neck. No. Not Butter mints.

Just two nasty old cherry cough drops fuzzy with Paw-Paw's pocket lint.

"Icky."

I stepped back. Made a face. Someone said, "Don't hurt Paw-Paw's feelings. Take the candy."

"Mind your manners. Obey your elders. Play nice."

Swallow pocket lint?

The Little Green Fairy wrinkled her nose.

Somewhere in the process, I found myself up on Paw-Paw's lap. Once there, Paw-Paw put an arm under my knees and another behind my neck. He pressed my face and knees together; I cried out, struggled for breath. Paw-Paw's old smothering trick, disguised.

Paw-Paw loved tricking us in plain sight of our parents. Public tricking, like taking Bayard to look behind the secret doors in his shop, or squeezing Duncan's hand in the photograph, meant getting away with "it" right in front of our protectors. Tricking, getting away with cruelty in plain sight doubled Paw-Paw's pleasure, proved his power.

When I squirmed or tried to get away, Paw-Paw increased the pressure, laughing at me. He egged the uncles and aunties on. They joined in, jeering and calling me cry baby right along with him. But then, they all still lived in fear of Paw-Paw. All his grown children, willfully dis-remembering their own childhood, looked away as Paw-Paw got over on his next unwary victim.

All except Mama. She took my hand, said, "Stop it." She lifted me off Paw Paw's lap. Mama somehow dared say "No" to Paw-Paw, the Lord and Master within the sacred walls of family. For a moment, Mama dared to be Uppity.

Mama stepped out of her woman's place. She went
against what Elise's fundamentalist religion decreed was
proper womanly behavior. She dared to wear "immodest"
city-slacks. She had to be regularly reminded, schooled, as
to her proper place in a recycled domestic tyranny handed
down father to son in Paw Paw's house.

I'll always be thankful Mama stepped up, and lifted
me off of Paw Paw's lap, in spite of knowing she would
later face the consequences for embarrassing her husband
in front of Paw-Paw, the unthoughtful husband who called
his wife Mule and laughed then tricked grandchildren in
plain sight.

Taken to look behind the secret doors in Paw-Paw's
shop, I understand why the photo shows Buddy pushing back into the safety of Sara's skirts. Cruelty creates
trauma, then cycles on.

• • •

All my life I have been claustrophobic. And now,
in old age, sleep apnea becomes a problem that cuts off
breath and requires oxygen in the night. Paw-Paw's smothering "trick" come home to roost? The body remembers,
rehearses its secret survival, checks the windows, and
drops the locks.

Meanwhile, Duncan has always been afraid of the
dark.

"Bring your blanket and get on my lap," Daddy told
Duncan, as though offering to rock a lonely little boy to
sleep in our big maple rocking chair. A Daddy, offering to
soothe a little kid he'd already made afraid of dark shadows in a tall gray house while our Mama was off working swingshift at the grocery store. Once on his lap, Dad
played his improved version of Paw-Paw's smothering
trick. He put his hand over Duncan's mouth, pinched his
nostrils then demanded, "Shut your eyes. Be still."

Darkness descended.

What better way to take advantage?

God only knows what my father's life must have been like as an also smothered little kid, but it's a legacy I want to expose and thus prevent, since much of my childhood felt like having my hand squeezed while being told, "Be nice. Smile pretty."

"Don't think about it. Don't make yourself unhappy."

But when was happiness, anyway?

The tragedy of my father's life was that as a little boy he was forced to smile as he swallowed pocket lint. Back then no one dared speak, no one dared come, like my mother came, to say, "Stop it." Silence reigned. Fathers were right. Children were wrong.

Full of resentment, jealous of his children, my father chose cruelty and the perfect pleasure of squeezing people, bullying and tricking them. Yet continuing silence, lies, and Puppy Stories only serve to pay cruelty forward.

Once we picked up clean uniforms,
Dad detoured to Julia Davis Park.

Chapter 16

When Dad moved the laundry in the early 1950s hoping to take advantage of the Korean War boom, the same malignant forces that drove Uncle Bernie to suicide were alive and metastasizing, this time out in the Southern Idaho desert.

As the Korean Conflict began, the Strategic Air Command, its B29s armed with live atomic bombs, took over the little reactivated army air base at Mountain Home. The military purge of commie spies, reputed homosexuals, political dissidents, and "subversives" continued. In the ongoing "Red Scare," it was only natural that General Curtis Le May should require his Air Force base be cleared of all the Commies, Queers, Perverts, and infiltrators he imagined lurking out in Idaho's sagebrush outback.

Even given the post-war paranoia, it's hard to believe that grown-ups actually believed that a reactivated little Army air base way out in the wilds of Idaho had somehow managed to become "the hotbed of commie activity," that Le May asserted. But then again, the State Department, Congress, and John Foster Dulles' Military Intelligence "investigators" were busily ferreting out and denouncing traitors everywhere. Why not Mountain Home?

The cold war had begun. Armed with the Dr. Strange-Love logic rampant at the time, many Red-Blooded Americans lately returned from the horrors of Hitler's Holocaust set about spreading homegrown fascism and white-pride far and wide.

Throughout the '50s, alarm spread. Pastors took The Book of Revelation as their text. Rapture, Armageddon,

"End Time" damnation was upon us. They preached the gospel of the dangerously deranged to fearful congregations. And the deranged, much like the man who murdered my Uncle Ernest, took action. The Idaho Daily Statesman threw gas on the fire, stoking "Red" hysteria and old-fashioned prejudice against "commie-perverts" and "Sissyboys" alike.

My family, like all our neighbors, believed the fear mongering. We read the Statesman from cover to cover every day. Meanwhile, Le May had armed nuclear bombs waiting in the big bellies of the B29s parked on the tarmac mere miles from my school.

• • •

Somehow news of a pending nuclear winter failed to make me feel safer. But then, I was just a stubborn little third grader who wished her friend Egypt hadn't somehow gotten lost out there in the seething darkness.

I was afraid the Spiteful Little Green Fairy might go the way of Egypt.

School and the joy of learning had, always before, provided a lifesaving counterbalance to the lurking fears and constant dread available at home. Now even school was scary. Teachers made us crouch under flimsy plywood desks and wait for "all clear" to sound after an imaginary atomic blast.

Our neighbors built bomb shelters, then said no one but their own family was welcome to shelter there.

We had no basement and no shelter.

What to do?

"Secret Reds" were coming for us in the night. Just one more scary reason for me to stay awake and watchful, to reread "Little Red Riding Hood" under the covers by flashlight. Not only did the Big Bad Wolf prowl the night, looking for "Little Red" but now? Now "The Reds" were invading!

Mama laughed, "You don't really believe that do you?"

Unconvinced, I locked and relocked our doors. Even on hot summer nights, when nobody in our small town thought to lock more than their screen door, I watched and waited.

Sometimes I was awake to hear the lonesome midnight whistle of the last freight train passing through our town. There I was, a little girl, alone and lonely, too young to escape. I wished I could hop aboard, go along to wherever that lonely whistle went. To Egypt, maybe? Maybe slip into Never-Never Land, or into Imagination with the Little Green Fairy never to return?

· · ·

Just as a vengeful Colonel had before used the military purges to take down my Uncle Bernie, jealous politicians in right-wing Boise began a purge of their own, aimed at taking down one of Boise's power elite—a powerful politician, a home-grown closet queen.

The investigator they chose to rid them of the "Queen of Boise" was an ambitious man, ironically code-named Bill Goodman. This Good-Man's biggest claim to fame, according to investigative journalism done at the time by Time Magazine, was that he had relentlessly exposed subversives in the US State Department and ferreted out "Perverts" within General Le May's command at Mountain Home Air Force Base.

So, with backing in high places, and the now-standard Military Article 125 sting operation, the witch hunt began. In the process of his investigative climb up the ladder to entrap Boise's un-trappable Queen, Bill Goodman grilled some 1,472 men. In a town the size of Boise in the '50s, the sheer magnitude of Goodman's sting operation could not have failed to strike fear, even without the dirty tricks their Good-Man employed.

Jim Brandon, at the time Boise's Chief of Police, was interviewed in 1965, and said, "That's why we got Bill. Bill had been in the State Department, and an undercover

agent in Washington, Europe, and the Mountain Home
Air Force Base. Got a lot of guys court-martialed, got
well acquainted with the techniques of that kind of operation." As quoted in "The Boys of Boise," (John G. Gerassi:
Page 22), Jim Brandon goes on to say, "It was this [Boise]
power elite that in 1955, went up the ladder after the
homosexuals."

John G. Gerassi's book quotes a man initially in favor
of pushing the investigation, as later saying, "It was dirty.
In their investigation, there were other names, big shots
involved, one very big name. But nothing happened to
him."

During his investigation, the Good-Man in this cha-
rade between good and imagined evil set about gaining
informants—hiring young men, most over twenty-one,
who sold themselves to perform various sexual favors for
interested men at the Boise YMCA and the public bath-
rooms in Boise's Julia Davis Park.

Goodman needed to churn up suspects: men with
whom his operatives could engage in what was referred to
as unnatural acts. Once ensnared, Goodman blackmailed
them. He threatened them with felonies and prison sentences, saying, "You know what they'll do to boys like you
in prison?"

Thus terrorized, some still refused to talk. Some
despaired, some committed suicide. Some gave up the
names of yet other men Goodman could sting and black-
mail as his investigation moved from the YMCA and Julia
Davis Park upward into the hallowed halls of power.

Men were charged. Men went to prison. Reputations
and families were scarred forever. In the end Bill Goodman
had to dodge subpoenas to avoid exposing his murky
methods. He avoided testifying as to his conclusions
regarding the name of Boise's powerful Queen. Much like
Lord Douglas' "love that dare not speak its name," to this
day, none dare speak the name of Boise's powerful Queen.

In the process, Bill Goodman terrified 1472 suspects, including my father.

Bill Goodman's sting, combined with a nice woman's ever-abiding dread of social exposure, nearly destroyed Mama.

All are dead now. Mama, my father, Goodman, and all his young "operatives" who prowled Julia Davis Park in the 1950s are, by now, all dead.

Even Boise's Teflon Queen is dead.

But I still remember.

• • •

I can still see the wide expanse of lush green grass spread beneath the towering maple trees shading the Julia Davis Park of my childhood. The park had picnic tables, paths, and tall bushes trailing green fingers into the cool waters of the Boise River flowing silently through the park. In our usual 105-degree summers, the park was a cool, inviting haven in the arid Idaho desert. Twice a week my father, my brothers, and I crossed forty miles of scorching sagebrush desert to reach that lush green oasis.

I dreaded those visits.

Twice a week, my father left Mama to manage the laundromat. He'd put us kids in the back seat and rocketed along in his little hatchback Nash down the narrow two-lane highway between Mountain Home and Boise. Dad's stated aim was to drop off the dirty uniforms customers left at our laundromat, pick up dry cleaned uniforms left on a previous trip, and return home in record time.

But once we picked up the clean uniforms, Dad detoured to Julia Davis Park.

He had a routine. First, Dad took us to use the public restrooms while he scoped them out. Afterwards, he took us across the Park to the little zoo and left us.

"Just wait."

I hated waiting.

While we waited for Dad's return, I was expected to entertain the boys; keep them safe. Warned never to talk to strangers, I held my brothers' hands and led them around and around the sad, smelly little monkey cages waiting for Dad's return. Sometimes we "just waited" a very long time.

In those days, public zoos in towns like Boise weren't much more than old boards and chicken wire nailed together. In contrast to the wide, cool park, the "zoo" was stinky. Poor little monkeys reached out beseeching hands.

Every week, twice a week, we three walked around and around and around. We "just waited." My brother Duncan says he too remembers the endless waiting. He remembers being led around and around. Young as he was, Duncan remembers feeling sorry for the helpless, hopeless little monkeys staring back at us. Trapped and waiting.

Finally, Dad reappeared. If we had been good—no giving up, no setting off to find him, no telling strangers we were alone—then Dad might buy each of us a Nehi Grape Soda at the filling station when he gassed up.

And then? We rocketed back in Dad's little Nash toward home and Mama. Twice a week.

• • •

Anxiety ran Dad. He seethed with "road rage" before they invented the name. He couldn't bear to see another car in front of him. As soon as Dad passed one car, he drove like crazy to overtake and pass the next. My brother Duncan says he still remembers those wild rides home, remembers lying amid the dry-cleaned uniforms staring up through the Nash's hatchback window, certain he was about to die, fighting back tears, afraid he'd never see Mama again.

Dad bragged about what "fast time" he made shuttling back and forth to Boise. He never said just what he was up to in Julia Davis Park, but then I guess Mama never dared ask. Maybe she was afraid to know. Anyway, no nice wife would dare broach such a subject.

That was Men's Business. A loyal wife did not suspect, dared not delve. Better to actively forget; to just dis-remember.

Still, choosing not to know generated dread. Mama must have read stories in the Boise Statesman exposing men discovered prowling the public toilets in Julia Davis Park. Seeing Mama's growing fear, knowing she was silenced, must have given Dad added pleasure, a sense of power. But Mama just didn't go there. She may not even have let herself know there existed a There to discover.

• • •

No matter, in the midst of Bill Goodman's interrogation of his 1,472 suspects, Dad suddenly stopped going to Boise.

Maybe Dad saw a familiar name when the Statesman began publishing the names of "perverts" charged, convicted and sent to prison. Men who didn't escape in time were publicly disgraced. They and their families were forever shamed and singled out as pariahs. In small-town America, social ruin was real. Reprisals continued so long as small town memory served to repeat gossip.

Dad saved his own skin.

Overwhelmed by the possibility of a very personal danger, Dad sold the laundromat. The sudden sale dictated a financial loss. Dad explained that laundry work was "too hard on the wife."

Suddenly out of the laundry business, Dad found Mama a job working as a checker in the grocery-hardware store where he worked stocking shelves. The post office job hadn't come through, not yet. Suddenly, we were very short of money. Mama hardly had a day off. At least there was no more waiting at Julia Davis Park; no more visits to sad little monkeys trapped in smelly chicken-wire cages.

Now, suddenly, trapped at home, alone with Dad while Mom worked swing shift, I dreamed that under cover of darkness, the Wolf roamed Julia Davis Park, drove our

little hatchback Nash back from Boise. Neon cat's eyes
lit up my dreams. I dreamed of poor little monkey hands
reaching out. Mushroom clouds and invisible radiation
seeped through my classroom walls. Knocking in vain on
the doors of fall-out shelters, the Little Green Fairy and I
held out silent, beseeching hands.

I shared my Technicolor dreams. Mama rolled her eyes.
"You don't really believe that, do you?" she said,
once again pronouncing me a child with far too much
imagination.

But Mama remembered Bernie's suicide. She too read
the Statesman. Fear, like static electricity running before a
storm, filled the air. Dad flew off the handle. Rage rained
down like arrows upon Israelites. With Egypt long gone,
even my over-active imagination refused to save me.

Only the Brave Little Fairy soldiered on.

· · ·

Finally, a vacancy opened up at the post office—but
the post master didn't hire Dad. At Dad's urging, Mama
called postal inspectors working in the Oklahoma City
Post Office—men still loyal to the memory of her brother
Ernest used their political influence to force the local postmaster to hire Dad.

It was not an auspicious beginning.

Later, when an opening came up for a lifetime appointment as a rural mail carrier, Dad again made use of
Mama's connections. Like Uncle Bernie's spiteful colonel,
the postmaster remained utterly unforgiving. Their mutual
antipathy fueled a vicious, decades-long battle fought in
the dusty, cluttered confines of the local post office long
before workplace shootings became common.

Dad came home in black moods. He flew off the handle. He kicked the cat. We kids walked on eggshells. Dad
took over bath time.

Mama caught the brunt of Dad's rage.

"Show him you're grateful. He's had a hard day," she said, "Your Dad doesn't mean it."

But he did.

We tiptoed. Even the Uppity Little Green Fairy tried to play nice. We all learned Sara's lessons. The only way to gain favor, to survive, was to please, appease, submit and stifle. We hoped at least, he wouldn't tease. I wanted him to stop telling Mama she had no sense of humor, but he didn't.

• • •

Every family dinner was an opportunity to be humiliated, another chance to earn yet another Good Spanking. Or two.

In spite of that, we were greedy eaters. Food and plenty of it meant love.

"Food," Sara said, "is the way to a man's heart."

Mama tried. When she cooked supper, she'd come to the living room door several times and ask my father what vegetable he wanted with his traditional meat and potatoes.

"Corn? Peas? Green beans, Carl?"

Dad would shrug. "Don't bother me. Can't you see I'm reading my paper?"

So, forced to choose, Mama sat down to dinner knowing that, set-up for failure, whatever vegetable she put on the table would be exactly the wrong dainty-dish to set before the King.

Wrong was wrong, wrong, wrong. Unforgivable. Sitting across the dinner table, Dad started in, "Fat slut. Old hag. Old bag. Stupid cow. Worthless old maid."

Enraged since childhood thanks to Paw-Paw, further enraged by his boss, Dad lit into Mama. It was safer. Besides Dad knew all Mama's soft spots.

I can still hear her trying in vain to say, "But Carl, I thought you might like green beans tonight."

It all got to be too much. Married twelve years, taking blame for Dad's failures, isolated from family and friends in Oklahoma City, absorbing her father's "No." Grieving her brothers' deaths. Twelve years of providing silent cover for Dad's reckless ways?

And now, added to all that, the fear of reading Dad's name published in the Statesman as one of Goodman's 1472?

Something broke inside my mother.

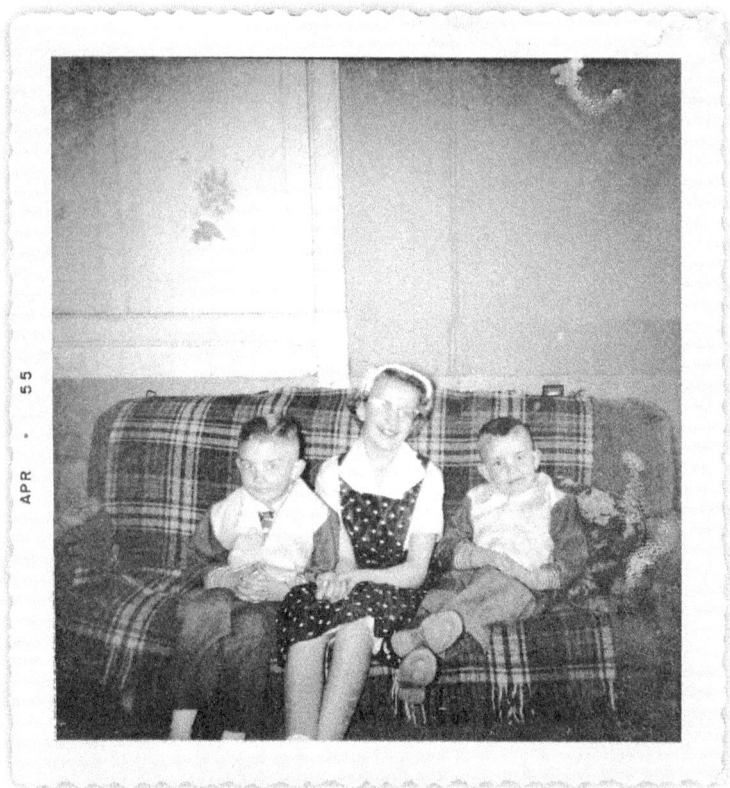

Like Lazarus, Mama rose from the dead, but something vital died on the maroon couch that day

Chapter 17

One fine day, Mama just stopped. She lay down quietly on our scratchy maroon-colored couch and she just stopped.

She even stopped noticing a stubborn little girl like me. Mama stopped noticing my little brothers, even when they came and leaned against the scratchy pillows, even when Buddy cried and Duncan called out to her.

Mama just lay there. Just lay there. She didn't notice when Daddy yelled, shook her, and shouted, "Get up!" She didn't notice, not even when Daddy flew into a rage and kicked the maroon couch.

Mama just lay there. After a while, even Daddy seemed a little afraid.

Maybe the King should have smiled and eaten his green beans. Allowed the Queen to enjoy bread and honey once in a while? Given his permission. Even said, "Sorry." Maybe even said, "Please" and "Thank You"?

Was Dad suddenly afraid people might think he had gone too far? Still, as far as my father was concerned, utility to his needs was everything. A nearly comatose wife was hardly useful. So he made arrangements. He decided to send Mama away to the state mental hospital in Blackfoot—the same sort of cold, gray place the Army had intended to send my Uncle Bernie.

"For evaluation," the Army had said.

"For evaluation," Dad said. A respectable way for a good husband to rid himself of a useless wife.

Because a wife's despair, like a brother's suicide, was a shaming thing, a family story to be told only in whispers.

Even a frightened, stubborn girl like me could tell that Mama lying there on the maroon couch day after day was not normal.

In the '50s, patients sent off to state hospitals returned dazed and incoherent from electroshock but supposedly returned to normal. Not "recovered." But compliant. Tamed. Readied like Elise to carry 100-pound sacks down dusty steps to the Home Place. Like "conversion" therapy today, shock treatments silenced patients, rendered them cooperative and ready to return to the same Father-Knows-Best status quo lives that had driven them "crazy" in the first place.

In the meantime, several too-nice, smiley-face women in our town circled round, anxious to help my "brave" father through his crisis. Just as Charley soon replaced his beloved Rebeka with another equally well-trained nice wife, my father looked around. Women were ready and willing to marry him. Some even claimed to be willing to take on his three poor, motherless children.

• • •

Dad had one small problem: Since my mother was not dead and had never committed adultery, the only avenue to freedom from an inconvenient wife was for my Father to get divorce papers signed and notarized then spend six weeks in Reno. But it suited Dad to be just a poor man unable to divorce. It prolonged the drama. A wife on electro shock or Thorazine in a mental hospital made for a good puppy story. His options remained open and he could still play those nice women against each other just as he played Mama and Elise, and Mama and I, off against each other, couldn't he?

Since Paw-Paw had taken his oldest daughter Carrie to do for him in Black Tower, maybe Dad considered me old enough to fill in for Mama. However, even though I was Big Sister to my little brothers, I was just a scared young girl forced to play "house" in the real world. I had no desire to emulate the aunties.

• • •

I wanted my Mama.

I was terrified and heartsick. I felt guilty.

If I hadn't made my Mama cry . . . If I hadn't been the "most stubborn girl" Mama had ever seen . . . If I promised to be good now, maybe Mama would smile. Maybe she'd rise up like Lazarus in the Bible story, take up the old plaid blanket and walk away from that scratchy old maroon couch where she lay day after day?

Still, women came calling; came smiling; came bringing Daddy peach pies straight from the oven. I hated them all.

Heck Fire! Mama was not someone to be replaced by a flirty, flirty stranger.

I would not have it!

The forever Spiteful Green Fairy and Stubborn, Contrary Singular ME, prepared to do eternal battle against all comers, interlopers, and sneaky peach-pie-bakers.

Things went from bad to worse.

Singular ME and the Spiteful Green Fairy lit candles to St. Jude—the saint said to side with hopeless causes. Both of us secretly feared maybe St. Jude was just another silly boy dressed in long robes, but we lit candles anyway.

I said, "Pretty please."

The Little Green Fairy shut up and agreed to light another candle.

St. Jude came through.

• • •

A miracle of kindness saved us all: St. Jude sent a kind country doctor who said "No" to Daddy. Our family doctor refused to sign the commitment papers my father thrust at him. Absent the doctor's signature, Daddy, couldn't send Mama away.

That done, the doctor pulled up a straight chair beside Mama as she lay inert on the couch. He spoke gentle words. He reminded Mama there were small children to live for; young children who needed her.

He made Mama believe in hope.

Revived by his simple kindness, Mama sat up. There was a blindness in the way she swung her feet to the floor, pushed back her hair. She looked around. After what seemed like an eternity, Mama absently picked up the old plaid throw that had slipped off the couch and began to fold it. She took a spoonful of soup, then another.

Mama rejoined our family.

She went back to work checking groceries again. She helped out.

Once again Mama stood in the doorway. She asked Dad which vegetable he preferred. She stopped fighting back.

She accepted "No" as the answer to freedom.

Like Lazarus, Mama rose from the dead. But something vital died on the maroon couch. Just as a woman called Mule must have died long before. Just as a little boy died up in the loft on the Home Place. Just as we might have died growing up.

But, shrapnel wounds sewn closed, life went on. We pretended nothing was wrong. Eventually, an icy winter became a chilly spring. Then summer came, and Grandma Sara stepped off the train.

Life dared to feel safe again.

· · ·

Later that summer, my father wrote a letter to Paw-Paw and Elise. In the letter, Dad says he is happier than he has ever been. Reading the dusty letter, discovered in Pandora's Box, I suddenly realize Dad made no mention of my mother's illness, nor did he write of Mama's miraculous recovery.

To this day, both my brothers say they don't remember, never knew, Mama lay inert on the maroon couch.

Certainly, I never heard anyone ask Mama how she was doing afterwards. Nothing to remember.

Nothing to tell Sara when she stepped down off the train.

In Dad's letter, there's not even passing mention of those terrible days before me and the Spiteful Green Fairy, St. Jude and the kind doctor saved Mama.

Dad's letter starts out:

"Dear Paw-Paw and Mums, Seems like an endless chain of work." Then the whole first page goes on to describe all the work Dad is doing to jack up the foundation of our old gray house with the maroon couch inside. "Will have to get another apartment rented to pay for all this. Sure glad Marie can work and help me pay for all of it. Believe we can make it without an FHA loan, too. Marie says she's happy to work and help out."

At a time when wells in Black Tower were drying up, and Paw-Paw and Johan couldn't make crops, Dad's letter continues, "Has been 106 here this year and sure seems hot. I'm sure it has been hot there too. It is dry here but we have plenty of irrigation water, and our well is sure fine. A well like mine down there would be worth three or four thousand dollars."

He then says, "I certainly have no desire to go back into that part of the country, except on a visit."

Although Dad's letter says nothing about Mama's health, Dad goes on to describe his own illness. "Seems like every year in August I have to have a spell of feeling rotten. The last couple of days I have been almost sick. I think I'll get another round of the Tetracycline. That sure seems to knock it for a loop. Should do something. It costs $1.00 per capsule and I take five or six a day. Anyway, I no longer have a spell of this for four or five times a year as I did for years."

...

*Thinking back, the first "spell" I remember was when
we lived behind the laundromat in Jerome. Newer "miracle" drugs like Streptomycin and Tetracycline* were later
developed, but Dad kept getting "re-infected"—or, at a
dollar a pill, maybe Dad took the medication only just long
enough to feel better.

Dad ends the August 1st part of his letter by saying,
"Grandma baked me a peach pie today. It's all gone." On
September 21, the letter resumes—Dad writes a page and
a half about all the work he is still doing to fix the house.
"We are putting in a propane gas forced air furnace with
a duct to each room. It will be an air conditioner in summer. It will cost us $47 per month for three years to do all
our remodeling and building, but Marie says she is glad to
work evenings like she is so we can get the house fixed up
sooner. Grandma is still with us and maybe if we 'make it
hot for her' she will stay longer than she now plans."

• • •

Of me, Dad writes:
"Janet is at the top of her class of 30, and she is a lot
happier and not so nervous since she got her glasses and
can see better."

"All the better to watch out for the Big Bad Wolf," said
the Little Green Fairy.

Dad's letter goes on, "Janet really is a different person
since she got glasses. Janet is just the height of Mom, and
she is quite a young lady. I used to say those brown eyes
would attract attention when she got to be fifteen or six-
teen but now I see the neighbor boys like to come over and
talk nonsense by the hour. They come looking for their cat
or want Janet to come fix their mother's hair or come over
to play with Bayard and Duncan hoping Janet will show
up before too long. She isn't nice to them, but they don't
seem to mind that, and I don't care at her age how she does
them."

I found a picture of us playing on the long cylindrical propane tank set up next to the house to fuel the "forced air heater" my Dad wrote of installing.

In the picture I'm a leggy pre-teen, wearing short shorts and holding someone's little girl—probably a child I was babysitting, but I don't remember. Knowing me, I was bossing everyone around. I made up stuff and "directed" while everyone play-acted out the imaginary stories I made up.

There is a tall boy standing there in the picture—one of two brothers who lived in the tiny rental house next door. His father breathed in mustard gas fighting in the trenches in WWI. Thirty years later, his father's labored breathing signaled the boy's father was busy dying. I don't remember that frightened boy as being much interested in me.

Even though Dad said he didn't much care, that's the summer Dad started tearing onto me, just as he tore into Mama. Screaming "fat slut, whore," his words told me no one would ever marry a bad girl like me. I can still remember my hurt and bewilderment. I didn't realize Dad's jealousy was talking.

· · ·

Reading back through his letter, Our World According to Dad, I am struck by the fact that my Dad tells his parents, "Marie sure feels good here," then writes, "I have never been happier." Well, why not? His wife was no longer comatose with depression; Mama professed herself happy to work and help him achieve his ambitions, while repeated doses of Tetracycline solved his sickness problem just as penicillin solved mine.

As Dad's letter shows, in our house, my father, like Paw-Paw before him, controlled the narrative. Dad had us "pegged," boxed-up and forever labeled: "Smart girl, needs watching"; "Oldest son, smart, but a mama's boy." "Duncan is going to be our Pecks Bad Boy"

It's Dad's description of Duncan that is most troubling to me. Of all of us, June-Bug was the most playful. Isolated, he tried for love and approval in a household where everything revolved around pleasing our father.

June-Bug liked to poke at you and run giggling. He wanted us to chase him, tickle him until he couldn't breathe. Then he begged for more. Dad's description of my brother as Peck's-Bad-Boy breaks my heart.

Duncan was a little boy lost in the shuffle. He, perhaps more than any of us, tried to win my father's approval, wanted his love. He certainly deserved a proud father. But Dad dismissed him as "Peck's Bad Boy." Dad played Duncan just as he played all of us. The King of the Castle, Dad advanced his own ends.

Dad's letter goes on to enumerate how many quarts of food we'd canned in preparation for winter. In a world where food came closest to love, Dad was happy. All was right with his world. Even the weather was cooperating. While Paw-Paw couldn't make a crop, Dad had a three–thousand-dollar well right on the property. Mama was hired out and earning.

Dad had only to elbow his sons aside and keep a vigilant eye on me.

• • •

Unfortunately, a degree of judicious violence, deliberately applied, was, it seemed, going to be necessary to keep me in my place. I was angry, mouthy, and opinionated. And stubborn to boot. I felt like the little girl with the curl right in the middle of her forehead.

Not a happy combination.

Not for a forever Uppity Girl; not in those days.

Each of us reacted to Dad's lust for control as best we could. Sometimes we even laughed. Once Mama rejoined the living, she had two favorite sayings. "Might as well laugh as cry." And "Tyrants make hypocrites." Both observations only to be used once Dad was safely out of earshot.

As for me, I resolutely hung reality out to dry. I disconnected, disremembered. I pushed more and more into outer darkness. Still, what to do with all the anger that a nice girl must not feel? I hated the Biblical injunction, "A soft answer turneth away wrath." The Spiteful Little Green Fairy absolutely refused to "Turn the other cheek."

I compromised. I made snarky comments but under my breath.

. . .

For escape, I read murder mysteries. There some sharp old Miss Marple, ferreted out the Big Bad Wolf, spoke truth. Then she set the world to rights, just like my Sara stepping down from the train. Angry, I wanted to disappear into some better place where lies did not overpower, and justice reigned.

My anger spurted out. My mouth caused me no end of trouble. Chastised, I was afraid that no Prince Charming would chose a not-nice, mouthy girl like me.

Trapped there within my father's orbit, forbidden to criticize, afraid to speak, I dreamed of growing up, of creating a magically happier family than the one I witnessed every day. I dreamed I'd reach escape velocity and disappear into Sara's perfect Happily-Ever-After.

Someday.

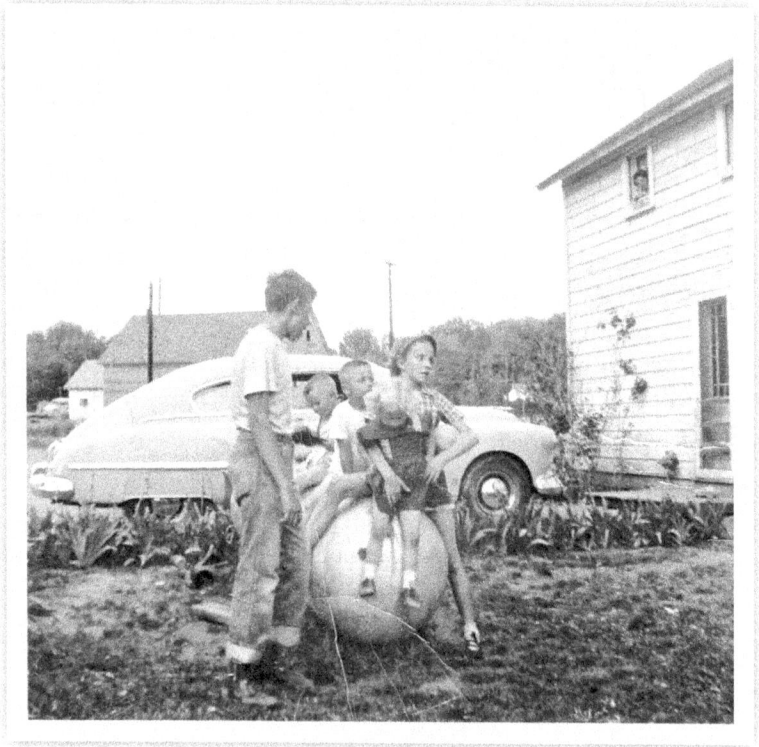

So much for the most stubborn little girl of all.

Chapter 18

My *dreams of escape began in earnest with a beating.* Our family was eating lunch, all of us sitting around the same round oak table upon which my father had written his letter to "Paw-Paw and Mums"—the same oak table where Sara said my mother once took her first baby steps into Bernard's outstretched arms.

In our house it was a female's job, my job, to spread the cloth and set the table. It was my job to fill all the glasses with cold milk. I had to make sure my father's place was set with his favorite knife and fork. A perfect table was set with bread and butter, salt and pepper, and Sara's blue sugar bowl. The relish tray must be filled with olives and celery, and Dad's favorite pickles, all present and accounted for in the middle of the round oak table, waiting for Daddy to sit down.

Dad said grace, but when he looked up, there was a frown on his face.

"Where are my pickles?"

I reached to pass the pickle dish across to him.

"No." He frowned. "I said my pickles."

I got it. These pickles were the wrong pickles.

I got up and returned from the kitchen with a different jar.

"No," he said. "Go back. Bring me my pickles." He tried to frown, but by now his smirk was showing. I knew that look. Like when Mama asked him what vegetable he wanted her to cook for his dinner.

Wrong. Wrong again. Wrong, wrong, wrong.

My brothers, alert to angry cross-currents, caught Dad's drift. He egged them on. As I watched, the boys tentatively nudged each other, stifled giggles.

Danger, like electricity, filled the air. Like when Paw-Paw held out his linty old candy toward me, played his tricking game and the aunties froze.

"No," Dad said. "Go back and bring my pickles."

Stung by the little boys' laughter, I went back a third and then a fourth time. I ignored Green Fairy's rebellion. I trudged back to the kitchen, opened the icebox. I tried to find the right pickles, I did. I tried but I was running out of choices. And behind me, in the dining room, I heard Dad and the little boys laughing.

Like the aunties, my brothers were afraid not to join in. Like all those brothers up in the loft so long ago, the little boys were afraid if they didn't go along, the bully's abuse would swing their way.

Caught like Mama, I knew whatever jar I chose would be, by definition, "Wrong."

Dad was openly laughing at me. Even the boys were beginning to laugh.

The humiliation stung. Back and forth. Back and forth. Sending me on a fool's errand, playing cat and mouse. Basic training for girls. Basic training for little boys, too. "How to treat a girl like a girl" unless of course a youngster wanted to be "treated like a girl" and called Sissy-Boy himself.

Stung, I sat down.

"Go back again," Dad said. "Get my pickles."

"Get them yourself."

Dead silence. The world held its breath.

"What did you say?"

"Get them yourself."

Suddenly I felt Dad's steel grip. He dragged me into the downstairs bedroom and locked the door. He paused only long enough to set my expensive new glasses carefully aside. Then he used his knee to pin me down. He climbed on top and began punching me, over and over and over. Methodically. Picking his spot: a controlled burn.

"Stop, stop!" Crying. Begging. I couldn't breathe. Smothered. Panicked. Trapped down between the bed and the wall. I couldn't move. Smothered. Like all the other times I got a Good Spanking. But worse.

Mama was pounding on the door, pleading, "Carl! Carl!" I could hear both my brothers outside, crying now.

Dad's face, ugly with rage, filled my world with hurt. Just as carefully removing my glasses had shown prudence, Dad chose where to hit. He avoided punching my face. Just as when he hit Mama, my bruises weren't meant to show. Bruises covered by clothes don't count.

Dad hit and hit and kept on hitting.

Forever.

The Wolf smiled. The cat purred. Shoved down between the bed and the wall, I could not breathe.

Still, I vowed to be the most stubborn little girl.

Dad went on and on.

"Carl, I'll call the police," Mama's voice came through the door,

I couldn't breathe. I was dying.

Terror took me.

"Daddy. Stop, Daddy! I'll be good!"

"Say please." Punch. Punch.

"Please Daddy, please, please! I'll be good."

I heard Wolf laughter.

"I'll go get your pickles."

Too late for pickles.

"Now" Punch—"say"—Punch—"say Pretty Please."

Even the Wolf was breathless.

"Say it!"

The ginger cat batted the tiny pink mouse one last time.

Daddy seemed strangely excited.

"Carl, stop it! Stop, or I'll call the police." Mama's voice broke. "I mean it, Carl."

"Pretty please, Daddy, pretty please! Pretty Please, Daddy . . ."

Laughter spurted out. Climaxed.

"Pretty Please, Daddy . . ."

"That's more like it."

Sexual excitement ebbing, Daddy climbed off, unlocked the door, screamed at Mama, hit her, then he shoved both of the now weeping little boys aside.

Mama had threatened to call the police. He wouldn't forget. She'd pay. For weeks. Until she said "Sorry." Said the Wolf was right. Until Mama too, said, "Pretty please."

· · ·

The next day I wore a short sleeve blouse to school. Deliberately.

I didn't point. I didn't tell. I knew better. Still, there was no way the teachers missed my bruises. Angry red bruises, shading to purple turned my arms to chartreuse then to yellow in the days to come.

The other children looked away, some no doubt remembering their own beatings. Back then, none dared speak up. Not in that small town. Not back in those never-ask, never-tell, stifle-yourself, days. It would be a long, long time before even adult women dared speak out and openly say "Me too."

Back then, the equation was simple: the worse the child, the worse the spanking. Spare the rod and spoil the child. In that world, fathers took off their belts and said, "This is going to hurt me more than you," then whaled away.

No telling what bad thing I must have done to force my father to give me such a Good Spanking.

No bruises marred my face though.

"Don't make yourself unhappy," Sara said. "Just don't think about it."

Bad children grow up and go to prison. Bad seed. Tainted blood. Forever bad. Once labeled, no welcome back. Ever.

So much for the Most Stubborn Little Girl.

Just thinking about it made the Spiteful Green Fairy's head hurt.

...

After that last Good Spanking, I knew a frontal approach was too dangerous. Instead, I focused on growing up, on escaping to a Happily-Ever-After Marriage of my own making, as though such an escape automatically ensured safety.

It never occurred to me that such an escape might only result in same song different abuser.

In the meantime, I tried to please.

I well knew, no nice girl would think of hating her father.

So I said, "I hate this town." "I hate these stupid people."

I never said, "I hate my Daddy."

I never said, "I wish I were dead."

Nice girls can't think such things. They never show anger.

Instead, I read.

I took to my bed.

While the ginger cat crept about hunting small frightened things, an electric current of stifled rage shaped itself into dreams of bloody murder.

Patricide, like incest, does not spring from thin air.

Patricide wafts from black holes, bubbles up in the simmering silence created by "Just don't think about it."

"Don't ask."

"Never tell."

"No dots to connect? Good girl."

Once he divided the first house into apartments, Dad needed cash to buy the next – our Sunday drives were his solution.

Chapter 19

There's an unhappy passage in Frank McCourt's memoir, "Tis," where McCourt says, as a child, he was afraid his friends would turn against him for telling the truth about his family:

"If I go on writing about my miserable childhood they'll say, 'Stop. Stop. Life is hard enough; we have our own troubles.' So from now on," McCourt writes, "I'll write stories about my family moving into the suburbs of Limerick where everyone is well fed and clean from taking a bath once a week."

Unlike McCourt, my own family never quite made it to Limerick—but we were well fed, and, for the Wolf's pleasure, my little brothers were treated to frequent baths.

Shortly after my last Good Spanking, our family began to trek from house to house in the same little town; moving from one fixer-upper to another, sawing, painting, remodeling.

Once pronounced done, Dad divided every papered-over fixer-upper into tiny apartments and rented them to military families.

"They'll rent a remodeled chicken coop," Dad laughed. He had indeed figured out another way to take advantage of the war boom.

"Flipping," they call it now—except Dad, like Paw-Paw with his lust to own 1,000 acres, never sold. Once the rewiring was done, the wall board nailed up, and the last crack papered over, the renters moved in and our family moved on, into the mess and dirt of yet another fixer-upper.

"When I marry, my house won't have wall board stacked behind the living room couch," I told the Spiteful Green Fairy. "My children won't be ashamed to bring friends home." Stuck in Idaho's outback, I longed for my own version of Frank McCourt's Limerick, shining and safe on the corner of Emerald Isle and Nice Family.

During the Korean War, the Cold War, and the Vietnam War, civilians like my father struck it rich. But, to start with, Dad needed cash to prime the pump.

Once he divided the first house into four rentals, he needed cash to buy the next. Having already defaulted on an FHA farm loan, getting a bank loan posed a problem. With the money from #2211 Pawnee spent on good times, the money Mama inherited from Uncle Bernie's death used to fund the laundry, Dad had no reserves to draw upon.

• • •

Our family's Sunday Drives were Dad's solution.

One Sunday in 1954, our whole family piled inside the little hatchback Nash. Dad drove like mad up the hilly, graveled, back roads toward Toll Gate. He drove faster and faster, cutting up the hilly curves, driving like a madman.

"Dad! Dad!" Mama said.

But Daddy stepped on the gas, cut more uphill corners, in search of disaster.

"Dad!" Mama reached out, touched his knee.

"Dad!" her terrified voice begged "Slow down."

But begging only encouraged my father.

Even then I knew Mama should have shouted, Faster! Faster! Then Dad might have slowed down. Watching Mama out of the corner of his eye, Dad began to smirk, then laugh. Seeing her fear, he stood on the gas, more reckless by the minute. That day, not just my brother Duncan expected to die. We all did.

But not Dad. Thrilled by risk, searching for reward in disaster, our terror merely added to his pleasure.

Dad cut sharp left just as a car filled with teenagers crested an uphill curve.

Thank God for the instant reflexes of the young. The youngster pulled quickly to his left, into the lane where Dad's Nash should have been, thus narrowly avoiding a head-on collision. The teenagers' car hit us on the passenger side. Mama's head broke the windshield. She bloodied both knees. We kids were shaken and bruised. Dad stepped out unscathed.

Unfortunately for the quick-thinking young man, he and his passengers had been drinking beer at the reservoir above Toll Gate. My father, a "stable family man," told the sheriff's deputy that he, not the eighteen-year-old, had quickly pulled into the wrong lane to avoid a head-on collision.

The police believed my father.

My lucky father received a substantial insurance settlement. The icing on his cake? Money for another fixer-upper. My father's risky plan paid off. Handsomely.

I begged off any further Sunday drives.

I wasn't in the car in 1956 when my lucky father was again awarded a substantial sum of money as a result of a similar accident.

Duncan remembers that second car crash because Mama was holding him on her lap in the front seat. Only Duncan's body prevented Mama's head from breaking through the windshield. Duncan's front teeth were knocked out.

Duncan still says Dad didn't care if he killed us all.

Meanwhile, the new windfall came in handy. Over my mother's objections, Dad bought yet another fixer-upper and moved us in.

...

Our "new" house had ancient, rusted plumbing, bare bulbs, and primitive "knob and tubing" electrical wiring. In the freezing, high-ceilinged bathroom, rusty water left brown stains in the chipped tub. The kitchen stove provided the only heat.

Narrow tongue-and-groove paneling covered the kitchen walls and the twelve-foot ceiling. Years of coal dust and dirt sifted down through the tongue-and-groove paneling. It smudged floors, smeared Mama's dishes, blackened white tablecloths and children's faces.

Even the scratchy maroon couch turned gray. Life competed with ancient dirt and fresh sawdust, with hammers and nails, wire clippers and rolls of electric wiring.

At 13, the very idea of having a friend see inside our front door was beyond humiliating. My first boyfriend walked me home then stalked off, insulted, when I refused to ask him in. I'd rather have died than tell him my secrets.

By then, I was Daddy's go-fer when it came to remodeling. I loved the geometry of carpentry. I loved the elegance of math. I loved the way story problems figured out the truth. In Home Ec., I loved cutting out dresses, loved seeing shapes cut from flat cloth turn into pretty dresses. I loved watching Sara build a Wedding Ring quilt. It was geometry created with a needle and thread and scraps of cloth. Carpentry was just building snug little houses instead of prom dresses. Only the tools were different.

I spent months, years, as Dad's go-fer, running, fetching, watching. I aspired to be a carpenter, a builder. I knew I could do it. I knew I could be more than Dad's go-fer.

But Dad said, "No."

In his universe, girls were helpers, plain and simple. Dad expected nice women to help out, have babies, polish the veneer, and provide cover for Men's Business. Women could never "Be" anything in their own right.

The Spiteful Green Fairy rolled her eyes. She flounced off. Sick of go-fering, she washed her hands of the whole mess, vowing once again to reach escape velocity.

And the Wolf? He issued orders, hammered away, hoping to out-own Paw-Paw someday.

...

Anger boiled behind my smile. I couldn't imagine
even June Cleaver, with her pearls and perfect hair, making breakfast amid the sawdust and soot of our makeshift
kitchen. Mama tried, but Limerick was never Daddy's
dream. Dad aspired to own 1000 rentals. He'd out-Paw-
Paw Paw-Paw! He'd show him! The obsessed little five-
year-old shook his fist at past injustice and cycled on
toward Black Tower.

Still, once upon a time, we did visit Limerick.

Mama said, "Carl, can't we at least go look?" We piled
into the car, and off we went to "just look."

The tidy little house had an attached two-car garage,
white trim, and a white picket fence. A For Sale sign beckoned in the freshly mowed lawn. We were entranced. All
except Dad.

No matter how much I might dream of Happily-Ever-
After, Limerick disappeared the first time the Wolf's shadow
fell across my bed. The first time silence was imposed,
safety was lost. Long before, when Andrew disappeared
and no one spoke, Paw-Paw's legacy closed over.

And the Mackies? They changed their name but
remained forever on guard counting on the fragile protection of a respectable veneer to shield them from abiding
prejudice. Had their world been safe maybe Sara's Bernie
wouldn't have chosen suicide.

No, I never lived in Limerick.

Even today I cannot imagine who I might have become
had I been safe.

Had I grown up in a snug little house, might not my
children, and grandchildren, too, have enjoyed a different
legacy?

But then, maybe not. According to the Center for
Disease Control, 1 in 4 girls and 1 in 6 boys report they
too were molested in childhood. How many children still

live in fear, silenced behind the closed doors of even snug little houses?

As for Dad, he looked the little gray house over.

He said, "I'll think about it."

We all got back in the car. I pressed my nose against the window. Dreaming in daylight, I waved "Goodbye! Goodbye!" as Daddy turned the corner and we drove away forever.

All these years later, that little house still stands dreaming somewhere in a childhood just out of reach, on the corner of Limerick and Happily-Ever-After. It still waits for the little girl I might have been to find her way back and move in.

Dad said "I'll think about it."

But as soon as we got home, he went out and bought yet another dilapidated fixer-upper—this time an old farmhouse on seven acres at the edge of town.

My father clearly had different dreams.

Dad drove us up to the dilapidated old farmhouse. We got out and started over.

Dad secured the rural postal route he coveted. Mama went back and forth to work. My brothers and I changed schools. I walked home every day to help Dad out.

• • •

Then Dad bought three more fixer-uppers in quick succession and had them trucked to his seven acres. They formed a disheveled row next to the old farm house. It was late fall when backhoes dug the basements, concrete mixers poured the foundations, and movers dropped off the houses. We kids raked the leftover piles of dirt out across dead weeds and vegetation, creating muddy yards and driveways in front of each sad house.

When winter arrived, muddy driveways became furrowed sheets of ice—which, when winter turned to spring, melted into the slushy goo of freeze and thaw. Tromping in and out, we tracked the sticky black mess all through

Mama's house, adding yet another layer to the sawdust and chaos we forever lived in.

The Spiteful Green Fairy seethed, but after that last Good Spanking, that last "Pretty please!" I knew better than to openly rebel. At least at school, I could forget home, where the wood stove smoked, and the Wolf lived.

Stifled rage bubbled up. After school I excelled at not helping. If I could only hope to be Dad's forever gofer, never a real Carpenter, why bother?

Once home from school, I snuck off to the bathroom, locked the door, and comforted my thirteen-year-old rage by reading tales of bloody murder in the best traditions of Miss Marple and Sherlock Holmes.

I loved Miss Marple, a smart old lady much like my Sara. Miss Marple stepped into mayhem, restored order, made it safe to breathe again—she possessed integrity. Miss Marple set things right; something that never seemed to happen at our house.

I graduated from being a stubborn little girl to a sullen teen, forever egged on by a Spiteful Little Green Fairy.

Mama sighed. "You are such a joy."

The Spiteful Green Fairy glared at Mama and planned mayhem. In secret dreams, I plotted bloody murder in the best traditions of Miss Marple.

• • •

Mama's mantra, "You might as well laugh as cry," mocked us all in that first terrible winter out there on the muddy seven acres. Depression tracked in with the mud on our shoes, entered with the cold before we could slam the back door shut to protect what hope was left.

Mama tried. Since food meant love in our family, Mama dug out her Fannie Farmer Cookbook. She said we should "eat healthy" to keep from taking sick in the cold.

She cooked polenta. She baked lasagna and whole-grain brown bread. For a few minutes, the house smelled like heaven.

Mama spread a clean white cloth over the old round oak table. She set out elaborate dishes. She tempted us with love right there in that muddy kitchen with its sink propped up on two by fours and electrical boxes and wiring hanging down from the ceiling.

When Dad came home, she presented him with casseroles of green beans and mushroom soup, Irish lamb chops and garlic potatoes. Then she stood back, waited expectantly. Each dish reappeared only if Dad smiled.

Afterward, Mama washed the dishes and waited to gather energy and courage enough to spread her white tablecloth in the midst of mud and misery—hoping next time she'd find the path to Daddy's heart.

Even today, my throat closes up at the unexpected sight of a green bean casserole. Turning the pages of Mama's worn Fanny Farmer Cookbook, I see Mama's handwriting and remember the courage of her white table cloth spread against our winter of despair.

That winter I tried to bury despair. I forted up in the bathroom and read murder mysteries until the Spiteful Little Fairy appeared, muttering and glaring. She went underground, weaving all my buried rage into clever plans of patricide, a taboo at least as ancient as incest.

"A taboo necessitated by incest," the Spiteful Little Fairy insisted.

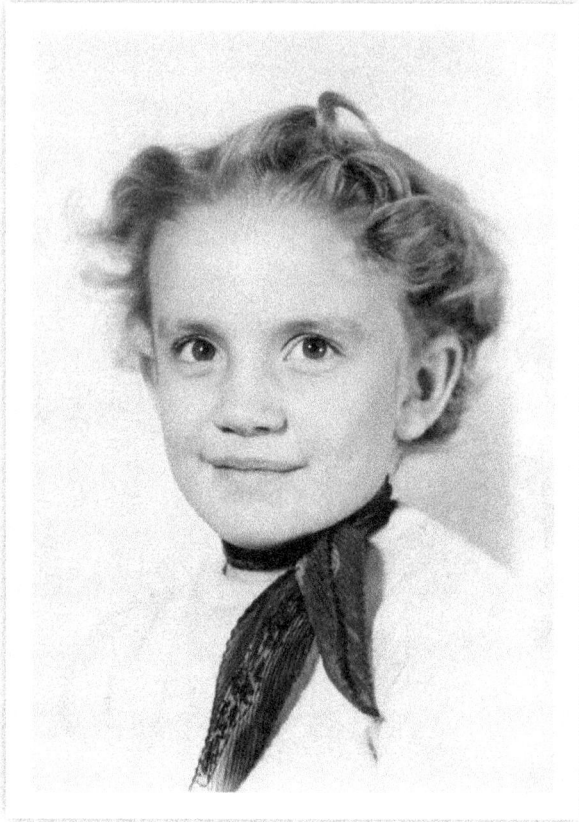

Plotting and planning, the trail of clues led unerringly to the wolf whose ambitions were plainly intended to kill us all anyway.

Chapter 20

There in the dark recesses, the Little Green Fairy and I plotted and planned bloody murder most foul.

"First," she said, "You must steal Daddy's insecticide from the shed. Then slowly, slowly poison Mama's food, because, in our house, food is the closest thing to love.

"Once Mama sickens and dies, leave hints for the kind doctor, point out the trail of poisoned crumbs left for the detectives to follow. Point out that Dad is the only one with a key to the garden shed where he stores his poisons.

"Remind them, Daddy is the husband who, once before, tried to rid himself of his inconvenient wife."

Planning and plotting, the trail of clues lead unerringly to the Wolf, whose ambitions were plainly intended to kill us all anyway.

Let the Sheriff and the autopsy point out the killer.

Let the judge and the jury sentence Daddy to "hang by the neck until dead."

And then?

"Then," said the Spiteful Green Fairy, "You step in."

"Don't kill my Daddy, kind sir,"

The Judge's heart will melt.

He'll say, "Well then, rot in prison, you Big Bad Wolf, you!"

Bang. Bang!

"Forever and ever. World without end. Life without hope; a fate worse than death," intoned the Little Green Fairy.

Slow death in prison. Slow death by insecticide. Poison, like food, is a woman's weapon. Poetic justice. Death by poison-peach pie: the path to Daddy's heart.

"Easy-peasy," said the Spiteful Green Fairy.

Then one night I dreamed the Green Fairy's plan into action.

Imagining murder in the best Miss Marple fashion, I dreamt I slowly, secretly, poisoned Mama. I laid down the Green Fairy's trail of clues. Each crumb lead detectives straight to Daddy. The Wolf convicted, I begged the judge's mercy. I graciously accepted Daddy's gratitude. Cruelty cruelly avenged.

The Spiteful Green Fairy celebrated. I smiled a sweet smile. Getting back at Daddy, getting away with murder was, indeed, a risky pleasure.

· · ·

But then I remembered, Mama lay cold and dead in her coffin. I awoke brimming with remorse. All-enveloping guilt washed over me.

What had I done?

Not easy-peasy after all. Pocket lint for me!

Maybe I should have said, "No," to the Little Green Fairy's bloody dreams?

Who knew that I possessed integrity, an inconvenient conscience?

The Spiteful Green Fairy threw up her hands and stalked off.

Relieved to realize my perfect murder was but a dream, I wrote a short story for the school literary magazine. The teacher read it. She rolled her eyes. Bloody dreams of patricide weren't exactly the sort of stories journalism teachers dared publish back then. But then, maybe mine wasn't the first twisted tale ever submitted for publication?

Thankfully, some small-town dreams, once imagined, are rejected.

"Two wrongs don't make a right," Sara said.

The Spiteful Green Fairy and I gave up childish hope of vengeance.

"Daddy hurt me first" was not an excuse that could fly anywhere except perhaps in a grown-up world peopled by Paw-Paws, predators, and still-angry little boy-men intent upon proving that their own rape had not somehow unmanned them.

Sometimes I wonder, what lights the rage that makes school shooters choose to kill their parents first, even before moving on to murder half their middle school?

Maybe some dream dreams of revenge only to wake up filled with remorse, only to discover an inconvenient conscience? Maybe most, attracted by revenge, awaken, and stop themselves before rage takes advantage?

In my case, all I felt was overwhelming guilt, followed by enveloping remorse. I recognized murder as an unwelcome fantasy to be avoided. Just so, I wish my father had recognized "taking sexual advantage" was risky business to be refused not re-enacted.

Integrity. Who knew?

Afterwards, I bided my time. I put off escape.

Silence reigned. We walked a minefield. It wasn't only that at our house cruelty might reappear at any time; there was the unbearable dread stretched in between the act and the inevitability of next time.

In those years of cold and dirt, I knew wherever normal was, it wasn't where I lived. Unable to cry or even laugh, as Mama advised, I vowed not to think about it. I knew I was too young to escape on my own. I needed Daddy's permission to cross the street.

Instead, I chose the role of provocateur. I decided Mama must leave and take me with her.

· · ·

"Leave him. Take us all to California," I begged.

Mama refused. She had once entertained dreams of escape. But her father said, "No," then both her brothers died. And in the long years afterward, Dad, his face red and dangerous, spittle showering from his mouth, convinced her otherwise. His never-gentle hands, his balled-up fists said leaving was too dangerous. She got the message. She couldn't win: He'd kill her children, disappear us then come for her. Even Limerick couldn't promise safety. But then, when had we ever been safe anywhere?

I know now that it wasn't simply fear for herself. My father obviously had reason to keep his children close because once away . . . well, who could say? Since Dad forbad her to take us with her, maybe Mama loved us enough to stay behind.

"But I'll work. I'll quit school. I'll take care of you," I promised.

She smiled. She shook her head. "No."

Even after the rentals made money, when they were, indeed, very well off, when leaving became possible, Mama still said, "No,"

I suspect that as years passed, Mama stopped seeing the husband who stood before her, wolfing down her life. I'm sure Dad's well-timed confidences tore at my mother's heart. Long after they married—in spite of indignity, and long after we left home—Mama stayed to mother Elise's lost five-year-old, still refusing to hurt the lonely little boy Dad had once been by abandoning the man he had chosen to become, the man who chose not kindness or self-control as antidote to cruelty but, instead, chose to re-enact the role of his abuser.

Better none of us escape than Mama should leave that little five-year-old behind.

. . .

In the end, Mama's world was whatever Dad's Good Husband story claimed it was. When she could no longer get around by herself, Dad took Mama to the Senior Citizen Center. There, just to get a rise out of Mama, he danced with all the old, lonely women who smiled and clung, praised and sympathized with him over his poor wife. Maybe some even baked a peach pie for him. Who knows?

Right to the end, Mama hoped Dad would buy her the gold wedding band he'd promised to give her once he made good. A ring would say they were married; a ring would tell the world she'd found the path to Dad's heart.

Dad danced and danced but he never gifted Mama with a gold wedding band.

• • •

Dad's lessons taught me to stay safe on the smiling surface. I dreamed only the approved dreams; the small-town dreams of a Happily-Ever-After-Believer. I got a job ushering at the movie theater. I babysat weekends. And, of course, I helped out. I gofered. I hated that a girl could never actually "Be" the action-hero who moved the arc of her own story forward.

But so be it.

I dated a local boy. A senior with a car, a very necessary accessory in those days. He was a nice guy. He took me to the local hangout and bought me a root beer every day after school. I hated root beer. But, as an aspiring "nice girl," I couldn't just say, "Thank you. I'd really like a Nehi Grape Soda, pretty please." So when I couldn't stand to drink another root beer, I dumped him.

Had I married him, I might still be living in that isolated town out in the sagebrush desert. Maybe I'd be in a snug little house on some corner, drinking root beer and telling my grandchildren the same Happily-Ever-After stories Sara told me. I'd still be waiting for my husband to come home for dinner; working up the courage to ask for grape soda. Like Mama, waiting for permission to breathe.

My brother said the last time he was back home, that old boyfriend asked him about me. Maybe he did care. Maybe he'd have said "Yes" to grape soda if I'd possessed courage to speak up?

Unable to prevent boyfriends, Dad started bringing
home young Airmen, ones he said I could date. I don't
know where Dad picked them up or just whose boyfriends
they were exactly. But after I dumped one, Dad took him
out to dinner and then gave the guy a ride back to the base,
returning late at night.

"Just to cheer him up," Dad said when I protested. In
our family didn't we close ranks against outsiders?

Dad laughed, shrugged, blew off my hurt.

Apparently I was focused on the wrong betrayal.

Dad's jealousy lashed out: Fat slut! Bitch! Whore! In
Dad's mind, I deserved it. Wasn't I betraying him by hunting for Prince Charming in order to escape Dad's control?

Mind games gave him the power to impose and dispose
of our reality. He controlled the narrative. Nothing could
be real if he said it wasn't. My hurt didn't exist if he said
he was only joking.

Neither Mama nor I knew the half of it.

Mentally distancing from him, escaping the bubble,
establishing boundaries, discovering confidence in my own
judgment, none of that was possible unless and until I realized that the received reality I learned in childhood was not
my reality but his.

It took far too many years to understand whose boyfriends those boys were.

People ask, "Was your Dad homosexual?" "Was he
minor-attracted?" Was he…?

I think Dad's gyroscope was so splintered by childhood trauma, he had no idea where his own true North
lay. More likely he was a sexual omnivore, an opportun-
ist prowling around, searching out whatever risky business
might serve to shore up his uncertain ego in the moment.

For self-respecting adults, "attraction" isn't the over-
riding factor. For example someone may be "attracted" to
his best friend's wife. That doesn't mean he automatically
gives himself permission to have sex with her and betray

his friendship. That doesn't mean he blames her for attracting him and thereby absolves himself of responsibility.

The same with people who are minor-attracted. Most choose not to act upon their attraction. They choose not to indulge their "attraction." Instead they make ethical decisions and choose not to abuse their power as adults to take sexual advantage. Self-respecting adults exercise the power to choose whether or not to act upon "attraction" even when making the ethical choice means denying their own needs. Integrity indeed.

For my father utility to his needs, whether sexual or financial, I think, came to be his only real "attraction." My father used us to meet his sexual needs then blamed us, saying we "attracted" our own sexual assault. Just so, he must have come to believe he had somehow "caused" his own abuse as a child.

Damaged as he was in childhood, denied real opportunity for help, Dad believed he was his label. Accordingly, Dad gave himself permission to devour whatever easy prey crossed his path. I think, for him the power to overpower, the opportunity to dominate and take advantage, became the over-riding attraction. Gender or age mattered little so long as his needs were met.

Doing harm, getting away with it in plain sight—such betrayal was the icing on his cake. Just as Dad relished our fear before the car crashed, even before the insurance pay-off came rolling in, he also relished my dread before a Good Spanking and my confusion afterwards as he passed Sara's delicate blue sugar bowl across the breakfast table.

It took years to recognize and finally unlearn family lessons skillfully taught, for it wasn't only Dad's narratives but Sara's romantic formulas that shaped my life. Afraid of shame and blame, we lived inside a bubble of sexual abuse in a family, in a country where "Don't tell!" "Don't think about it," is a legacy that continues to silence lives and ensure the cycles of transgenerational trauma continuing to harm families like my own. We dare not connect the dots. We fail to learn lessons a bigger picture might teach.

Still, in spite of set-backs, the Green Fairy urged escape, but after the last beating, after the aborted patricide, I insisted Green Fairy stay safe with me inside the bubble.

"Just don't think about those boys Dad brings home," I told her. "Don't make yourself unhappy."

· · ·

Having made escape my life's ambition, college should have been heaven. Instead, I was a fish dangerously out of water. With my head still inside the bubble of Dad's reality, I experienced devastating loneliness. I was completely unschooled in the normal give and take of friendship.

I was smart, but the stepped-up competition of college blew away what little self-confidence I had. I earned a "C" on a story I turned in to freshman English and knew, then and there, I'd never manage to "Be" a writer.

Instead, I majored in political science. There I discovered another wonderful teacher—an old Jewish man who had barely survived German concentration camps, as had his wife. He said, a world that produced men like Eichmann had to change.

In his classes, I first learned of Hannah Arendt's ideas about the sheer banality of evil. Arendt pointed out that great evil was often accomplished by aggressive but very conventional men consumed by their need to control.

Still, I assumed such aggressive men were only be found in the out-side world. They couldn't be Paw-Paws presiding over very conventional families could they? To imagine dots connecting Paw-Paw and Hitler was silly, wasn't it?

By the end of my freshman year, I was drowning in emotional crazy glue. Flying blind, I barely passed.

Dad's "smart daughter" had failed to make him proud. Given my failure, Dad balked at paying my tuition out of pocket.

"Anyway girls only go to college to get their Mrs. don't they?" Dad joked.

Mama insisted I return to college. She found me a job checking groceries in the store where she worked, so I could save money and pay my own tuition. Instead, I fell in love with a man strangely like my father. I chose Sara's tried-and-true, escape route: the trap door always open to nice girls hoping to reach escape velocity but afraid to cross the street; I fell in love.

"We just clicked,"

With the arrogance of the young, I told myself of course I'll be a better mother than my mother. And my husband will certainly be better-than my father.

It was a long time before I realized better-than isn't much of a criterion. It took longer still to realize my own Prince Charming was not the kind hero of Sara's Fairy Tales but was, indeed, a man strangely like my father. Absent a seismic shift to gender equality, my own marriage could be no different than the patterns of female subservience I'd been taught since childhood.

It took me years to realize my own Prince Charming was a man strangely like my father.

PART IV: AND THIS MY PRINCE CHARMING
COME TO RESCUE ME

Chapter 21

"Candy, little girl?" The handsome stranger grinned and slid a roll of cherry Life Savers across my checkout counter that summer.

"Cherry?" I wrinkled my nose, reached out and took one.

Seeing my expression, he laughed. He looked me up and down. Considering.

"Nice!" he said. "I'll be needing a couple of packs of cigarettes, too."

"What brand?" my voice sounded strange.

"Marlboro."

I smiled.

The Wolf smiled back, this time from behind a stranger's eyes.

Smiling, laughing at my confusion, he returned, and returned, again and again.

"Candy, little girl?"

I looked and then looked again.

"Nice! He thinks you're nice," the Green Fairy whispered.

The Little Green Fairy preened. She rearranged her gossamer wings just so.

My blue-eyed blond Prince Charming sported a military haircut. Here an oh-so-cocky warrior in an immaculate uniform and spit-shined jump boots, come to take me away. My Knight in Shining Armor, my Marlboro Man come to rescue me.

"Candy, little girl?" It was our joke now.

He slid candy across the counter. He bought cigarettes and held out his hand, "Matches little girl?"

I handed him matches and for lingering minutes his hand held mine in thrall.

An electric current ran up my arm; a shiver ran down my spine.

The fire was lit.

Prince Charming returned, bought another pack of Marlboros.

He lit more fires.

He smiled. He watched. He waited.

As nice girls will, I told myself, "He loves me!"

Mama's dreams for my better future didn't have a chance. Prince Charming's shiny blue Chevy matched his ice blue eyes!

My Marlboro Man picked me up after work. We rode around and talked for hours. He joked. I laughed.

He bought me a root beer. I said, "Thank you." Maybe I liked root beer after all.

He talked. I listened.

He told puppy stories. I heard wedding bells.

His Mother was still in a mental hospital due to post-partum depression. I said I understood about mothers and depression. Ben had been in a group home before his Dad remarried.

Ben said his wicked stepmother saw sex in every harm-less smile, in every lingering glance, every denied gesture that passed between a teenage Ben and her young daugh-ters. She imagined things. Ben said "I meant no harm. It was nothing." Nothing. Blended families with four teenag-ers—two stepbrothers, two stepsisters.

His wicked stepmother imagined things.

"There were problems," Ben said.

I understood.

By now the Spiteful Green Fairy didn't seem all that convinced, but I knew better. All Ben lacked was an understanding, loving, nice little wife.

Ben said his wicked stepmother never understood.

According to Ben, the attraction grew between Ben and his stepsister, love ensued—not rape as his wicked stepmother claimed. Well maybe someone had climbed into bed unannounced while a step-sister slept but?

But our love? Now that was different.

We were different.

The Little Green Fairy rolled her eyes.

Ben's wicked stepmother reported Ben.

The authorities came. Ben was unfairly detained.

"Pending further investigation," the policeman said.

The Green Fairy and I both agreed, Ben's tale did sound a little uncertain around the edges, but hey, even so, the step-sister was to blame.

She attracted him.

"Of course she wanted it."

"Takes two to tango."

Nice girls wait. Learn the tango after marriage.

Anyway, all Ben lacked was an understanding wife for life to be perfect.

Ben had been enticed. He said so.

And the detention center where they sent Ben after his wicked stepmother had her fit? Well, Ben said, Steilacoom was replete with older, experienced males, on the prowl for innocent young detainees awaiting a judge's decision.

Ben's puppy story reeked with resentment. He was the misunderstood, terrorized, bullied, and abused young boy summarily locked away in a cold and dangerous detention center by his wicked stepmother. What they did to him was worse than anything he'd ever done!

Besides, Ben swore the charges were a figment of his wicked stepmother's fevered imagination.

I sympathized. I'd heard puppy stories before.

Confused and in love, I told the Little Green Fairy, "No wonder Ben is mad at his family. No wonder he came home from detention even angrier than before."

The Green Fairy frowned.

"Don't you think?"

After that, Ben said, the court decreed, "Prison or the military."

Then as now, nothing much was done to prevent the future.

"Prison or the military" the Judge said,

Faced with "enlist or else," Ben chose the Air Force. Stationed at Le May's little Air Force base, he asked the million dollar question, "Candy little Girl?"

We drove around. Ben's ice blue eyes smiled at me across the seat of his shiny blue Chevy. I smiled back. We touched.

"We just clicked."

I was glad Ben trusted me enough to tell me his secrets. I'd make it all up to him. Wasn't that what Sara said a good wife did? Wasn't that what Elise and Mama tried?

I forgot my own experience. My Secrets stayed private. I asked Ben no penetrating questions. I stayed out of Men's Business. I trusted Ben.

But it seemed Mama and the Spiteful Green Fairy, much like Ben's wicked stepmother, distrusted Ben.

I sided with Ben.

What nice girl imagined her Prince Charming did things like that anyway?

"Just don't think about it," Sara said.

I didn't.

I didn't even tell anyone the story of how Ben came to enlist.

Bent on marriage, intent upon reaching escape velocity, dreaming of a better-than marriage of my own, I followed Sara's advice. I didn't make myself unhappy. Instead, I listened as Ben told Puppy Stories about his bad childhood.

I kept my own counsel. I listened, but I knew to keep my own Secrets secret.

"Thinking makes your heart hurt," the Green Fairy warned.

• • •

As a nice girl, I knew Ben only lacked an understanding wife, and I only lacked a Prince Charming. We understood. We fit, hand in glove.

We agreed, "No divorce in our family."

"Never? Ever?" The Little Green Fairy frowned.

Ben proposed. I accepted. Ben drove me to the jewelry store in the shiny blue Chevy that matched his smiling blue eyes. We picked out our rings. I paid for my gold wedding band with my college savings. Ben took me home. I showed Mama my ring.

• • •

Mama was devastated by the news. I can still see her sitting, weeping, on the old maroon couch. Protesting, trying to get Dad to back her and say "No" to my marriage to Ben. Maybe Mama heard the sound of another lock dropping, foretelling disaster.

Dad stood by. Watched Mama plead and weep. Then took my side.

From that day forward, Dad bent all his efforts toward widening the rift between Mama and me, isolating us and dividing us against each other. There would be no dangerous "telling," no old secrets spilled, no long, confiding phone calls between mother and married daughter after marriage. Widening the rift was his protection.

Dad won. Mama lost.

Ben and I married in Mama's living room.

But maybe Dad was so intent upon the pleasure of defeating Mama once again that it didn't occur to him until too late; Ben wasn't one of the Airmen Dad had brought home.

I was escaping Dad's control.

. . .

On our wedding day, before I even changed out of my wedding dress, Dad stepped inside the downstairs bedroom and shut the door. He was red-faced and angry. Too old for a Good Spanking; a Good-Talking-To would have to do.

"Well, young lady," he said, his never-gentle finger poking me in the chest, "you made your bed. Don't think you can come crying home to me when Ben dumps you."

Every hissing word accused me of betrayal. It was all too clear: no matter what happened between Ben and me in future, Dad would say, "No!" to divorce just as Bernard once had, but for reasons of his own.

Shaken and bewildered, I told myself it didn't matter. Ben was clearly better-than my father, who hit, shouted and abused.

I would never need a divorce.

I'd be a better wife than Mama.

Awash in Sara's romanticism, I knew if I just followed Sara's script to the letter, if only I was sufficiently understanding, loyal, thrifty, supportive, submissive, silent, and of course loving enough, well, my husband would love me back. I knew we'd sail through even the darkest days.

It's the Wolf's eternal bargain: if a wife is just loving enough, she'll have power to melt the hardest heart. He'll be sorry, vow to love her better. He'll make it up to her. A good woman's love is magic. If she just loves enough, their children will surely never suffer harm. And if a husband still looks elsewhere? She just hasn't yet loved him enough to keep him from being forced to look elsewhere. But elsewhere in his own house? Inside a child's little yellow bed?

Just never connect the dots.

And should Ben turn out to be but a smiling Paw-Paw? A young man with ice-blue eyes dressed in jump boots, not my hero? Well, whose fault was that?

· · ·

No matter.

The Cuban Missile Crisis blew up.

Honeymoon interruptus.

The Air Force expected Ben to help guard the Free World's nuclear missiles, all armed and rearing-to-go in silos dug in Idaho's sagebrush outback.

Dad slammed out of the downstairs bedroom.

Ben left.

I finished changing out of my wedding dress and spent my honeymoon alone in one of the two-room apartments Dad rented to enlisted men and their young wives.

Just me and the Spiteful Green Fairy watching Kennedy on TV; expecting the world to end with a bang, not a whimper.

Kennedy and Khrushchev stared across the nuclear abyss for an unlucky thirteen days. The world escaped but, afterward, Ben came home with tales of a new, secret Southeast Asian conflict. Vietnam, it seemed, was morphing into what promised to be the hot war of our generation. But where in the world was Vietnam?

Even the Green Fairy couldn't figure that out. I vaguely remembered Mama telling me that when my Uncle Ernest "flew the hump" back in WWII, the Army Air Force landed planes at a French foreign legion air base built somewhere out in the Mekong Delta.

Ben and I got out yellowed WWII maps of Japan and looked for Vietnam.

"See?" Ben said, "Across that tiny finger of blue water?"

"Yes."

"That's Tonkin Bay."

"And there's the Mekong Delta." Full circle.

On our map, Southeast Asia was yellow. Communist China was pink. Pink?

"But didn't our president say Southeast Asia is crawling with Reds?" I tried to joke. Not funny.

Generals opined on TV, "Dominoes are falling." It seemed only US military intervention could save the Free World from threatening foreigners living on far off shores.

General Curtis Le May, right out there at our little Air Force Base, offered to bomb the Reds in yellow Vietnam "back into the stone age." John Wayne donned a green beret and convinced us, one and all, that what was happening was shadowy, top-secret, and of course, oh so romantic.

The hated French Foreign Legion decamped from Vietnam, and America took over. War boom ad infinitum. Some young Americans took off for Canada. Other's claimed they had bone spurs.

But not us.

Ben and I imagined we were making history. Just like in the Hollywood movies.

Mama's family were never draft dodgers. My uncles fought every war until Uncle Bernie was defeated by prejudice and Uncle Ernest murdered.

"Choose prison or the military," the judge told Ben.

Ben enlisted.

War, like power, like sex, was Men's Business. Married women should follow their husband's lead.

"Don't bother your pretty little head," John Wayne drawled.

Through it all, the Spiteful Green Fairy maintained radio silence.

Meanwhile, I fed the cat and waited for my hero's return, as lonely and isolated as Mama out there on the farm, or Rebeka waiting for her absent fly-boy's return.

With Ben gone long hours guarding America's nuclear missiles sites, and me whiling the time away day after day on the home front, the excitement of married life began to drag. How many times can you make the bed, sweep the floor, check the time, look out of the window, and not feel trapped, like Elise, behind glass? Or, like me, alone in a room, listening to the tic-toc of the clock, playing patience, watching and waiting for Ben?

Maybe making a baby would help pass the time.

. . .

Afraid pregnancy might, indeed, be my next wifely project, Mama seized her opportunity. Still cherishing hopes of my return to college, she relied on irregular warfare. In Ben's absence, Mama took me to a doctor willing to prescribe the then-new birth control pills. "But," Dr. said, "only to married women; only with their husband's permission."

Apparently men were not prepared to trust the women who'd been having children since the world began with control over their own bodies.

With access to affordable birth control pills, a woman could say how often, how many and if, she wanted children. It was a revolutionary concept. Weaponized, pink pills won the battle of the sexes, a battle always before won by aggressively conventional men upon the battlefields of women's bodies. It was a freedom Elise certainly never enjoyed.

Mama's male doctor hemmed and hawed.

Faced with Mama, he finally guessed it would be okay.

Back then they said once females gained access to the magic pill, lost their fear of unwanted pregnancy, all of them (loose women and little virgins alike) would suddenly run amok and lose "it" well before they lost "it" to their husbands.

Ben assured me that once little virgins experienced "it" they became sexually insatiable.

The Green Fairy demurred; rolled her eyes.

Apparently, guys believed such guff.

Religion-in-service-to-patriarchy fought the battle of the vagina from pulpits everywhere.

"No little pink pills, no irregular warfare, no 'choice' for you!"

"Ever?"

"Never! Women's bodies must always and forever be open to life."

So pregnancy must always be a crap shoot? What about all my "virginal" experience? Did rape, did incest, count? Had Aunt Carrie become insatiable?

"I wouldn't know it was sex if it wasn't with you," I told Ben. He agreed.

That solved that.

The Green Fairy frowned.

What about the story of God, the father, who impregnated the Little Virgin Mary?

Insatiable?

Miraculous, the priests explained.

I hadn't lost faith. Not yet. Miracles could happen.

"You don't want to start a family just yet, do you?" Mama said.

Oblivious to the freedom of choice my mother offered—I secretly thought a baby might help pass the time. I just never thought about the eighteen-year consequences of producing a real, actual baby. But no matter, with Ben gone so much, having a baby sounded like fun.

So I swallowed the pink pills Mama's doctor gave me, but just long enough to please Mama and foil small-town gossips bent on counting the months between marriage and the birth of a first child.

Once I stopped swallowing pink pills, I was almost instantaneously, with child.

Pregnancy was exciting.

. . .

Suddenly, I belonged. I was one of the Sorority of Pregnant Military Wives. It was a military town, and every young military wife I knew was either trying to get pregnant, already "large with child," or comparing tales of childbirth and nursing. All of us were focused intently on the sheer physical experience of being with child. Military wives in every stage of pregnancy occupied endless rows of benches set out in the halls at the base OB/GYN clinic. We were an assembly line attesting to male potency. Each girl waited hours to see her doctor, "hers" if only for her allotted five-minute appointment.

Afterward, we sat around in each other's kitchens, talking, comparing notes: "Well, my doctor says . . ." "Well, mine says . . ." We exchanged "pregnant clothes;" we swapped old wives' tales. We passed around ancient remedies: for morning sickness, gingersnaps; for heartburn, ice cream.

Who knew?

We were all so young, so innocent, and so ignorant of life. The Sorority of Military Wives welcomed unformed, unconscious, nice girls like me into the fold. Sara's Chinese foot-binding all over again.

This time, herded together into mandatory "New Wife Orientation" meetings led by skinny colonel's wives, it was plain we were on sufferance. The base commander spoke—told the same joke at every New Wife Orientation: "If the military wanted soldiers to have a wife, the military would have issued them one. Ha, ha, ha!"

The too-skinny officer's wives obediently joined in their fearless leader's laughter. On cue, we too laughed, carefully obedient to military expectations. If a military wife failed to snip off any offending bits, failed to conform as expected, her husband wouldn't make rank. So, smile. Default to nice. Get skinny. Stay skinny. Laugh along with the Commander and the officer's wives.

Well-schooled by Sara, well-groomed by Daddy, I knew the drill.

. . .

Barely nineteen, unconscious of any feminist revolution aimed at freeing my mind and body, I wasn't ready to understand that little pink pills spelled freedom of choice, offered power to shake ancient foundations, maybe even win the Battle of Roe vs. Wade.

ERA? Someday. Maybe. But only if my husband said so.

Priests said swallowing pink pills was a sin so I took pills and went to confession.

Mama's male doctor delivered a parting shot: "Prolonged abuse of birth control pills will render you infertile."

"How long is prolonged?" I wondered.

• • •

Years later, still married to Ben, by then a mother of three children and working a demanding job as a Child Protective Services investigator, I quit going to confession but continued taking the pills. It was a catch-22 religious women faced. How refrain from sin, space our children and keep our jobs? Today many see access to pink pills as the best solution. Forced to choose between an abortion, an adoption, or a Zika baby, no woman kills her unborn child without reason. But then, what mother can bear to carry her father's child 9 months only to give it away like my Aunt Carrie?

But, at nineteen, when I found myself with child, nothing dampened the pure joy, the all-consuming intensity of that first pregnancy. I loved the costume my new role offered, those cute little tents both announcing and hiding my condition.

I was "in a family way." Eating for two was okay.

All eyes on me. "Butter mints all round."

Safely married and heavy with child, I was prepared to perform three roles: Perfect Mother, Selfless Wife, and perhaps even Working Woman and Good Provider. I watched, perplexed, as some men and women began the long adjustment to "more-equal" unions. It was a paradigm shift I couldn't quite grasp, raised as I was on Sara's perfect wife stories.

Some feminist revolution.

The Green Fairy sniffed and resumed rearranging her gossamer wings.

I did promise Mama that Ben and I would finish college. Someday.

I was standing barefoot and very pregnant in my mother's kitchen, ironing and re-ironing Ben's olive drab uniforms to perfection, when news of President Kennedy's assassination came on the TV.

Walter Cronkite reported the stunning news to a reeling nation.

All of America watched Kennedy's funeral, witnessed Little John's salute and wept. A First Lady like Jackie did all "forever nice" wives proud.

The Spiteful Green Fairy pointed out that Jackie, unlike me, never even spoke much above a whisper. Jackie never even mentioned Marilyn Monroe. Journalists like Walter Cronkite didn't break the 1st Commandment. They, too, didn't "tell."

Back then, before #MeToo, no one wrote president and pussy-grabber in the same sentence.

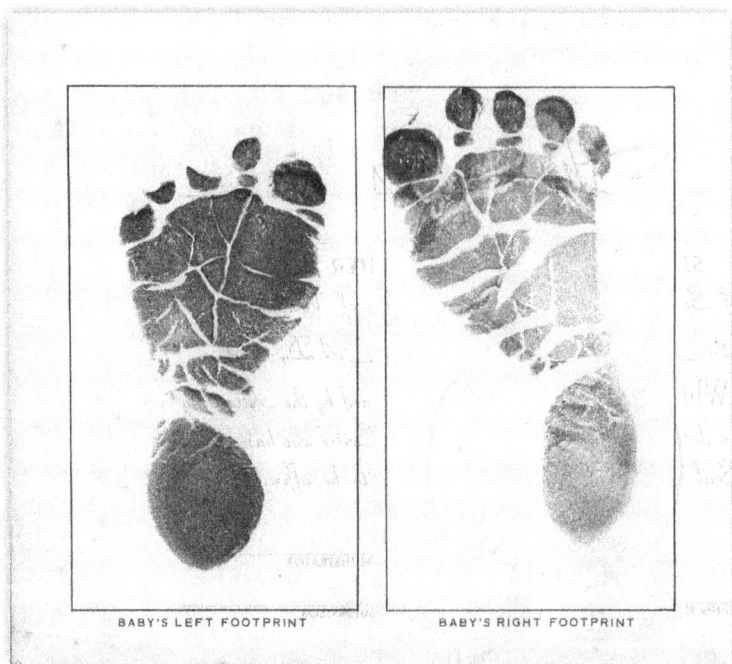

BABY'S LEFT FOOTPRINT   BABY'S RIGHT FOOTPRINT

Sometime in that long lonely night I heard a girl's voice crying out,
"I want my mama, I want my mama".

Chapter 22

W*eeks later, my daughter Carrie Marie was born at the base hospital. Emotionally, I was still about ten* when I walked from Ben's shiny blue Chevy into the base hospital at 5 p.m. that December day. A girl already in the throes of labor, my husband carrying my overnight bag, my situation must have been obvious even to the orderly lounging behind the front desk.

"Wait just a minute." He pushed around papers. "We're in the middle of a shift change. Someone will be here to check you in shortly."

My water broke while the orderly was making excuses.

"You know husbands are not allowed beyond this point don't you, sergeant?"

Ben nodded.

The Green Fairy bristled. "How come no one told me this before?"

I looked down at the floor. Where had that puddle come from? A child raised on euphemism and cliché, I had no words to describe amniotic fluid.

Military rules: "No husbands. No Ben" they said.

"A labor room is no place for a military man."

What about the military man's wife? "If the military had wanted him to have a wife. . ."

Their military fighting man hastily dis-encamped.

I faced the long night alone

I was scared and as ignorant about the process of giving birth as I had been about birth control and the politics of motherhood. Virginity of body and mind, old wives' tales notwithstanding, I only knew that babies came out "down there." I did not know, had not looked up forbidden words, not even in the Bible.

To look, to let on you knew such words, marked a girl as "too experienced." The Bible said the little Virgin Mary "brought forth her child . . ." Feminists said girls should get a mirror and look at themselves "down there," but even had I been brave enough to look, or even to figure out how to pronounce clitoris—well, clitoris was another word I knew a good girl should never know.

I was unacquainted with myself down there, frightened by my mother's tales of a cigar-smoking country doctor who laughed at her hours of pain but finally agreed to "deliver her" using forceps. Left alone with my fears in the darkened labor room in a military hospital. I labored to "bring forth" my first child.

I'd never felt such pain.

A nurse examined me. She said I had to dilate to eight centimeters before my baby could come out "from down there." Then she left.

How big is eight centimeters? How many more centimeters do I have to go?

After another forever, the shift changed. A different nurse came in and looked down there.

"You are slow dilating," she said.

My accuser walked away.

Well, I certainly would have speeded things up down there if I had only known how.

· · ·

Sometime in that long, lonely night, I heard a girl's voice crying out over and over.

"I want my Mama. I want my Mama."

To my bewilderment, I realized the voice I heard was mine.

The Spiteful Green Fairy poked her nose around the corner. "Stop whining. Grow up! You're gonna Be Mama now."

Embarrassed by my ignorance, I resolved to pull up my socks and get on with speeding "it" up.

Great. But how?

My daughter Carrie Marie finally arrived at 9:00 a.m. Monday morning. I was indeed the Mama now. An orderly called our house, woke Ben up, and told him he was Daddy now.

. . .

Carrie Marie was indeed, Monday's Child. She arrived gorgeous and tiny and fair of face. Her skin was incredibly soft. Her eyes were the navy blue of a new baby peering out at the world for the very first time. She had blond peach fuzz like strands of gold forming a halo around her head. Following her birth, I learned the joy of feeling a tiny head snuggled between my chin and shoulder and the inert, sleeping weight of a small snuggled child warm against my breast.

I learned my own joyful response to her searching little bird's mouth and waving pink starfish hands; her sudden, contented silence when she found my nipple, her primal greed at the breast. Maybe motherhood was heaven.

I chose to nurse her, no bottles. But after a few greedy moments, Carrie Marie always fell asleep and then, about the time I tried to go to sleep, she awoke hungry, rooting around, her little bird mouth open, ready to nurse again.

The nurse said, "Tickle her feet. Keep her awake."

I tried. Carrie Marie curled her toes, smiled in her sleep. Good luck with that.

I had hoped for a little girl. All the nine months this five-pound, thirteen-ounce new being was growing inside me, I'd been excited to meet her, looked forward to getting acquainted. And now this tiny bit of humanity, this little bit of female fluff, had arrived, complete with a personality and a mind of her own. I couldn't tell if, like me, she'd come armed with her own magic Green Fairy, but it soon became plain that she had come armed with her very own sleep cycle.

I had never experienced anything to compare with the overwhelming primal love I felt when, at long last, I held her.

But once Carrie Marie was born, everything changed: I was no longer praised for "being large with child."

• • •

The male doctor said, "Lose the baby fat."

But the nurse warned, "Eat for two, or your milk will dry up."

I looked in the mirror and wept. I was fat, fat, Fat. Even the word was ugly.

No skinny Military Wives Club for me.

I weighed myself in the hospital. Delivering a five-pound baby girl definitely had not, magically, returned me to sylph-like teenager status. My body had changed, irrevocably. Filled with shame, I got on the pay phone down the hall and called Mama. This time I didn't brag about my gorgeous new baby, I bawled my eyes out.

"I'm fat! Fat! Faaat!" I lamented. Then I bawled some more.

Mama laughed. It wasn't funny. Food was love, but for a woman to be fat was to be unlovable. My job was to be perfect. Before and after childbirth, a nice wife must look good, be attentive, please her husband in bed, and, preferably, produce a son next time.

If I failed, it would be my own fault if Ben was forced to seek risky attractions elsewhere.

"Lose that baby fat before your next checkup," the young doctor ordered.

Fat Chance.

Growing up, I'd seen my father's face twisted with contempt as he spat out, "Old fat cow," "Fat slut," "Fat bitch"—fat, fat, fat. Hard words, like hard fists, tearing Mama down, his eyes wandering toward me. Blaming a fat wife excused many a risky pleasure. Neighbors shrugged and looked the other way. "What did she expect? She let herself go."

I knew in my bones that since that young male doctor said I was fat, it meant I wasn't just fat, I was at fault. I must magically slim down, or Ben would be right to reject me.

"Lose the fat." But how?

To say "I'm full," to refuse food, even green beans, was to refuse love. But only skinny women could be perfect wives. I pointed all my accumulated self-hatred at my fat self and pulled the trigger. A starvation diet was the magic bullet to reach perfection.

I'd just not eat.

• • •

My breast milk dried up. It became necessary to bottle-feed Carrie Marie. Thus set adrift, unhooked from the very source of the maternal closeness I so cherished, I hated myself. I sought out baby books, all written by male pediatricians, to tell me how to mother. Ben was even less experienced. No matter. I took Ben's advice.

With no firm boundaries, anyone's opinion suddenly mattered more than my own. I knew only a skinny woman could be the perfect wife, the perfect mother to a little bit of female fluff named Carrie Marie, the longed-for baby daughter I'd just met.

Once, late at night, when Carrie Marie finally stayed asleep longer than the usual few minutes, I panicked. What if she's dead? I woke her up, just to be certain. She cried. Ben laughed. But it didn't feel funny to be so afraid, so uncertain, as a mother. What about my "mother's instinct?"

Carrie Marie was born just before Christmas. We took pictures of her, an angelic little pink bundle, under our Christmas tree. A Christmas present left just for us. A sweet little girl-child, perhaps armed with her own Good Little Green Fairy?

• • •

Ben got orders six weeks after Carrie Marie was born. Months before, Ben had volunteered for training to become a forward controller, whatever that was.

The classes were at Keesler Air Force base in Biloxi, Mississippi.

The Green Fairy objected, "Too soon for a little bundle of pink fluff to make a cross-country journey in a January ice storm."

Then there was Mama, "Wait. Don't follow Ben to Air Traffic Controller School. Stay here. Go back to college." She smiled down at Carrie Marie. "I'll take care of the baby."

I ignored everyone's advice.

Intent upon being a Good Military Wife, Ben and me, plus tiny little Carrie Marie makes three, packed up and prepared to set off cross country. Ben tied a chest of drawers stuffed with diapers and tiny pink baby clothes onto the top of the new red Corvair he'd bought just for the trip.

We were young. Vietnam was heating up. It seemed adventurous, patriotic even, to set off in the middle of winter with a six-week-old baby in tow.

The Air Force needed forward controllers. Ben had volunteered to cross-train. How could we know that forward controllers were being killed on the battlefield faster than the military could train and fly them out to die in the rice paddies and rain forests of Vietnam?

Americans are indeed staunch believers, in love with a hero's hubris. War looks exciting, at least on the big screen, so long as War is "over there."

Ben had his orders.

After Idaho, even Biloxi, Mississippi seemed exciting and patriotic, my chance to escape and put "back-home" behind me. My chance to see the world as Ben's Military Dependant. I imagined Real Life had finally begun. A trip of a thousand miles seemed far enough to leave incest and my father behind as we three hippity-hopped from motel to motel on our way down to Keesler AFB and a hoped-for bright, shiny future.

...

Hearing Carrie Marie's frantic cry in that motel room in Mississippi where we'd stopped for the night, I hurried to get up and turn on the light. Instinct told me no baby cried like that without reason.

I was right.

A huge black cockroach crawled out of Carrie Marie's receiving blanket, scuttled away down the baseboard and disappeared into the motel's still-dark bathroom.

The next day I mentioned cockroaches to the motel manager. He was silent for a moment, looking at me as though I was some Northern Bug he didn't much like. But then, suddenly, southern hospitality spread like winter sunshine from ear to ear.

"Little lady, them's not cockroaches; them's Water Bugs. Jest water bugs is all."

Thus dismissed, I smiled back. I defaulted to "Nice."

The Spiteful Little Fairy, not so polite, glowered. In her book, a cockroach was a cockroach was a cockroach. And a Water-bug by any other name? Still a "Cock-a-roach," the Green Fairy insisted.

Raised on euphemism, I didn't argue. But Mississippi in 1964 felt as dangerous as Mama's house at midnight. That year the Freedom Riders—"Northern agitators," the Ku Klux Klan called them—descended upon Mississippi. It was the era of civil rights marches, voter registration and a dangerous hostility toward "Northerners."

As we drove toward Keesler, good ole boys yelled and honked and cut in front of our little red Corvair with its Idaho license plates. The closer we got to Biloxi, the more the southern chill deepened.

The danger wasn't just a feeling. As in Bonanza in 1906, there was 'unrest' in Mississippi in 1964. Lyndon

Johnson was president, and by June, after sixty days of fili-
bustering, Congress passed The Civil Rights Act. No matter. The Un-Reconstructed Old South still relied on night
riders and the hanging tree to keep "Nigrahs" in line.

Before we left Biloxi, three civil rights workers—
Goodman, Chaney, and Schwerner—a black man, a white
man, and a Jew, were ambushed and murdered by the KKK
led by a local sheriff. The bodies of all three "Northern
Troublemakers" were eventually discovered buried in an
earthen dam 200 miles from the same Water Bug Motel
where we'd stayed on our way Down-South.

"Well, they got what they was askin' for, coming down
here. Causing unrest," my white neighbor said, blaming
"race hatred" on Blacks and northern agitators.

"Well, you can come Up-North any time; create most
any sort of unrest you want, and I can guarantee you won't
be taken out and buried in some northern dam," I told her.

The woman frowned like I was some Bug she didn't
much like.

I still don't know if it was the Green Fairy or me who
spoke up. But that summer, as all of America watched the
violence on TV, I think a majority just stopped using the
N-Word. The balance of opinion began shifting away from
long standing prejudice to a seminal recognition that Black
lives do matter. Seeing feverish white faces twisted with
hate, most Americans began to realize just how sick Jim
Crow really was.

That summer in Biloxi was humid and damp. Our
trailer was bug infested.

The Little Green Fairy spotted danger around every
corner.

To make matters worse, an unwelcome undercurrent
also flowed through my personal life. Darkness, postpartum depression, was headed out past the honeymoon stage
and into uncharted territory by the time Ben, Carrie Marie
and I reached Biloxi.

A stubborn Happily-Ever-After Believer, I didn't realize I'd need to triumph over more than just the slew of cockroaches infesting our little, rented trailer. I didn't know I would have to deal with a bug-infested internal darkness scuttling through my thoughts, hiding in every dream, in every drowning pool I'd created by "just-not-thinking-about 'it'" since childhood.

• • •

Air Traffic Control School started before 5 a.m. Ben spent his days on important stuff, Men's Stuff. After school, he played baseball with the guys.

Mornings, I did mommy stuff. I dragged my still-fat, still-hated self out of bed. Alert to Stranger Danger, I checked and rechecked all the locks. I shook out Carrie Marie's blankets. I looked for bugs. Then I made formula, washed diapers, and ironed Ben's uniforms to perfection.

Isolated and alone in a strange place, coping with a new baby and old fears, I counted the minutes until my husband's return. Ben's homecoming promised an adult presence, an end to wifely isolation. But most times, Ben just came home, ate his dinner, watched TV, set his alarm clock and went to sleep.

"Can't be late for class. 4 a.m. comes way too soon."

Of course, Ben was right.

Women in Mississippi, like women everywhere, insist romance novels must end with wedding bells. No one admits married life goes on. No one says romance doesn't triumph over all the water bugs infesting real life. Fairy Tales still end with, "And they lived happily ever after."

So, how dare I be unhappy? It was my fault. Any way you looked at it, "unhappy" was a betrayal of Sara, of Rebeka and the Military Wife's Code of Conduct. Obviously, I ought to be happy, and more supportive of The Mission.

But how?

• • •

Looking back at my fearful, twenty-year-old self down there in Mississippi, I wish I could gift that young mother the happiness she so desperately hoped to achieve. Unwelcome thoughts ran like the cockroaches scuttling through our trailer between the present and the past, the past and the present. I tried not to think about cockroaches, past or present. I tried to do as Sara said.

The Little Green Fairy complained of whiplash.

Happy as I was with my new baby, I was unprepared for the effects of long days of isolation and sleep deprivation—unprepared for my sudden slide into postpartum depression.

The Little Green Fairy sniffed, "Just some new-fangled way to say crazy?"

Finally, inexplicably, I couldn't drag my fat self out of bed except to feed and change Carrie Marie; except to wolf down double chocolate brownies snatched from the jaws of water bugs by the pale light of the open refrigerator in the dead of night. Food, after all, was love. I indulged then hated myself by turns.

But "Why?" I asked myself, "Why? What is the matter with me? I'm supposed to be happy."

When Brer Rabbit was trapped, caught on the fence and about to die, I made Mama stop, "Turn the page! Turn the page!"

In Mississippi, I was once again, a child too frightened to endure more.

Why couldn't I just turn this page? I knew I ought to be happy. Prince Charming arrived just in time. We married. I had a gorgeous baby. So why, oh why, all the unbidden tears?

Bewildered, I told my still fat self over and over, "Smile. You should be happy."

Instead, when my baby woke at night, crying for her bottle, I dreaded clicking on the kitchen light. I dreaded the inevitable cockroaches escaping like sudden clarity back into another refused memory.

A childhood of hidden fear inhabited every Biloxi night.

. . .

Depression is painful—and my depression seemed all the more frightening since Ben's real mother had been institutionalized and my own mother, although never sent away, had periodically drowned in depression.

I was ashamed of myself for dragging around. Why hadn't I succeeded in creating a happy family all my own? What was wrong with me?

Professional help cost money. Besides it would reflect badly on Ben's military career. PTSD? Postpartum depression? Still not part of the military fighting man's vocabulary. And to be fair, not words I had ever heard either.

I told my fat self, over and over, "There's nothing to be unhappy about. If you'd just lose the baby fat, if you'd just emulate Jackie, life will be perfect."

Failing perfect, I fed my stupid-fat-self double chocolate brownies and cold spaghetti straight from the refrigerator in the middle of the night while waiting for Carrie Marie's bottle to warm. Always, of course, keeping an eye on the Big Bugs, medium sized "regular" Bugs and Tincy-Wency-Baby-Bugs as they scurried away in droves, up the water spout, down the sink, and off into cupboards each time I clicked on a light.

Mornings I berated myself, "Pull up your socks. Get on with it."

I shook out Carrie Marie's blanket for the hundredth time. I warmed another bottle. I got out the ironing board. Again. Nice women might not be happy but they certainly lead safely repetitive lives.

"Remember, Stupid, you're Mama now," I told myself.

It never, ever, occurred to me that my objection to "Water Bugs," like my rejection of euphemism in general, might actually be proof of near-sanity in a crazy-making world like Biloxi in the '60s.

...

Winter in Biloxi meant interminable drizzle, broken by an afternoon downpour—or three. Humidity turned everything clammy. I rushed to wipe condensation off the inside walls of our trailer house before it ran down the walls and grew the black line of mildew running between the inside walls and the carpet's edge. The bold black line encircled the inside of our trailer and cut me off from the outside world like razor wire encircling prison. But that was silly. Too much imagination.

I imagined the encircling black razor wire was the crack in the universe where "Bugs," big and small, laid eggs and reinvented themselves. That crack in my universe was where darkness entered, where razor wire became a fact of life. Bugs, like all the other disremembered things scurried around just out of the corner of my eye, hidden there in the mind's darkness, just beyond knowing.

Half serious but afraid since childhood to say aloud what my heart knew was true, I laughed.

"Might as well laugh as cry," Mama said.

Such imaginings were, I told myself, over and over again, "silly."

Even so, I began a mental catalog, an imaginary database of Bugs. There were big Bugs—"Jest water bugs, little gal," the guy at the motel said." Okay, I'd just "pay them no mind."

The black, medium-sized bugs were harder to ignore. They flew straight at me when I cornered and tried to kill them. I shivered. These fears weren't as easy to overcome as when I faced down the fuzzy pink mouse eating up all the chicken feed out behind the little farmhouse in Colorado. Back then I didn't want to be scared like Mama.

I was Mama now. I was scared.

But, "no worries." Down South, it was routine to have the exterminator come in once a month.

"More often if bugs bug you," they said.

Yeah, Bugs did bug me.

The exterminator came and sprayed bug poison all over our trailer—poison became a regular expense, like paying the phone bill.

I wondered aloud if Carrie Marie was being poisoned by all the relentless chemicals sprayed around once a month. Southerners rolled their eyes at Yankee-me. In 1964, Southerners weren't about to go ballistic over "jest bugs,"—maybe "Nigrahs," "Jews," and "tainted blood;" maybe over "Northern Agitators," but not over "jest bug poison."

The Spiteful Little Green Fairy wondered darkly, as fairies do, whether bug spray and Exterminators were out to get her. After all, she had wings too. As for me, I threw poison, prejudice and postpartum depression on the slag heap of "Things-best-not-dwelt-upon."

"Pull your socks up! Get on with it Stupid. You're Mama now!"

• • •

Our kind landlady realized I was struggling. She saw I was way too focused upon my private plague of cockroaches. Like Sara's "Just don't think about it," the landlady's one size fits all, all-purpose solution was "Get right with Jesus."

Pray postpartum depression away.

And if that doesn't work?

Try Elise's solution, "Pray harder. Work harder. Submit."

"Marriage takes work?"

Ben agreed. Ben's secret ambition was to someday be in charge of an obedient little flock all his own. I couldn't think of anything worse than someday belonging to the Perfect-Pastor's Wives Club. Worse even than submerging yourself in the Military Officers Wives Coven?

After many invitations, I gave in. Ben and I left for Sunday services, our landlady and Carrie Marie in tow.

The preacher wept and shouted warnings. Death was about to fall upon one and all—"Eternal hellfire!" "Sweet Jesus!" "Save us!" Caught up in the Spirit, begging, pleading, the preacher leaped and spun across the stage. He paused briefly between long red velvet curtains to pray for us sinners.

The trombone, the electric guitar, and all the flower-hatted white ladies "Amened" in chorus as their preacher, a true showman, used his microphone to shout, whisper, intone and generally scare the hell out of backsliders. His shouted warnings awakened Carrie Marie.

Carrie Marie added her frightened cries to the commotion.

Just listening to the preacher, buried memories of childhood wafted up. I saw another Pentecostal preacher, another Church, set out in the wide alfalfa fields of Colorado. I remembered being dragged out to the car, remembered the Good Spanking in Daddy's truck.

Sweet Jesus!

Heck-Fire!

Remembering unfortunate connections, I was suddenly more scared than Carrie Marie. After that one foray into Thank-you-Jesus-land in Biloxi, I refused to return.

Thanks, but no thanks.

Their insistence that I give in and accept their version of Salvation didn't feel like compassion. It invaded boundaries, demanded conformity. It refused to take "No" for an answer.

Back to the crack in the universe with you, girl!

After church, I returned, babe-in-arms, to my little bug-infested trailer, renewed in my determination to wipe down walls and try harder to fulfill the role of Smiling Military Wife and Brave New Mother. I'd just pull up my socks and all would be well.

Just to make sure all my bases were covered, the Little Green Fairy and I lit a few candles to St. Jude praying Ben's classes would end soon.

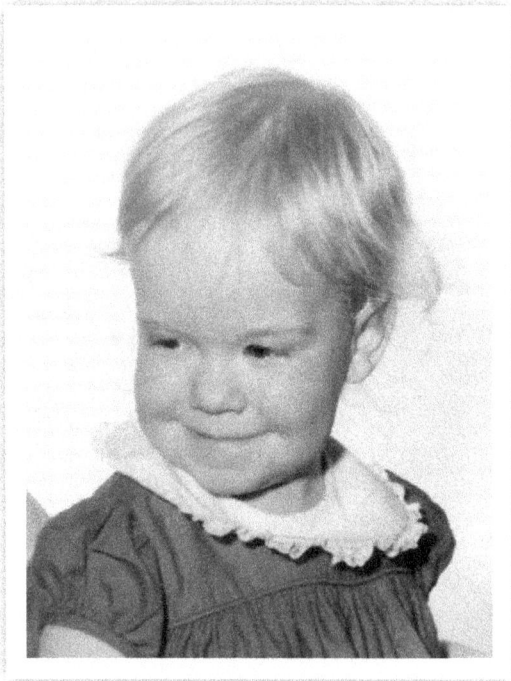

A little girl hiding herself in the night in a trailer house in Oklahoma City.

Chapter 23

Finally, finally, Air Traffic Control School ended. With the US Air Force's usual indirection, Ben's orders were not for Vietnam, but for Tinker Air Force Base, Midwest City, Oklahoma. Promoted and assigned to the control tower, Ben worked three day shifts, three swing shifts, three night shifts, and then three days off.

Tinker was, probably still is, a military suburb of Oklahoma City. Ben and I bought a ten-foot-wide, thirty-six-foot-long trailer house. The trailer court, like every base hospital, was full of young, pregnant, military wives. Like Ben, their husbands were often away. We were too-young wives engaged in parallel play, playing house and dreading the day when our husband's orders said, "Vietnam."

I had Carrie Marie and was pregnant once again. I fit right in.

The Green Fairy perked up.

The Officers' Wives Coven backed off. Officers all lived on base anyway.

In Oklahoma City, I met my mother's childhood friend Leone, long-lost Jimmy's sister. Full circle back to Mama's past? Safe on my island in Midwest City, I didn't reach out. I barely remembered stories of my Uncle Ernest's murder. Mama's past life was, I naïvely assumed, irrelevant to my present.

Absorbed in my second pregnancy, I didn't even drive past Sara's house.

In Midwest City taking care of Carrie Marie, cooking for Ben, ironing uniforms, I was a nice wife looking out windows, pregnant and barefoot, awaiting my next baby.

I gained more weight. Eating double-chocolate brownies and cold spaghetti for breakfast was okay. I was eating for two.

My phobia subsided.

I grew "large with child."

In Midwest City, I made friends with other stranded young mothers in the trailer court. We were small islands of pregnancy and self-absorption, awash in a sea of diapers. We couldn't distinguish ourselves from our mommy roles.

Was there a difference?

• • •

Ben became my expert in all things. He read and interpreted Dr. Spock's baby bible to me. Just like those young male military pediatricians, Ben always knew better.

Worried? Ask Ben.

Still worried? Eat another brownie.

I'd have been better off relaxing, cuddling, and enjoying Carrie Marie. Instead, I listened as Ben pointed out what he said were my all-too-obvious failures in mothering. Ben told me what I wasn't doing right, what I ought to have done.

He and Dr. Spock both knew better.

Disconnected since childhood, I believed what others told me even when it somehow felt wrong. What did I know? Following Ben's confident directions, I took the path that led away from me—I abandoned myself and, in so doing, I abandoned Carrie Marie to Ben.

I couldn't get Carrie Marie on schedule. No matter what Ben and Spock advised, Carrie Marie slept and woke up on her own time, not mine.

The minutia of motherhood consumed me. The diaper bucket was forever full. Like me back on the farm, my Carrie Marie refused even to consider using her cute little flowered potty chair. Just breathing, she created mountains of laundry. Why couldn't I keep all the balls in the air? Wasn't I the Mama?

Nearly two, Carrie Marie's favorite word was "No." She spit out the peas and carrots Spock said she must eat. A little bit of pink fluff, she pooped and smiled, giggled and cooed, stomped her foot and shook her head. Carrie Marie was perfectly imperfect. But then, maybe she had a lot of the Little Green Fairy in her, too?

On the other hand, as Carrie Marie's mother, I knew Carrie Marie deserved better. Ben, Spock, and the Baby Bible all agreed: Fathers know best.

Back then, I didn't understand that mothering isn't a quantifiable activity. No A's, no report cards. No Baby Bibles. Back then, I thought I was lucky to have such a patient, knowledgeable husband. Ben told me what I should accomplish while he was at work. Then he came home, gave me C- and took over.

• • •

Suddenly, Carrie Marie began to leave her bed at night to hide herself here and there in the darkened trailer.

Mornings I'd find Carrie Marie hidden behind the couch, squeezed into a corner, asleep tucked inside a kitchen cupboard. As a child, my brother Duncan had been afraid of the dark, tried to hide from the wolf shadows he, too, saw coming down the hall before an ungentle hand held his eyes shut, pinched his nose. Now, my own Carrie Marie, crept out of the bottom bunk to hide herself away from shadows coming for her in the dark. Oblivious to the obvious pattern, I turned to Ben.

What to do?

Ben said, "Consult the Baby Bible."

The baby bible diagnosed Carrie Marie's hiding-in-the-dark problem as sleepwalking. Ben and Dr. Spock said something must be done. Carrie Marie couldn't wander around in the night. She must not hide herself behind living room curtains.

Confined to her own room, in her own bed, Ben said she'd be safe.

Where Ben could safely locate Carrie Marie quickly and easily without fumbling around or falling over furniture in the dark?

According to Ben, the solution to Carrie Marie's sleepwalking problem was to put a screen door on her bedroom and drop the lock. Then she couldn't wander, hide, or get hurt in the dark.

Ben installed the screen door.

Trapped, Carrie Marie had to stay put in her room. She couldn't sneak out and hide herself anymore. Problem solved.

But whose problem? What made Carrie Marie afraid?

"I'll just go in and check on her," Ben said.

"What a good father," I said

"Just to make sure she's okay," Ben said.

I never imagined. Never said, "No I'll get up and check on Carrie Marie myself." I never thought to investigate further. Never thought just to cuddle her, make her safe on my side of the bed for a few nights.

Besides, Ben said I couldn't do that because Spock said, "No children allowed in bed with their parents."

Not ever?

Did mothers really smother their toddlers just rolling over them in bed? I never flipped that question over and examined the underbelly: What if it was not the child but the parent crawling into a little girl's bed? A father smothering her cries? I never thought. Never asked. I trusted the Ben-Spock bible.

"I'm so lucky to have a husband who takes an interest."

In Midwest City, I was Mother. Yet I never entertained dark suspicions.

What might happen if I actually posed such questions? I could just hear Ben.

"Who do you think I am? How could you think such things?"

Followed quickly by my own, "I'm sorry. How could I have thought that, even for one second?" My bad.

"Well, if you don't trust me, then . . ."

Like Mama, I didn't think the unthinkable. I never dared broach the question.

Ben took the lead, and together, he and Spock solved every child care problem. By the time Ben fastened a screen door to Carrie Marie's room, he'd fastened me securely into position as well.

• • •

Years later I heard another tale that revealed what Ben was actually up to all those nights in Midwest City. Hearing Ben's tale, I was heartsick to realize that in Midwest City, little as she was, Carrie Marie hid in the dark to escape her own Big Bad Wolf prowling around in the dead of night.

"I was just checking on Carrie Marie. Go back to sleep," Ben said as he crawled back into our bed, his skin cold against mine.

I, like my mother before me, went back to sleep. I'd never really woken up at all.

Many years later Ben told a third party a story about a father hunting a small daughter at night. Ben said the father searched the little silver trailer in order to molest his daughter but was frustrated when the little girl, only a toddler, managed to hide from him.

Ben's version said it was my father who'd fitted a screen door to his daughter's bedroom door to prevent her escaping his abuse. Ben recounted his version long after we moved out of the trailer in Midwest City, long after our divorce, when there was no one except me left to dispute his tale. Even then, I only heard his version by accident.

Ben rearranged the truth, retooled it to better suit his purposes, just as he had rearranged my perception of "the sleep-walking problem" at the time. Ben's version is masterful. In one fell swoop, Ben's story displaces his guilt upon another.

Like Ben's tale of his wicked stepmother's spite, Ben presents himself as the to-be-pitied, long-suffering victim, this time the victim of his adult daughter's mistaken accusations of ongoing incest, as though Carrie Marie's tales of sexual abuse were not true. As though Carrie Marie's molest should be dismissed as the lies of an ex-wife.

Ben explained to his listener that I was the only one who was actually molested as a child, but bitter over our divorce, I caused Ben's own daughter to accuse Ben of molesting her in childhood.

Ben's tale ties it all up. Like all puppy stories, Ben's tale engender's sympathy, shifts guilt and affixes blame elsewhere.

Unless you already knew the truth; unless you knew that the trailer Ben described in his story was the trailer Ben and I bought when we lived in Midwest City; unless you were there when Carrie Marie hid; unless you already knew that it was Ben and Spock who diagnosed sleepwalking; unless you saw Ben install the screen door, and drop the lock to make incest quickly possible nights when Ben got up to check on Carrie Marie, nights while I slept, you, too, might believe Ben's puppy story and shower him with sympathy.

Unless you knew the truth.

• • •

One day, just before our first son, Benny, was born, Ben came home and volunteered to help out. Ben said from now on he'd take over bathing Carrie Marie. Carrie Marie loved bath time. Once they out grew their plastic baby-tub, I bathed my kids in the kitchen sink. Our trailer in Midwest City only had a shower stall. Ben took Carrie

Marie into the shower with him and said Carrie Marie'd just have to get used to showering with him

Shortly after Ben's offer of help, I awoke from a Saturday afternoon nap to hear Carrie Marie's frantic cry. It was a piercing cry for help. I hurried to save Carrie Marie just as at the Water-Bug Motel.

I found Ben standing naked in the shower, holding my also-naked daughter, water splashing off them both.

Carrie Marie saw me and cried even harder. She squirmed and reached out. I reached to take her.

"What's going on here?"

"Nothing," Ben said, "nothing. Go back to bed."

Carrie Marie cried harder, her little pink starfish hands beseeching me.

"Go away," Ben said. "See? She's just afraid of a little water. She'll get over it."

But Carrie Marie had never been afraid of water before.

"Go away. You coddle her. Can't you see you're just making things worse?"

I turned away. I accepted Ben's explanation. I told myself, "She's just afraid of a little water. I'm making things worse."

It sounded reasonable, but Carrie Marie kept crying, kept reaching for me.

"Go away. You baby her too much. Close the door."

It did seem I was making matters worse.

"You spoil her. You're the problem."

Maybe so. By now Carrie Marie was crying harder and harder.

To this day I can hear the peculiar quality of her cry. It was the same cry I heard when the cockroach scuttled out from her blanket and off into the bug-infested Mississippi night when she was tiny. But that other night I got up. I saved her.

This time, in broad daylight, I turned and walked away. I left Carrie Marie behind. I abandoned her to her father's abuse.

I ignored my own instinct.

I told myself Ben and Spock knew best.

But my baby's cry, the scene in the shower lingered, lingers still. Another memory to forget at 3 a.m. now that it's too late.

I know. I know. I know.

Too late I know. Too late I regret.

I should have reached out and taken Carrie Marie away from Ben. Knowing what I know now, I should have divorced Ben then, never to return. No child cries like that if not in danger. If not in pain. What was Ben doing? This husband, so strangely like my own father; so like the father who insisted upon bathing his sons?

But divorce?

"No woman in our family ever divorced."

"Don't think you can come crying home."

Ben never hit. Never did the obvious things I'd seen my father do. I told myself my marriage was still better-than.

I never asked myself "Better-than what?" Like Elise, like Mama, I went on believing that if a nice woman just loved her husband enough ...

I was perfectly trained to be Ben's wife.

• • •

I have no idea how many have listened to Ben's retooled version of the screen door story, nor do I know how many other tales Ben has retooled and told. When I heard Ben's reworked screen door tale I recognized our trailer in Midwest City. I realized the truth Ben's version sought to cover up. I was heart sick. Ben's screen door story confirmed Ben intentions and my suspicions the afternoon I awoke and heard Carrie Marie's frantic cry from the shower.

That day, I saw Carrie Marie stretching out her little starfish hands to me as she tried to squirm away from Ben's grasp in the shower.

Yet I ignored instinct.

I obeyed Ben.

I turned away.

Heard years later, truth clicked into place. Ben's tale unwittingly revealed the lies he'd told back then—confirmed realities I failed to pursue when our "Happily-Ever-After-Family" lived in Midwest City just before our second child, Benny, was born.

· · ·

In May, Benny was born at the base hospital. His birth was much like Carrie Marie's, only this time a darling boy arrived. I'd produced a son and heir at last. Ben was proud. Benny was beautiful. All seemed right with the world.

Soon after, Ben came home with orders, still not for Vietnam, but this time for Lakenheath Royal Air Force base, Suffolk, England.

Ben had dodged a bullet. I was happy. I still wanted to travel and see the world. I'd follow Ben from air base to air base just as Sara's perfect Rebeka had once followed her Charley all over the place.

The US Air Force allowed Ben thirty days leave to move his family. We'd sell our trailer. Then the plan was for me to return to my parents' house with the kids and live there until I'd paid off the rest of our bills. In six months, I'd join Ben. I'd fly to England, a baby on each arm, diaper bags and baby wipes in tow.

I'd see the world just as Air Force recruiters promised.

It all sounded so simple.

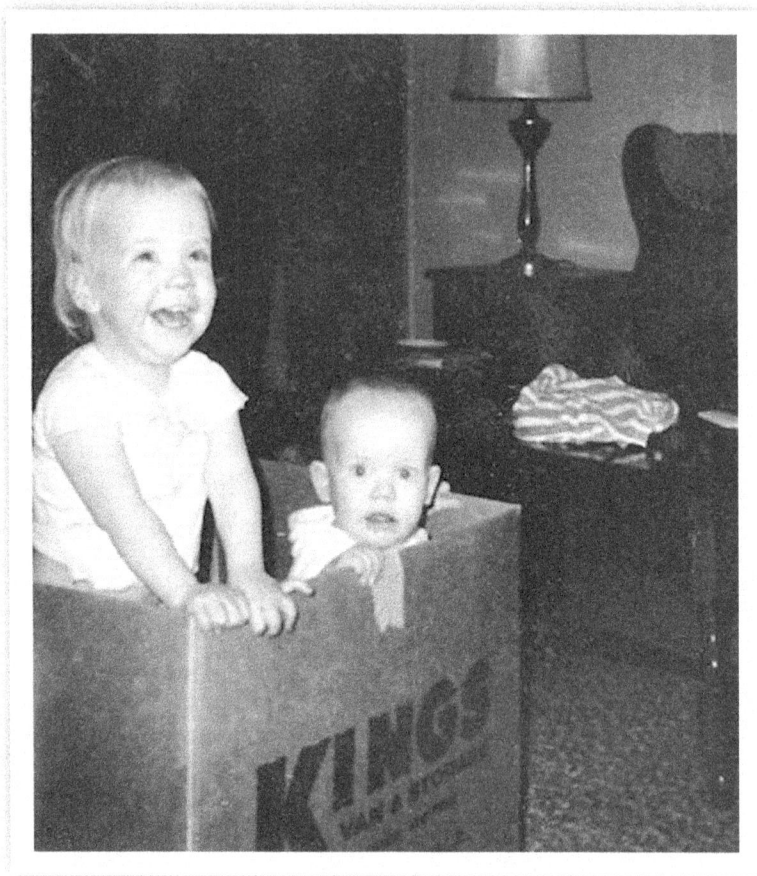

I set off to join Ben in England, a toddler on each arm.

Chapter 24

Arrived at my parents' house, we had one double bed and two cribs cramped together in the downstairs bedroom.

In the thirty days before Ben left for England, Carrie Marie continued to climb out of her crib and hide at night. Searching for her one morning, I saw two little feet sticking out from beneath Mama's living room curtains. When she saw me, Carrie Marie began to cry inconsolably.

I insisted we take Carrie Marie to emergency at the base hospital.

I just knew something was terribly, terribly wrong. But the young Air Force pediatrician on duty didn't examine my little girl.

Instead, he agreed with Ben's assessment. The doctor diagnosed me. I was an anxious, overwrought, overweight young Air Force mother. Two children, three moves in three years? What could anyone expect?

Ben said Carrie Marie's problem was sleepwalking. The young Air Force doctor agreed. Ben told him Carrie Marie cried inconsolably because, when she woke up, she was afraid of the dark. The doctor nodded wisely.

"Yes," he told Ben, dismissing Carrie Marie and me, "sleeping pills will help the little mother worry less, and mother better." He wrote out a prescription for me. Ben and I drove home. Ben brought me a glass of water. I took my sleeping pills. I slept through the night. The doctor and Ben knew best.

"All better now?" Somehow the Little green Fairy didn't think so.

. . .

Years later, my father told his visiting nurse the story of what he witnessed in Mama's living room late one night just before Ben left for England.

Awakened by Carrie Marie's piercing cry, Dad got up to investigate. He witnessed Ben sitting there naked on the living room couch, caught in the act.

"Doing nasty things," Dad told his visiting nurse, "to Carrie Marie."

According to Dad's story, Ben held a naked Carrie Marie on his lap. She was squirming, protesting, and crying out as she tried to push herself away from Ben.

At the time, my brother Buddy was still in high school. With so many extra people in the house, Bayard had been relegated to a sleeping bag on the floor in the darkened dining room. That night, Bayard confirms, Carrie Marie's sudden, piercing cry woke him too. Peering from his sleeping bag into the living room, Bayard saw Carrie Marie crying out and hitting at Ben's erection, attempting to push Ben's penis away and squirm off Ben's lap.

Bayard still remembers seeing Dad standing over Ben. He remembers hearing low, angry voices telegraphing accusation and denial. Unlike Bayard, Dad realized what he saw. But then Ben and Dad were kindred spirits but on different sides that night in the living room. Ben shook his head, protesting innocence and denying what Dad could see with his own eyes. All the while, Bayard says, Ben's stiff erection, sticking up between his legs, stood in mute contradiction of Ben's denials.

Although Dad confronted Ben that night—although Dad witnessed Ben in the act of "doing nasty stuff" to Carrie Marie—Dad kept Ben's secret. Dad never spoke of that night to me. He, like me, did nothing to protect Carrie Marie.

Perhaps what Dad witnessed was just too close to home. Perhaps he wondered whether I had kept my childhood secrets secret. If not and Dad reported Ben, might not Ben just turn around and accuse Dad instead?

Bayard says he saw, he remembered, but he never really put the pieces together until years later when Dad told the story of what happened that night in Mama's living room to the visiting nurse.

But I was "Mama."

How is it that I, too, saw Ben with Carrie Marie those other times yet never put the pieces together? How was it I went on blindly trusting lies, not realizing, dis-remembering? I protected myself. I, like Mama, like Elise, lived "right there" while the Wolf roamed through yet another night, another house, a different time.

Unless we overcome fear and speak out, unless we dare put the pieces together, admit there is a larger picture, how do we forgive ourselves for what we did, or failed to do?

In any case, for whatever reasons, Buddy didn't comprehend, and Dad didn't tell. The next day, Ben's thirty-day leave was up and he flew off to England. Six months later we three joined Ben at Lakenheath's Royal Air Force base.

• • •

In the six months following Ben's departure, as I focused on paying off our bills and rejoining Ben in England, Bayard and Duncan took turns tickling, feeding, and entertaining Carrie Marie and Benny. It was my brother Duncan who first discovered that at nine months and not yet walking, my son Benny was, indeed, spouting words. Armed with language and as yet unsilenced by nights filled with the threat of trauma, Benny took his place as the center of his own noisy, resilient universe.

Uttering three-word sentences, Benny gave orders. He stuck his Curious–George nose into every corner, used up the first of his nine lives and amazed us all. Delighted, we became his willing gofers, learning to fetch and carry at his command. Benny translated for Carrie Marie, whose only spoken word was still a stubborn "No."

Benny and Carrie Marie were fast friends, Bobbsey Twins.

"Really something!" Mama said, shaking her head.

Living there with two babies in the barely controlled emotional chaos of my parent's home, I longed to join Ben in Miss Marple's green and pleasant England, Happily-Ever-After, I thought, would surely save me once we finally arrived.

Mama was no doubt relieved when we three left and silence reigned.

It had been a very long six months for us all.

Happy to escape, I vowed I'd try harder, get it right. This next time would be different. Ben and Spock would see. I'd be the perfect wife and mother.

No need to wish for Limerick.

England, the Fabled Shining City on a Hill, sat just across the English Channel from Elise's Danish fishing village. If at first you don't succeed, try, try again.

Happily-Ever-After in England's East Anglia would do nicely.

. . .

Like my father, trekking from one place to another, I imagined all happiness lacked was a new location and renewed effort. Bound for England, I boarded the plane, a twenty-two-year-old mother carrying a toddler on each arm. A diaper bag bulging with binkies, bottles, baby food, broken Oreo cookies, and teething rings was slung over one shoulder. A purse bulging with shot records, passports, and the kitchen sink dragged down my other shoulder

Dad dropped us off at the airport and waved "Goodbye." His expression said good riddance much as on my wedding day.

Carrie Marie didn't walk, she ran—in whatever direction she was facing when I was foolish enough to stand her down on her own two feet. Benny weighed as much as Carrie Marie, but imperious Benny refused to walk at all.

I carried them both, on and off every plane, from Idaho to England.

Eventually our military plane, seats packed with exhausted young mothers and whiny little kids, took off from New Jersey, circled the North Pole and finally, finally landed at Lakenheath RAFB in Suffolk, England.

• • •

Ben kissed me. Then he piled us bag and baggage into a little black beetle of a car left over from WW II movies. We drove out to a rented red brick duplex set in an enclave inhabited by the families of American enlisted men.

Our half-house had two bedrooms, a living room, a kitchen, a front hall, and what the English called a water closet: a tiny room housing only a toilet. Next to that was a bathroom with only a sink and a huge deep cast iron tub. A couple of times a day, I filled a free-standing heater with kerosene from a large fuel barrel perched outside on a rough wooden stand in the corner of the yard. Once filled, I moved the heater from one cold room to another throughout the day, shutting doors behind me as I went, trying to keep warm.

Those were cloth diaper days. With no laundromat nearby, I filled the claw-foot bathtub and washed, rinsed, and wrung out diapers, towels, sheets, clothing, and uniforms by hand for our family of four. That done, on good days, I hung everything on clothes lines strung across the backyard in the fond hope that our wet clothes might dry in the pale East Anglia sunshine.

When it poured rain, I hung the wash inside on lines strung across the bathroom ceiling. Then I moved the space heater into the bathroom, shut the door, and crossed my fingers that all would dry in time to iron Ben's uniform for the next day.

Next day I began the wash-dry-iron cycle all over again in hopes of more clean, dry diapers before the two dirtied the last clean one. "Mother" was an occupation I had been raised to expect. But with two toddlers in diapers and an English climate, "washerwoman" was more to the point.

As usual, Ben worked three days, three swings, three nights, and three days off just as he'd worked at Tinker Air Force base. Cooking for Ben felt like chasing him around the clock with a frying pan.

All the while, I tried to maintain the Spock–approved daytime schedule for two toddlers. I tried to keep the toys picked up for when Ben came home. But, by now, both toddlers were running around dragging stuff out of drawers, and emptying their toy box in near record time. Carrie Marie scaled the cabinets. Benny, a budding Picasso, rejected coloring books. Crayon scribbles appeared like magic on all the once-white walls.

The Spiteful Green Fairy egged them on. She loved every minute.

. . .

As for me? Like Mama out on the farm, I couldn't wait for my kids to be potty-trained.

Neither diapered little kid showed much interest in fulfilling mommy's dearest wish. Oh, they loved to hang over the edge of the toilet, swishing toys around, speaking jabberwocky and giggling themselves silly. When the last yellow rubber ducky was swallowed up in a rushing vortex of toilet water, they wept crocodile tears, giggled and ran off to raid the toy box searching for yet another defenseless ducky to sacrifice down the toilet.

But, having watched so many Duckies disappear in the vortex, both Benny and Carrie Marie were quite understandably reluctant to actually sit on the toilet themselves. Flushing Duckies was okay, but their own poop seemed way too personal a contribution. Besides, what would happen if one of them fell in? Why tempt fate?

"No." Both kids shook their heads.

I washed more cloth diapers and decided maybe I should have listened to my mother and taken those pink pills she offered. I resolved to space my future children.

While I enjoyed their curiosity, laughed with them at their endless antics, the two were obviously one step ahead of me. What one didn't think of, the other did.

Once, while I napped thinking they slept, both kids woke up and played hide and seek with my glasses. What fun.

I woke up. No glasses.

"Where are they?" Blind as a proverbial bat, I felt around.

The kids chortled and rolled around on the floor.

"Where are they?"

"Jabberwocky."

"I'm gonna kill you both!"

Unfazed and unafraid, they giggled hysterically, elbowed one another and watched me feel my way around the house in search of my glasses,

More "Jabberwocky."

Even the Green Fairy chortled. "You'll have to call Ben home from work."

Not Funny!

Ben's work was important, landing planes and saluting. Ben came home. "This is your emergency?"

Ben discovered my glasses perched on the middle rack of the broiler oven.

Unimpressed with minutia, Ben sighed and went back to doing John Wayne stuff.

Benny and Carrie Marie's innocent expressions said they had no idea what all the fuss had been about anyway.

I went back to imitating June Cleaver living in a little brick half-house situated in Green and Pleasant England.

My whole world was jabberwocky.

. . .

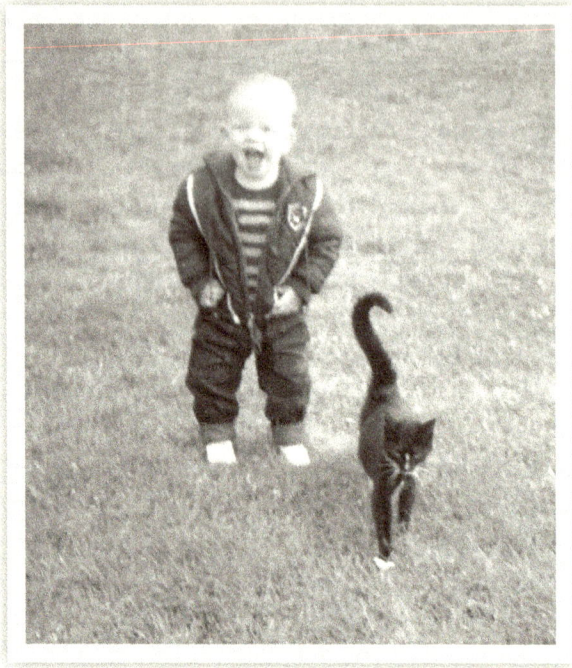

The little boy with 9 lives.

My ever-curious Benny learned to turn the kitchen door knob. He escaped out the back door and drank kerosene dripping from a barrel sitting in the corner of the yard.

Ben had to come home again.

We rushed Benny to the base emergency room, where the young pediatrician sighed and said, "You must watch your son more carefully."

"More carefully?" The Little Green Fairy bridled.

"If I wasn't super watchful," I protested, "Benny would have blown through all his nine lives and been dead before he figured out how to get out the back door and drink kerosene."

The pediatrician raised his eyebrows and looked at Ben.

Both looked at me.

What was I thinking, talking back to a doctor?

"But Benny's into everything." Even June Cleaver protested.

The young pediatrician, Ben, and Spock all saw I was a June Cleaver failure.

No matter how defensive I sounded, I also blamed myself.

"No Butter mints for bad mommies?

"Just pocket lint and nasty old red cough drops?"

Ben sang "The Bad Mommy Song." Spock and the little base pediatrician harmonized. June Cleaver agreed and hummed along.

Meanwhile, Carrie Marie was waking up at night again. Carrie Marie wept inconsolably. I insisted we take Carrie Marie to the base hospital. Something was very wrong. Ben pointed out that the same pediatrician who said I had endangered Benny would most likely express the same opinion in Carrie Marie's case.

June Cleaver's children never cried like this. It was me.

"And, anyway, if they make us wait at the hospital," Ben said, "I'll be late for my shift in the control tower. If the lieutenant writes me up, I won't make rank."

Out-voted, I did not insist. Life cycled on.

• • •

Huddled together in England, we Air Force wives tried to prove that we were Military Issue. But even filled with patriotic pride and propaganda, as we were, the specter of death in the jungles of Vietnam hung like a pall over us all. Meanwhile the Air Force promised reenlistment bonuses and promotions to family men who volunteered to go first.

Lakenheath's Base Commander, a WWII ace, volunteered. Word came back: his plane had been shot down. He had, indeed, been "first to go."

Ben talked as though he couldn't wait to get orders for Vietnam. Ben said he was a 20-year man.

As for me, I was, for all intents and purposes, confined to quarters.

I didn't have a European driver's license. There was no public transport out where we lived. The only option for even a brief escape was to go next door and ask if I could please phone for the black, WWII-vintage taxi. I could barely afford the fare. In any case, I'd have to go next door just to ask.

Sometimes Ben came home late. Spending time at the Non-Commissioned Officer's Club after pulling a shift was just another macho, Military-Guy thing. Ben drank. John Wayne drank. They all drank. Some even made rank.

Then, in 1966, De Gaulle withdrew from NATO and kicked the American military out of France 20 years after the end of WWII. The US military sent cargo planes and air traffic controllers to France to pack up U.S. bases. Ben was sent TDY for 90 days to help move American bases off French soil.

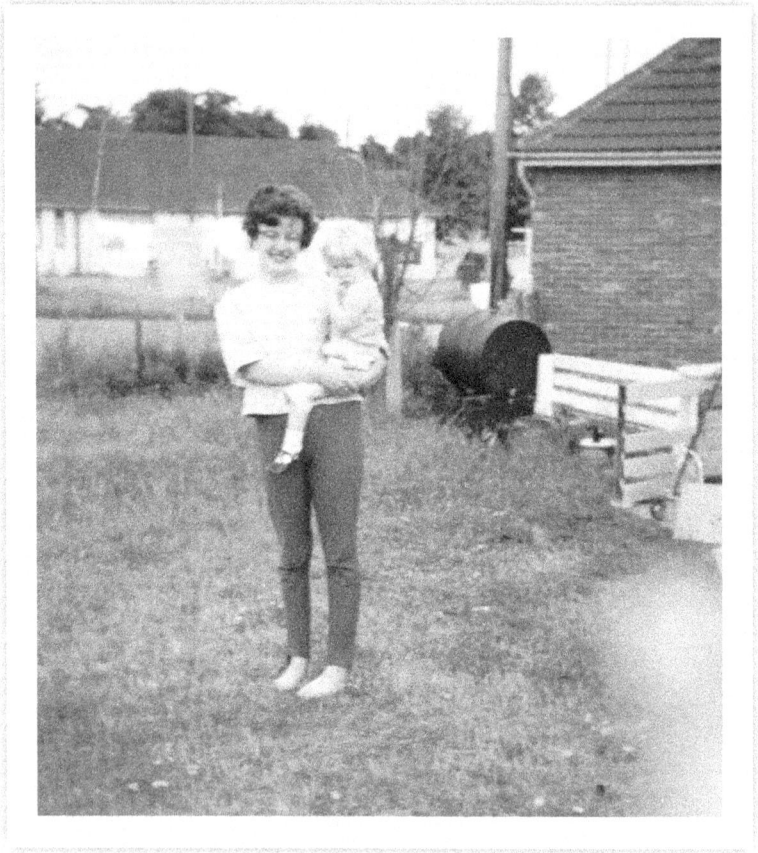

Once back at our little half-house, the bottom dropped out.
Despair pulled the trigger.

Chapter 25

*With Ben in France, I was alone 24/7. No adult. No
break in the minutia. Solely responsible for two children,
I could cope days. Nights were terrifying. I couldn't sleep.
I checked the locks on every door. I checked every window twice before I went to bed.*

When I did doze off, I startled awake, got up, checked
the locks again, lay down, got up and then checked again
and again.

I tried to keep calm and carry on.

I tried. I really did.

I knew what was expected of military wives. The Little
Green Fairy thought the cloistered role of Bravely Waiting
Wife was just too much. But I'd grown up watching movies, hearing stories about brave wives: pretending, smiling,
and waiting. Forever?

Movies and magical thinking could not erase the pain
or calm my fears nor could they light my ever gathering
darkness.

The Military Wives' Club had obviously failed to clone
me into a heroic military wife and mother focused solely
on maintaining a perfect "home front." Days, I had my
hands full with two rambunctious toddlers. Nights were
spent protecting us all from wolves and things that went
bump outside in the English night.

Fear took over. I knew I'd never be good enough, no
matter that I loved my children. Trapped in the crazy glue
of self-blame, I hated myself. I thought in absolutes. The
tyranny of The Perfect took over.

. . .

Before Ben even left for France, I was deeply uneasy about my Carrie Marie. She began to throw temper tantrums, tantrums which seemed to me to be way beyond what Spock said to expect of the "terrible twos".

Ben and Dr. Spock decided upon a course of action: I had to put Carrie Marie in time-out whenever she threw a tantrum.

"Just shut her in her room. Close the door and leave her there until she stops crying," Ben said, "I'll give her a talking to once I get home."

"You baby her too much."

Where had I heard that before?

I hated the Spock-Ben solution. I just knew something was very wrong.

Once again.

So, once Ben left, I scraped together enough money to call the WWII taxi and take Carrie Marie to the base pediatrician hoping he'd know what had gone wrong.

The doctor who saw us was indeed the same young pediatrician who'd chastised me regarding Benny's care.

He did not examine Carrie Marie; instead, he questioned my motives.

"And why do you imagine there is anything the matter?"

"I just have this uneasy feeling," I said. "It's nothing specific, not really."

He rolled his eyes. He looked at his watch.

I stumbled on, "I, I just have this uneasy feeling. I just know there's something really, really wrong."

"You just have this feeling?"

I nodded.

"Well, your husband's gone TDY in France. Do you expect me to have him sent back here just because you have a feeling?

"No, that's not it. I just. Well, it's hard to explain."

Throughout it all, Carrie Marie sat there, smiling, looking perfectly healthy and happy. She sat quietly on my lap;
a little shy, perhaps. But no tantrums, no baby tears. Carrie
Marie smiled winsomely, waved to the doctor, and then hid
her face against my coat. No frowny-face for her pediatrician. Carrie Marie knew how a nice little girl behaved. It
was only Mommy who imagined stuff.

"But her tantrums?"

"Anger in a toddler is normal." The pediatrician
sighed. "You don't really want me to contact your husband's commanding officer, do you? Do you want to ruin
your husband's career?"

Reminded that a wife with problems could block a
man's promotion, I backed off.

"Well, no. I'm probably wrong."

"Anyway, what do you imagine is the matter?"

I caved. "Sorry. Of course, it's just me. I'm imagining
. . ."

I picked up Carrie Marie and fled. Once the taxi
arrived back at the little brick house, the bottom dropped
out. Despair pulled the trigger.

I was a Perfect Failure. Always would be.

Done trying.

· · ·

*At home alone that night, I planned the perfect
suicide.*

"I'll lock myself in the bathroom, fill the big Victorian
claw-foot tub to the brim, and swallow sleeping pills. Then,
like Uncle Bernie when he shot himself and died of carbon
monoxide poising, I'd make doubly sure. I'd slit both arms
from elbow to wrist, lay back and bleed out.

"I'll die peacefully while the water turns a nice rosy
pink," I told myself.

Nice touch. I could just picture it all. Just like when
the Green Fairy and I plotted bloody murder. And when
someone found the body? I wouldn't look too fat. I'd been

dieting, so I'd probably look quite nice. Naked and dead, but very nice.

"Wait! Wait! What do you mean 'When someone finds you?'" The Little Green Fairy frowned, "But when will someone find you?"

"Not soon." No one but our Polish milkman ever came to the house.

So, who will finally find Carrie Marie and Benny?

And, more to the point, When?

How could I leave two little kids cold, hungry, and alone for days with their mother's dead body floating around in a claw-footed bathtub? Never mind all that rosy water, that perfect suicide, this was not a Miss Marple mystery.

Carrie Marie and Benny were my kids.

I was "Mama" now, their Mama.

How could I?

"No, no, no! I can't do that."

Some still-sane part of me balked, flatly refused. I'd just have to pull up my socks. I'd have to keep on keeping on for the sake of Benny and Carrie Marie. Maybe mine was the same decision Mama made when she arose from the maroon couch? Maybe mine was the same decision Elise made day after day when she was so ill after Rosie was born and Carrie went to California?

Once I decided against suicide, the hissing voice didn't stop. The familiar voice hissed on and on at me from the darkness inside my head. Every night, the voice spewed self-hatred. It cataloged in minute detail my every failure, demanded perfection.

"You can't even pull off your own suicide."

The hissing went on and on, excoriating, deriding, and taunting me. For what seemed like weeks on end, I was afraid that the hissing, badgering voice would catch me in some unguarded moment. Before some saner-self arrived, I'd try to commit the perfect suicide.

In daylight, I went about taking care of Benny and Carrie Marie. At night, my semi-sane-self tried to stay awake, be vigilant. The arguments went on and on until finally, exhausted, I'd had enough. My sane-self gathered courage.

Using my children as a talisman, I told the hissing voice, "Do your damnedest. I'm sick of listening, tired of being afraid. I'm going to sleep."

"Yeah! Heck-Fire," the Spiteful Green Fairy chimed in, "Me too."

I lay down. I slept through that first defiant night. When I awoke the next morning, the sun was shining, and I was fine. The hissing voice vanished.

• • •

Years later, after Mama's death, my father called me over and over in the dead of night, hissing, telling me, "You're a bad daughter."

A bad daughter, he said, when I refused to drop everything, quit my job, move home, and devote myself to taking care of him for the last years of his life. With Mama gone, Dad, like Paw-Paw, demanded that a little replacement wife appear. Instead, a visiting nurse came. Then came the old woman who cried at his funeral, telling anyone who'd listen, "I loved that old man."

Listening to Dad's nocturnal phone calls, I suddenly recognized the hissing voice I'd heard in England. It was my father's voice, hissing down the long halls, echoing out of the darkness of childhood: "This is your fault, all your fault. You tempted me past all endurance. It's all your fault."

Over and over, making me want to die.

• • •

Back in the little brick half-house, after the hissing voice subsided, I woke up to a rare day of English sunshine. I somehow knew that whatever sort of imperfect mother I was, I did love my kids. Since I was the only mother they had or were ever likely to have, Benny and Carrie Marie were, for better or worse, pretty much stuck with me, warts and all. I'd always and forever be an imperfect June Cleaver, a mother, like my Mama, who failed but still loved us enough to rise up from the scratchy maroon couch and keep going.

The Tyranny-of-the-Perfect subsided. At least for a while.

I was never going to be a natural at this motherhood stuff. I was who I was. My children, too, were who they were.

Yet just vowing to try, try again didn't answer why my tiny little Carrie Marie cried inconsolably and flew into towering rages.

I was still Mama. I would not abandon them.

I vowed to persevere. Carrie Marie, Benny and me would keep on keeping on, we'd muddle through motherhood and childhood together.

We survived but I, like Mama, only went back and tried the same stuff, harder. Caught in the loop de loop of the Happily-Ever-After-Believer, I was afraid to die, afraid to live. Afraid to know. Afraid to tell.

My resolve to return and try Sara's formula over and over and over again changed nothing. It only kept the secret legacy of despair going. It never protected my children as promised. For me, back then, Happily-Ever-After and my place in it, was an article of faith. How dare I not believe when Church, family, and the Officer's Wives Coven said dis-belief was unforgivable sin?

Didn't Dad say, "All that nasty stuff comes from your mother's side?"

The Green Fairy rolled her eyes.

But what if despair, forever triggered, re-experienced, but isolated and silenced, never heals? What if despair is the pain handed down to silence succeeding generations?

What if, "What's the use?" is the legacy at the heart of abuse?

And what of those who, like my father, find no help, but go on to re-enact their own abuse? Perhaps they too give up? Loose hope of every being listened to? Never welcomed back? In their pain perhaps they mistook cruelty, even sadism, as the risky antidote to their own despair? Perhaps each one of us hiding behind silence, thinks, "If you really knew me, you wouldn't like me."

Who could bear to show themselves to a husband, a wife, a pastor, a friend or even a therapist, only to find not kindness but cruelty, bias and rejection?

In the meantime, trapped in our isolation, we deny our pain. We pretend. We pass. Like the Mackies, we spend our lives trying to assimilate. "Say you're one of them. Act normal, and they'll think you are normal," is the mantra of the marginalized.

To be pronounced "Normal" is the line, the razor wire crack in the universe, between acceptance and social death, between respectability and abiding contempt for 'those people' forever disenfranchised in America the Beautiful.

Try "conversion therapy." Pretend better.

In my experience, small children victimized close to home hear the hissing voice. Once grown up, we all know the drill: Don't ask. Don't tell. Dis-remember. Don't think about it. But even dis-remembered, despair still lurks beneath the dark pool of forgetting.

No matter. Times up. Much like my brother Duncan seeing the snapshot of Paw-Paw holding his little boy hand and instantly feeling the pain of Paw-Paw's iron grip all those years later, the body remembers what the mind swears it's forgotten.

* * *

As for me, living in that little half house in England, an inexplicable sadness dogged my days. Relieved of the tyranny of the hissing voice demanding my perfect suicide, darkness yet remained. Waking up to sunshine did not suddenly make taking care of two rambunctious toddlers easy. I discovered being a "Perfect Mommy" club of one was not a breeze, not even for a doggedly Happily-Ever-After Believer.

Grief welled up.

Stubborn tears made despair visible.

One day, not long after I banished the hissing voice, I was washing dishes when Benny and Carrie Marie started arguing. I stopped washing dishes and made the two sit on the floor with their backs to the kitchen door. Timeout: the perfect Dr. Spock solution. Then, with the kids a few feet away, I went back to washing dishes.

Looking down, I realized that small drops of water were splashing into my dishwater.

Tears? But whose? What's causing all these tiny splashes?

Still, the tears fell unabated.

Curious, divorced from myself, I found a mirror and looked at my face. I touched my wet cheek with wet hands. Could it be? I dried my hands and felt again. Yes. Endless tears bathed my face, dripped off my chin, splashed into the gray dishwater below.

These inconsolable tears were not Carrie Marie's. They were my own. I was at a loss. I had no more idea why I wept than I had answers for why Carrie Marie cried inconsolably.

I felt no sorrow. I felt nothing. Yet those inexplicable tears kept coming. Despair splashed down into my dishwater.

Wasn't I trying to do everything a good wife and mother was supposed to do? Wasn't that supposed to make me happy? Wasn't the sun supposed to shine?

And yet the body remembers, weeps endless tears.

Isn't childhood where all the lonely people come from?

• • •

I brushed sadness aside.
"I just need to get out of the house more."

So I scraped a few shillings together, and decided to make a weekly journey to Lakenheath Air Force base; just me and the Little Green Fairy, and two little kids bumping along together in a little black WWII taxi.

I dropped the kids off at the base nursery. But once I paid for the taxi and held back money to pay for daycare, I was too broke to buy anything at the Post Exchange or see a movie. Instead, I went to the base library. I read and soaked up the quiet for a couple of hours. Reading was my safe haven re-discovered in the green and pleasant East Anglian countryside.

Just as I had, once before, escaped Mama's sadness reading Alice in Wonderland in Colorado, in England, reading at the base library grounded me. I discovered space to begin deciphering what my life was telling me.

I discovered the, I thought, radical psychological theories of Karen Horney. Unlike Sara's Alice-in-Wonderland, or the inscrutable story of Little Red Ridinghood, Karen Horney made sense. Unlike Freud, who discounted the sexual victimization of his female patients as hysterical lies, Karen Horney honored women's experience with a separate dignity. She thought women should be the movers of their own story arc.

I shudder to think what might have happened, had Freud, instead of the kind country doctor, been summoned to Mama's side as she lay immobile on the maroon couch. "Hysterical" would undoubtedly have been the "scientific" label affixed to dismiss the common cruelties yet another controlling, conventional man visited upon yet another nice woman.

Just another once "nice" but now "hysterical" woman, beaten, frozen in place, driven to despair, only to be labeled and sent away, discarded as useless, unless, of course, she managed to silence her despair in time to conform to expectation.

At least Karen Horney did not dismiss female aspiration to achieve a separate dignity, as merely frustrated penis envy. Maybe she even thought someday too-nice women might throw off all the limiting beliefs demanded of them since childhood and be carpenters in their own right?

Discovering Karen Horney's ideas changed my life. Her ideas about the psychology of women at least gave me hope that there were "dots" to connect. And if so, I too might discover the dots connecting me to a self that didn't automatically believe girls couldn't be good at math because the Ancient Greeks said women possessed wandering uteruses.

Provincial and untutored as I was, I really can't say I understood Karen Horney's dense paragraphs. I remember being a little shocked to find that a book other than the Bible contained dirty words and spoke openly of sex.

I read on.

Perhaps, I thought, if I follow these dots down their untraditional rabbit holes, I'll discover something to make sense of my woman's life? Drawn back and back to the base library, I vowed I'd return to college, just as I had once promised Mama.

Heck Fire! Why not major in psychology?

Great idea.

I hadn't yet heard the joke about all the Psych 101 students who diagnose themselves with every malady in the book. Me and the Spiteful Green Fairy, well, we had plenty to work with. There was hope that someday, someone might even figure out what motivated the Big Bad Wolf, might listen instead of label, and might figure out how to intervene before despair and risky business took over and the Wolf cycled on?

"Rape isn't about sex; it's about power. It's about control." the feminists insisted.

The Little Green Fairy understood.

They called it, "consciousness raising."

What about the rape of childhood? Incest was hardly mentioned. Stranger Danger was the all-white feminist's focus, that, and the pervasive domestic violence used to keep even those nice women fixed in place.

It would be way too many years before I got it.

For growth, I'd need to know there were tears falling off my chin without having to stand before a mirror to see that I was weeping. I'd need to find the courage to unearth feelings, drowned in silence long ago beneath those same salty tears. To prevent the legacy's continuation, I'd have to find courage as a woman, a wife, and a mother to break the silence, raise my voice and begin an honest conversation. Even about incest?

Yes.

Otherwise, crying inside, retooling woe-is-me stories, even true ones, I'd just be inventing puppy stories of my own. Like Dad's stories, they'd be tales motivated by resentment and self-pity, stories meant to elicit sympathy, manipulate, and make myself feel safe by gaining control of the bodies and emotions of others.

As such, they'd be worse than lies.

Used in such a context, a child's suffering becomes the adult's smoke screen. The erstwhile powerless victim, the hungry ghost, transforms—siphons off power in the act of telling true lies and becomes the next betrayer of childhoods, past, present, and future, the next unconscious mother allowing the sex offender's legacy to cycle forward.

Perhaps, like Paw-Paw, like Ben, like my father, some might get away with gaslighting, with retooling and retelling tales exonerating themselves. But how heal the wounded child, how give hope to the boy or the girl, "treated like a girl" before the legacy repeats itself in yet another generation? The required paradigm shift certainly can't be achieved in silence or by misdirection. But who wants to tell or listen to such raw truth? Who dares risk attack for telling "unseemly" stories about a woman's life?

• • •

Living in England offered me a chance to grow my thinking, to examine the world from a different vantage point. Before England, before Karen Horney, I had no inkling that I'd lived my entire life bound by Sara's romantic tales. I had no clue that Sara's-script was handed down from ancient times when "invade, rape, pillage and enslave," first convinced women the wisdom of submission to save themselves and their children. Dark times when Paw-Paw's bragged, "a woman, a dog, and a walnut tree, the more they be beat, the better they be." Beatings meant women had to accept "No" as the answer to freedom just to keep themselves and their children alive through dark times. Just to live to fight another day.

In dark times, the wisdom of "just don't think about it," the art of dis-remembering, made survival possible between onslaughts. Still, until I dared think about the social constructs which ruled my own life, my children and my grandchildren too, would remain in danger. A danger which I, their supposed protector, was still powerless to recognize or remember. Just another determinedly unknowing mother, living right there in the same house, yet too blind to see; just a grown-up child, still dis-remembering, still accepting "No."

• • •

Finally, the long months passed and my blue-eyed Prince returned from France. Rapunzel let down her long hair and found herself magically rescued from isolation. I felt grateful for Ben's return. I was "saved" by Prince Charming. Absent Ben's guiding presence, I was convinced I could never manage motherhood on my own.

By the time Ben got back from France, we had dodged orders for Vietnam twice. But, if Ben re-upped, he would almost-certainly be sent to the "hot" war in Vietnam.

Politically, Ben was all in favor of the war. He was an air traffic controller with the skills and experience to be a forward controller in the jungles of Vietnam. But now, after eight years in the Air Force, Ben told his Captain, I had fallen apart while he was in France. Ben said he didn't think I'd make it if he went to Vietnam.

"Family comes first," Ben said.

Fully convinced that I was incapable of raising Benny and Carrie Marie without Ben-Spock guidance, all I felt was immense relief.

We came home with plans to work and pay for college using the newly enacted government college loan programs. I would major in psychology, maybe minor in social work and Ben would be a teacher. Ben said working with kids was his calling.

With my childhood safely dis-remembered, I imagined that returning to my parent's house might give me a chance to make friends with both my parents.

"After all, I'm a grownup now."

The Green Fairy rolled her eyes.

Time for civilian life. This time, of course, everything would be different.

We bought an old green fixer-upper and took in foster kids.

PART V: HAPPILY-EVER-AFTER:
TRY, TRY AGAIN… AND AGAIN AND…

Chapter 26

Home from England, we settled in for the summer. We were, of course, expected to attend church with the family.

The Green Fairy demurred. She hated church, remembered unfortunate connections. And all that stuff about how God-the-Father got some little girl, named Virgin Mary, pregnant? Well!

"Stuff and nonsense! Gives me a splitting headache," she said.

Only the Spiteful Little Green Fairy would dare say such things aloud.

But, in spite of The Green Fairy's objections and the Virgin Mary's obviously unfortunate connections, we all trooped off to church.

Back home from church, I found myself alone with Dad.

"I'm glad to be home again," I told him.

Dad smiled.

"Dad, I love you," I said.

Dad went stone still.

The Wolf looked me up and down, considering, calculating.

A chill ran up my spine.

He does terrible things to people who get too close.

I took an involuntary step back.

How had I forgotten?

After three years away, I had somehow imagined that as a married adult I might be able to put the past behind me, start anew with my parents.

Instead, Dad's face, the Wolf's cold eyes?

The hair stood up on my arms.

The little boy abused out there on the Home Place had been wolfed down long ago. The man didn't have it in him to allow love. He couldn't tell pocket lint from Butter mints.

But, no worries, Dad, after that one attempt, you were safe from me.

After that, benumbed and fearful, I also didn't try to make friends with my mother, who by then was an isolated, lonely woman slipping further and further beneath a husband's control. She slipped too soon away, into darkness and old age.

The last time I saw my mother alive, she was in bed in the nursing home. I stayed all day without any sign of recognition.

Suddenly Mama opened her eyes, smiled across at me and said, "That color lipstick looks pretty on you." Then Mama closed her eyes and disappeared back into darkness again.

• • •

Over the years, my father joined and departed several churches based upon what he perceived to be the "correctness" of their doctrine. Just after we left for England, Dad moved to a new church.

This time, conversion came with what my father believed was a calling to "preach the Word." The parent church asked him to serve as a lay pastor to a struggling "mission" church located in a tiny farm community some miles distant. Dad was "well off" and newly retired with full post office pension and medical benefits.

Dad accepted the position, bought a double-wide trailer, moved it and Mama to the tiny farming town, and assumed control of a fundamentalist flock of faithful women.

Such Preachers confess, "I was lost but now am saved." Dressed in sack cloth and streaked with the ashes of repentance, preachers in such churches claim God heard them, "turned their lives around," and told them to preach.

It's an all too familiar narrative.

But the exact details—what, precisely, the preacher's "sins of the flesh" amounted to—that's lost in euphemism: "Saved by the Blood" is formula enough.

A congregation must not inquire too closely. Correctly professed, a magic formulaic repentance closes the book on the past. Repentance does not, of course, guarantee a temptationless future. Back-sliding may be expected as suppressed but still festering compulsions reawaken. If caught out, more sermonizing, more saving magic becomes necessary.

Looking back, I feel both immensely exasperated with and somehow deeply sorry for my father. As Catholic bishops, pedophile priests, wives—and, alas, the children—of many sex offenders know, confession may well be good for the soul, but repeated repentance without necessary change, does not long exorcise the thrill of risky business and sexual obsession.

Even a heart-felt "I'm sorry" is only the beginning. For omnivores, or even those directly minor-attracted, taking responsibility for past acts and in fact choosing to stop, to change behavior, to deny impulse its expression is a long, sometimes painful, learning process that requires self-honesty and continued self-control over a lifetime.

Too many therapists are unable to get past their own euphemistic "scientific" labels and their own implicit bias and offer real help but real help is out there. It's certainly more available today than during my father's lifetime when shame, blame and silence reigned.

Today, no one need accept the fixed role of "forever victim." Nor must anyone live life "forever a predator." There is a third path that chooses self respect and kindness

over recycling cruelty. Restorative justice means we break
the silence and consciously choose to use the power
assigned us as adults not to bully and abuse but to protect
and raise up each other and the vulnerable among us. For
some whose only real attraction is to minors, self-restraint
before they act becomes a life-long sacrifice of self for the
good of others.

Self-respect does not come cheap.

As for my Father, although he was obedient to the call,
as a preacher, he was no stem-winder. The sermons I sat
through were mechanical, legalistic, and sadly embarrassing. Meanwhile Dad's unresponsive little flock of farm
women and their children quietly made friends with Mama.

They gathered in each other's homes for prayer. Safe
with other women, they spoke aloud of trials and tribu-
lation. They practiced laying on of hands and prayed
with and for each other. The farm women who came to
Dad's little church were obedient, submissive women who
believed their station in life was decreed by God.

Like Elise, they prayed again and again. Some, like
Elise, even wore little white prayer caps. Some, undoubtedly, had their own Paw-Paws at home. Perhaps they too
disremembered unfortunate past connections. Like Elise,
they were stubborn Believers. To dare believe otherwise
meant they were destined for hell.

Whatever the sincerity of Dad's calling, after a few
years, sanity, reality, or maybe even Elise's God prevailed.
Dad suddenly gave up preaching and moved Mama back
into town.

• • •

Back in town, Dad continued to counsel sinful locals.
Whether to save the sinner or out of prurient interest, Dad
regularly visited and prayed over another sinner in town,
a man widely known to have long molested his young
daughter.

Later, when the young girl reached her teens, the girl's mother discovered the girl and her father "in the act"— but since, by then, the incested girl was a young teen, even her mother accused the girl of perpetrating adultery. Some agreed, the girl had taken unfair advantage of her father. Incest was never mentioned, of course, but loose talk of the girl's shameful adultery spread. Fewer towns-people mentioned that the same man also had a history of sexually assaulting his son. When the son later turned to alcohol to silence his pain, he was dismissed. He would never have amounted to much anyway. Didn't his father say he was gay?

Perhaps when Dad counseled the "adulterous" unthoughtful father, maybe they traced the daughter's original sin back to Eve, the original sinful female who tempted Adam beyond endurance? It's less clear if the two fathers mentioned the struggling young son silenced, virtu-ally emasculated in childhood by his father. My father was firmly homophobic. It was "Biblical," and nasty to boot as far as Dad was concerned. And Dad was always firmly against drinkers, another "nasty thing" inherited from Mama's side of the family.

Re-tooled and retold small town gossip overlaps, runs in cycles. Religion-in-service-to-patriarchy reminds us it's a sin to uncover the "nakedness of the fathers." Taken together they are road maps through time, pointing back-ward to silenced lives and toward a cruel future destined to cycle on if left unexamined.

Maybe that's why Dad gave me such a long, consider-ing look when I said, "Dad, I love you." Maybe the Wolf imagined the possibility of yet another adulterous cycle?

Perhaps he imagined I proposed more than mere friendship?

• • •

If I believed in heaven or feared hell as my father certainly did, I would hope for a merciful God who could extend forgiveness and grant his mercy unilaterally, even to a little boy eaten alive by Paw-Paw out there on the Home Place.

My father harbored a rigid fear that connecting the dots of his own childhood would not save but, instead, would surely unman and destroy him, perhaps prove he had wanted it, just as Paw-Paw told him back then. Accusing himself, believing he was a "pervert" in the core of his being, he thought himself unsalvageable no matter what Sigmund Freud or Elise's religion might offer. We were all still trapped in the old labels, the old language, the old "Biblical" prejudices. Perhaps there was little hope or help available to him even had he reached out.

The man who preached Dad's funeral said, on his deathbed, Dad refused to profess the correct magic formula to gain entry into heaven. The preacher said he could not testify that Dad was Saved-by-the-Blood.

I would hope for a God, not bound by human formula. A God capable of granting mercy to a man who, by then, couldn't tell the difference between pocket lint and Butter mints, who, in the end judged himself "beyond redemption" and refused to lie even to save his soul. As such, I would hope for a God capable of granting mercy to a little boy who grew up to be a father who saw little difference between, my "I love you Dad" and an invitation to adultery.

Sadly, even today, some still believe "once a sex offender, always a sex offender," and rather than set aside the legacy and commit to the work that might make real change possible, they vote to allow Paw-Paw's unthoughtful legacy to cycle on and on.

As for my father, thanks to Paw-Paw, thanks to the bullying and the ridicule heaped upon him as a small child, my father lived his whole life in the hell of a defiant and resentful isolation.

My father died alone, convinced that only in becoming a man like Paw-Paw could he recoup power enough to reassure himself of safety in a world full of Paw-Paw's. He never dared discover who he might have been. Still, how could a little boy so contemptuously treated have chosen to heap the same legacy upon so many others in order to relieve his own anxiety about how powerful he was, even back in the day?

Sadly, I never knew my father. We never made friends. I only knew the Wolf I tempted "past all enduring."

I told the truth when I said, "Dad, I love you."

But when I felt a sudden chill, I knew enough to step back from the Wolf's considering eyes.

Sadly I married a man strangely like my father but, still a Happily-Ever-After-Believer, I fondly expected our marriage would be better-than.

I am so, so sorry I never thought to say, "I love you," to Mama before she closed her eyes that last day in the nursing home.

• • •

Back home from England, Ben picked up side jobs, but mostly he spent his time tightening his grip on Benny and Carrie Marie.

I found a job teaching Head Start. At work, I glimpsed a competence, an unfamiliar self-confidence that I'd never enjoyed in the role of mother to my children. As Mother, my role was to agree and support Ben-Spock's perfect solutions. Undermined at home but still an inexperienced breadwinner, I didn't feel liberated. I had one foot in each camp. My life was splitting dangerously apart.

Summer ended, and so did Head Start.

With no jobs and no income, Ben and I decided it was time to enroll in college. We packed up our little kids and left Mama's house with all its unfortunate connections, bound for a college town in another state.

Mama pointed out, again, that a teaching degree would be perfect for me as well as Ben; I could work while my kids were in school and stay home with them in the summer. But I was needy myself, and afraid that being shut up in a room all day every day with thirty needy little kids would be infinitely worse even than being home all day failing to meet the needs of my own two children.

I remembered Karen Horney. Majoring in psychology might explain my life to me. I minored in social work. Like nursing and teaching, social work was a "helping profession" suitable for nice women, nice women who still didn't recognize that being paid less-than all your working life, meant poverty in retirement.

Ben said again that his "calling" was to work with children. He chose teaching.

· · ·

Instead of the tidy little house of my Happily-Ever-After dreams, Ben and I bought a big old green fixer-upper—a house with lots of bedrooms, a porch swing, and no central heating. There was room to take in foster kids. Ben was the expert with kids. Foster care money would add to our struggling budget.

A neighbor with children the same age as Carrie Marie and Benny agreed to babysit mornings while I went to college. Afternoons, I came home, cooked for everyone, took care of foster kids and my children, kept house, and did reams of homework.

I was sure "things" would magically work out if only I could just manage to stay awake and keep trying until the magic happened. Didn't Feminists say women could now have it all?

Looking back, I can't believe we dragged our two little kids around willy-nilly, expecting them to fit their growing up around our growing ambitions.

Exhausted, it took a stinging hot shower just for me to wake up and get myself going. Even so, I did sometimes wake up in the middle of the night and realize that Ben, who I'd thought was still in bed beside me, was just then sliding back into our bed.

Asked where he'd been, Ben always said, "Go back to sleep. I was just making sure the kids were covered."

I remember thinking, "What a good father," as I went back to sleep.

My son Benny now tells me that he remembers those nights when Ben would leave my bed and go, naked, into our children's bedroom.

First, Ben told Benny, "Turn over and close your eyes."

That done, Ben focused his attentions on Carrie Marie, sleeping in the bottom bunk. Sometimes, it seems, Ben then turned his attentions on Benny. Later Ben moved Benny into another upstairs bedroom.

Ben said the Baby Bible says, "Boys and girls that age should never sleep in the same bedroom." Ben and Spock's Baby Bible often agreed.

On the plus side, that arrangement left each child isolated and alone in separate bedrooms. Like the screen-door solution in Midwest City, the arrangement solved Ben's problem perfectly. The foster kids slept downstairs, but by then, both Carrie Marie and Benny were old enough to see what was happening to the other. What if one reported the pain the other was enduring?

Separate bed rooms were Ben's answer.

My blind trust proved disastrous for Benny and Carrie Marie.

Not satisfied with physical separation, Ben destroyed their friendship to protect himself. Benny and Carrie Marie had always been "best friends" but their friendship suddenly evaporated. Benny says, "Carrie Marie just stopped talking to me. About anything." When she was grown, Carrie Marie said Ben threatened to kill Benny if she talked to him.

About the same time, Carrie Marie's first-grade teacher called me.

"Carrie Marie is peeing down her leg at school," the teacher said, "Bring fresh panties to the school."

No one understood that a little first grader was hoping to call attention to incest, silently, publicly, pointing to "down there."

I took clean panties as requested. Problem solved?

Carrie Marie's actions, meant to speak louder than words, fell on deaf ears.

"Too big to pee your pants," we scolded.

Just as when I went to school and silently exposed my bruises hoping for help, no one listened to Carrie Marie either. I should have realized. But by then, I was far too exhausted to remember the cruelties of my own childhood.

• • •

Ben took a college class that required him to work as a volunteer, counseling young people in the evenings at a drop-in center in a large town nearby. After that, Ben started bringing his young clients home.

At first, we only applied for a foster care license. Social workers began placing runaways and youngsters with drug problems with us. We had plenty of room, and the added foster care payments helped feed everyone. Besides, just the title Foster Parents somehow endowed us both with instant "expertise." We told each other we were saving kids from bad parents, from bad families, from selling themselves to live on the street.

The middle-class culture war against drugs, hippies and "loose morals" was in full swing. We joined an army of naive helpers out to save the world from what we saw reported on TV. The unsaved and the unwashed were rioting at the Chicago Democratic Convention. They enjoyed themselves at Woodstock, held hands in Haight-Ashbury. They burned the American flag. They dodged the draft, took drugs and refused to go to Vietnam. How dare they?

Ben bought a VW van and grew his hair long. "All the better to fit in with the kids we plan to rescue," he said. Then we got licensed as a boy's group home.

I had somehow forgotten Ben's first stories about being sexually abused as a young child in foster care when his father returned from WWII, even before his father married his step-mother. Later, I wondered, given his bad experiences as a teenager, why Ben wanted to run a group home with himself in charge. Never mind, I still knew we were the good guys, middle-class emissaries from the religious right. The group home offered a bridge over troubled waters, for a price.

Besides, Ben said saving kids was his calling. Like preaching was Dad's.

To tell yourself you are called, to "make a difference" is a heady thing, somewhat like Dad being an unsalaried pastor. Once licensed as a group home, we took in more kids. I took on the added tasks of cooking and cleaning for a small army of foster teens, all the while juggling college classes.

Carrie Marie and Benny got lost somewhere in the shuffle.

· · ·

Ben graduated and turned our foster group home into a nonprofit business. The business bought a large house from a Catholic doctor with a lot of kids. Ben and I, our two kids, and all the teenage foster kids moved into the retired doctor's respectable neighborhood.

To protect Carrie Marie in a house full of teenage boys, I insisted she have the bedroom across the hall from our upstairs bedroom. In doing so, I gave Ben unobstructed nocturnal access to Carrie Marie.

Somehow, in the big middle of everything, Ben and I decided another baby would be perfect. I'd taken birth control pills for seven years. When I stopped birth control, I immediately found myself happily awaiting my third child.

Evidently seven years wasn't the too-long-on-the-pills that Mama's doctor meant when he warned too-long caused infertility? Apparently not only husbands, but priests and doctors and everyone, except the woman herself, had a right to say "Yes" or "No" when it came to control over a woman's own body?

Meanwhile, unbeknownst to us, our respectable neighbors were up in arms. They signed petitions aimed at kicking us and our group home out of their nice, middle-class neighborhood. Ejected from Limerick? Who knew? But then, a group home brought down property values, much like when "Blacks" integrated "nice" neighborhoods.

Our nice-neighbor's petition prevailed. The city council gave us thirty days to move across the tracks. It was my first experience of the reality of being cast out. Why had I always imagined I would be welcome in Limerick even if I ever I got there?

With our group home permit revoked, Ben found us a house in a working-class part of town. The move was a fear-filled jumble. Ben had already graduated from college. I was still juggling, cooking and cleaning for Benny, Carrie Marie and the foster kids, while driving back and forth every day, taking tests and trying to graduate before the new baby arrived.

Benny tells me that during this fear filled, anxious time
he was sexually assaulted.

Chapter 27

Benny tells me that during this fear-filled, anxious time, he was sexually assaulted. Benny says his assault was terribly painful. At seven, he says, he was too terrified even to look round at his attacker. Benny waited until the whole house was asleep, then he crept upstairs and stood on my side of the bed waiting for me to wake up.

Benny remembers I asked him, "What's the matter?"

What words would a little boy know to describe his sexual assault?

"I have a stomach ache," Benny whispered.

I opened up the covers on my side of the bed, and Benny slipped in.

Later, Benny says, I woke up again and asked him if he felt better.

"Yes," Benny said.

"Okay, Honey, go back and get in your own bed," I told him.

The Ben-Spock Bible decreed, "No kids allowed to sleep in a parent's bed."

Never, ever? Benny wasn't a baby. Sexually assaulted in 2nd grade, Benny was a little boy denied words to describe what was done to him. Benny was a scared little boy who waited until his father was asleep before he even dared whisper, "I have a stomach ache."

...

We applied for and received state and federal funding as a group home, and went from a mom-and-pop operation, to a business with an outside business office and paid employees. Ben, of course, was the Chief Executive Officer, a real life CEO. The business acquired a bookkeeper and a board of directors. The board opened several more group homes for boys and one for girls.

The whole thing turned into a dizzying blur.

In the process, I found myself edged out. Unemployed. I was suddenly not a "working partner" with authority of my own. I was demoted to Wife of the CEO. The kids and I moved back into the old house originally licensed for foster care. When I objected, Ben said there were concerns that I might try to use my relationship with Ben-the-CEO to try to influence business decisions.

Heck Fire!

Back when we were still a mom-and-pop operation, we had given each foster child a metal lock box so they'd have a private place to store important papers, pictures, and personal mementos. We stopped providing the lock boxes once we realized the boxes were often used to hide contraband.

Even after we stopped, Ben still retained use of his lock box. He was the Director.

Apparently Ben liked to revisit pictures of embarrassed young foster girls posed unclothed and "smiling pretty" for the camera.

Like a lot of men, Ben kept souvenirs.

. . .

As the group home business expanded and Ben worked longer hours. I became just another isolated pregnant wife and mother, relegated to watching, waiting, and welcoming my CEO Husband's return.

Meanwhile, my relationship with Carrie Marie careened downhill.

If I said "up," Carrie pointed "down." When I took her to buy school clothes, any garment I said looked cute on her was automatically the last thing she'd buy. If I insisted, it remained in Carrie Marie's closet until safely outgrown. Carrie Marie had gone from throwing temper tantrums to a passive-aggressive "you can't make me" attitude that I put down to growing pains.

My relationship with her resembled my childhood relationship with Mama, but worse. Luckily, Carrie Marie probably never dreamed of poisoning me.

But who knows? Maybe she did.

• • •

As the business grew, Ben started taking Carrie Marie with him on business trips.

"It'll give Carrie Marie a treat and give you both a break," he said.

When they returned, Ben said, "Carrie Marie was a good girl. Why don't you buy her a dress or a doll? Praise her for being good on the trip; it'll bring you closer."

Obedient to Ben's instructions, I bought the dolls and gave them to Carrie Marie. I praised her for being a good girl, for "doing what Daddy says." Ben said all this would help restore our mother-daughter relationship. It didn't.

As her doll collection ballooned, Carrie Marie's anger grew too.

Writing this, I shake my head.

Is it any wonder Carrie Marie assumed I already knew what Ben was up to? There was no need to tell me. After all, when they left, I said, "Now, be good. Do what your father says." When they returned, I bought her gifts. I rewarded and praised her. She must have thought I knew. And, if I did already know, why would Carrie Marie tell me what Ben was doing to her on all those business trips?

No need for screen doors. Gaslighting does nicely.

• • •

When my youngest son, Duncan, was born, I stopped college to stay home with him for a year. Duncan was pure joy right from the beginning. Named after my brother, he went to bed easily and woke up happy. He chortled, giggled, and spoke fluent Jabberwocky.

Duncan demanded the world take note. He loved being the center of all our delighted attention. Duncan's arrival moved my focus off the problem of dolls and trips, temper tantrums and stomach aches. I fell in love with my new baby son.

Morning found Duncan clutching the top rail of his crib, walking back and forth, crowing. When Duncan saw me, his eyes sparkled. Then he'd let go of the railing, plop down on his mattress, hold his legs up, signaling he was ready for a diaper change.

Laughing up at me, Duncan had me wrapped around his finger.

Duncan's joyous smile and bright curiosity lit up my life.

As for Benny and Carrie Marie, they both tried to protect Duncan. Benny insisted Duncan's crib stay in his bedroom. Years later, Benny still insisted Duncan share his room because Benny thought his presence would protect Duncan. Benny was probably right. If Duncan was never molested, he has only Benny and Carrie Marie to thank.

Duncan was nine years younger than Carrie Marie and seven years younger than Benny. Protected from actions he didn't know about, maybe Duncan felt not so much protected as excluded—isolated from a family dynamic that, had Duncan been in the loop might have helped him make sense of what happened several years later.

Instead, Duncan, much like my brother Duncan, was too often left to rely on his father's self-serving narratives as he grew up.

Ben was as good at telling puppy stories as my father ever was.

• • •

When Duncan was two, I went back and finished college. The older children were in grade school all day, but Duncan needed a babysitter. Duncan didn't see it that way. He raised such a determined fuss that the babysitter nearly refused to take him. What babysitter wants to take on the potty-training of a recalcitrant two-year old?

Oh, Duncan was cooperative, I told her. He just insists on solving the problem of potty-training his own way. Duncan says, "Icky," wrinkles his nose, then runs to bring a fresh diaper. He thinks his level of cooperation was quite enough.

"Icky." Problem identified.

Fresh diaper delivered. No need for potty chairs. Ever.

Problem not solved?

Fortunately for us all, Duncan's babysitter had a four-year-old daughter who assumed the role of the little mother in a house full of kids. Unimpressed with Duncan's solution, she resolutely and repeatedly took Duncan by the hand and ushered him into the bathroom. She expected Duncan to be a Big Boy—and soon he was, just to please her.

We all rejoiced. No baby tears.

But when I took Duncan for his first Big Boy haircut, and the barber gave me a handful of soft brown baby hair, I cried all the way home.

• • •

The year Duncan was two, my grandma Sara suffered her last stroke. Sara died propped in her wheelchair in a nursing home.

I felt nothing at Sara's funeral. Numbed out, I buried my grief at her death somewhere down there where I'd buried sorrow in childhood. Five years later, triggered, the damn broke. Sara's death hit me. I suddenly got up, shut my office door, and wept in great stifled gasps for hours.

Absent Sara's nurturing protection, I doubt I could have grown the resilience that allowed me to survive childhood.

Maybe I hadn't yet actually managed to survive?

The same spring Sara had her stroke, I graduated with a BS in psychology and a minor in social work.

In class, we'd talked a lot about the unrecognized "ele-phants in client's living rooms." I planned to work as a family counselor—you know, helping others remove their proverbial elephants. I decided I'd be an addiction coun-selor, correcting the dangerous obsessions infecting the lives of others.

I detected no splinter in my own eye, no elephants in my living room, thank you.

· · ·

Police armed with search warrants, suddenly appeared on my suburban doorstep looking for financial records missing from the group home business.

Unless you too have heard the police knock at your door—unless the police have come into your house and taken over—you probably can't understand how person-ally violated I felt.

Men in uniform poked through my underwear drawer, searched every cupboard, and looked under every bed. They discovered the group home's financial records hidden under a pile of junk out in the garage.

While the director's wife had been focused on Duncan, on a little girl peeing down her leg, and on a little boy whose stomach hurt, not to mention finally graduating from college, it seems the group home business had sud-denly developed cash flow problems. Put plainly, for some reason the group home business was hemorrhaging money.

For one thing, the business had grown too fast. Then the Feds changed the rules regarding the definition of a "billable" hour. Money ran short. And, surprise, Ben's new bookkeeper had a previously undisclosed police record for embezzlement.

Instead of getting auditors in to find out why the busi-ness was suddenly leaking green, Ben decided to staunch the flow by double billing for services not rendered.

Ben walked the hall ordering everyone to, "Bill, bill, bill!" He submitted fraudulent bills and cashed the over-large government payments as though rules for billable hours had never changed; as though no state auditor would even notice the sudden hemorrhaging, as though simple lack of cash were the underlying problem.

Financial fraud is a felony offense.

Eventually, Ben's solution brought police to our house with a search warrant. Never mind the bookkeeper's initial embezzlement, Ben's decision to commit financial fraud shut down the group homes. Social workers came and took the foster kids away.

The board of directors fired Ben.

Needless to say, we couldn't pay our mortgage. Our name was in the news. Neither Ben nor I could hope to be hired by any school or social agency in the area. The word was out.

As the Director's Wife, ensconced in suburbia, I was stunned, terrified, and outraged. I took the accusations personally. A loyal, supportive and indignant wife, I just knew Ben was innocent just as he said he was. Ignoring reality, I thought since Ben said he was innocent Ben couldn't be convicted. I was frightened. We'd already been cast out by middle class neighbors and forced to move the group home across the tracks, now with Ben's arrest, how could I maintain respectability, buy groceries and feed us until a jury agreed Ben wasn't guilty?

The district attorney's office said Ben was nominally "free to go" at least until his court date. So, once again, we picked up and, as usual, we asked for my parents' help. They came through. My parent's hired a lawyer to defend Ben. We moved into one of my parents' rentals to await news of Ben's fate.

Dad must have thought I hadn't paid attention when he said, "Don't think you can come crying home!"

The one true thing they say;
"Don't tell or they'll come and take you away."

Chapter 28

I *became a Child Protective Services Investigator by accident.* Once arrived back in my hometown with a disgraced husband and three children in tow, I went looking for work. I came armed with a college degree, a major in psychology, and a minor in social work but with the group homes in shambles and my husband awaiting trial, I could hardly use my past experience as a reference.

If a new employer knew about Ben, would I be hired? If hired, once found out, would I be summarily fired? Why take chances?

Still, someone had to bring home a paycheck.

I filled out the state application for the job of social worker. I was interviewed, and hired as a Child Protective Services (CPS) Investigator.

My work must have seemed exceedingly surreal to my father and husband. I have no idea what Carrie Marie and Benny thought, abandoned by a mother who went off to work saving other kids from what was going on in my own home, every day, right there under my roof?

I didn't give it any thought.

I went off to work leaving my children in Ben's care.

• • •

I was soon out investigating the numerous reports of incest, sexual assault, neglect and physical abuse coming into our local CPS office. Afterward, I wrote reports and made recommendations to juvenile court judges. As a result of my CPS investigations, some abusers were charged in criminal court, but only if the district attorney decided there was enough hard evidence to press charges.

Some men went to jail even then.

But, back then, many prosecutors dismissed child abuse cases because, like rape, they were "He said, she said" situations. No hard evidence. Messy stuff especially when "she" was too young to testify anyway. And we certainly never considered that abuse might "cycle" down.

In cases of father vs. daughter, the child often paid a steep price for telling, while the father sometimes paid little or no price for actually doing. Back then, child abuse and neglect cases were too often judged as Private Family Business that had unaccountably escaped into the public arena.

Like doctors who ignored sexually transmitted disease in the '20's, like educators who ignored a young girl wearing a short-sleeved shirt, the better to silently display her bruises, or scolded a little girl peeing down her leg in silent accusation, some Judges also just preferred not to see.

"Unfounded" accusations, like escaped genies, were quickly rebottled, corked and returned home.

Anyway, everyone knew it was only "those people" who did nasty things. A respectable white family man with enough money, hired an aggressive attorney, stonewalled and was guaranteed safety. Juvenile court records were sealed—for the child's protection, we said. Very often the child was sent back to the perpetrator's home, shamed, disgraced, punished and forever labeled "Liar" as a result of attempting to tell.

It became clear to me as an Accidental Social Worker that the crime (and hence the punishment) was most often a measure of prejudice, of status, of ownership, harm measured by how important the family man who did damage or how valuable the man's property that sustained damage. A man might go to prison for doing more than $250 worth of property damage to his neighbor's truck, but probably not if he successfully hid the grievous harm he did to his own child.

A man who proposed to the girl he raped was "exonerated" by a "shot-gun" marriage, unless, of course, he was her father or brother. Then other tried and true methods such as mother-and-baby-homes and adoptions applied. Girls like my Aunt Carrie still took lonely "trips to California" or the nearest large city back then.

Back then, too, people believed a husband couldn't rape his wife; he owned her. Holding fathers accountable especially for incest was a very iffy thing. On the other hand, if the father actually was not guilty and loose talk got out, innocence hardly mattered. Prejudice kicked in. Indelible labels were applied. Families of both the guilty and the innocent were ostracized.

"Once a sex offender, always a sex offender" was taken as an article of faith. No one considered even the possibility of intervention, prevention or recovery. Both perpetrator and victim occupied fixed roles in an ancient morality play. Neighbors with pitchforks and flaming torches gathered round, happy to serve as judge, jury and Greek chorus.

Then as now, who got blamed was often circumscribed by class and custom. "Those People' were never us. Good reason to maintain silence in small town America.

"Don't tell. They'll come and take you away," is the one true thing fathers say to the children they sexually abuse. Unless a child denies the evidence of their pain, they are, indeed, often whisked away by social workers.

Boys and girls left at home end up feeling bonded to their abuser, anxiously aware in the calm between crimes, that they may be re-assaulted at any time. It's a repeated process that teaches learned helplessness, much like the violence that left my mother bonded to my father in old age.

Oblivious to the psychic split my job required, my competence was directed solely toward protecting each separate child on my caseload. At home, Ben-Spock was expert. If asked, I would have said that everything I knew about incest, I had learned in state training workshops, from reading books, or had learned secondhand from working with my clients.

One thing I did know with unshakable certainty: no one, no child, no little boy or girl, would make up self-shaming tales of sexual abuse unless they were true. Unless molested, young children can't draw pictures of sexual abuse in graphic detail.

At work, legal definitions of crime reigned. For example, without "penetration" it wasn't rape, and if not penetration then perhaps not even incest, not groped, not violated; maybe "just" fondling? And what's more, perhaps the "merely fondled" child simply misunderstood a kindly Paw-Paw's intentions? So, it was a misunderstanding. No one was really lying. The child was wrong to feel violated, humiliated, demeaned.

Thus undercut, the confused child agreed. Ways were found to save face all round.

But then, what if the Accidental Investigator discovered pederasty? What if a man peed into his child's mouth, or the child into the father's? Was that "penetration," "golden rain" or just something so disgusting that the judge said "Ewuuu" and sent word back that he never wanted to hear tell of that nasty stuff in reports to his court?

Not ever?

"Besides," the judge wanted to know, "How does a nice female social worker even know such words?" What sort dares ask questions that might reveal uncomfortable facts? Better we all not-know than disturb settled sensibility?

• • •

Considered separately, my investigations made no unfortunate connections. Like individual incest memoirs focused only on describing the experience of a single victim, my investigations carefully revealed no patterns, extended no dots that led toward dangerous larger issues. Back then, CPS investigations focused on girls. We never asked little boys in the same family if they, too, had been sexually assaulted in their own home. For a little boy to raise his hand and say, "MeToo," was literally unthinkable. And for a young sex-curious kid to molest another? That was simply dismissed as "playing doctor" unless the "doctor" was forever labeled "Nasty Child." And guys in prison took care of kids like that.

"Perverts" were cast into outer darkness. Only after a plea bargain and prison sentence, are men allowed to open up in court ordered group therapy with therapists who, even today, are mandated reporters. Given the implicit bias and the scientific labels indelibly applied, is it any wonder that beliefs like "once a sex offender, always a sex offender" reigned? Still reign.

No matter. Absent wider understanding, everything began and ended with one incested female child. Thus siloed, individual cases were investigated, then closed. It was safer that way. The investigation was better-than in my Aunt Carrie's time, back before the advent of "Child Protection," but absent a changed perspective the results weren't much different for anyone concerned.

Judges preferred happy outcomes like "returned home," 'life in prison' or "adoption."

Smiley faces all round!

Gavel down!

Case closed.

In juvenile court, messy details ordered sealed for everyone's protection.

"Next up!"

. . .

I remember a case where a teenager reported she was molested by her father every day. Regular as clockwork. The girl's mother came home after work, locked herself in the bathroom, and took a relaxing bath between 5 and 6 p.m.

Every day, her husband used the free hour to molest his daughter. Every day. But not on weekends. The mother didn't work on weekends. Weekends, Daddy visited the bar. When

I told the district attorney her story, the DA said, "That's ridiculous. She's lying." Impossible. End of investigation.

Another time I received a report that a father regularly made his daughter drop her pants and bend over naked across the tailgate of his truck, all the better to discipline her with his leather belt. To teach her to be good, to never entice boys.

"Spare the rod and spoil the child," the DA said.

Other fathers defended their actions saying it was not sexual abuse but a father's duty to educate his daughter about sex.

Some daughters, older by then, realized their fathers, owned the obsession. They used his obsession as leverage and turned the tables. They demanded favors before bestowing "favors." Some escaped to the streets. Perhaps that's when the oldest profession began, back when a child first pressed her advantage and used his obsession against her abuser? Maybe like when Paw-Paw paid for my own Aunt Carrie to go to secretarial school?

The Spiteful Green Fairy was not impressed. "Stuff and nonsense."

From my own lowly place in the justice system, I was tempted to agree.

Such thoughts make your heart hurt.

· · ·

That same summer, I heard the perhaps-true story of a cute little blond eight-year-old girl who was sexually molested by her father, over and over, while her mother, a grocery checker, was away at work. Every day, the little girl's father stuck his penis, his fingers, his tongue, sometimes even her #2 yellow school pencils into her tiny vagina, into her anus, into her mouth, to amuse himself. She had undoubtedly tempted him beyond human endurance. It was her fault.

Shamed, the little girl hung her head, told her Accidental Investigator in a very soft voice, her lips barely moving,

"Sometimes . . . Sometimes it felt good on my body, but it never felt good in my head."

Who counts the price of being denied all right to say "No?"

"Yes" means less than nothing when boundaries are breached, when a person is denied all right to say "No."

The little girl was taken to a male doctor to be examined for sexual trauma. The doctor, like many doctors, was reluctant. He didn't relish the idea of wasting his time as a court witness. He gave the little girl a light once-over and pronounced her "not very much hurt." He did, however, notice that she had diabetes.

Without a doctor willing to testify to what the doctor felt should have been considered Family Business all along, the Judge's conclusion was likely to be "misunderstood fondling." So how to proceed? The DA was still willing to file but had only a shy eight-year-old child witness. Up against a respectable father in outraged denial, the DA backed out.

After some negotiation, the judge did remove the little girl from her home. He placed her just down the street with a maternal aunt—the same aunt who had first anonymously reported the child's sexual abuse, but later also declined to testify.

Meanwhile, the little girl's father remained in his own home just down the street. He was, after all, an adult. He had rights. No actual crime was definitively proven. Loose talk avoided, he maintained his innocence.

A typical case. Frustrated, discouraged, caught in the system, I gave up the magic role of Social-Worker-Savior-of-Children. "In future," I said, "I'll investigate, report and recommend as best that I can, but if the prosecutor backs out, if the judge fails to read the report, well, let it be on their heads."

As for the little girl's brother? Still blinkered as I was by convention, I never inquired as to what the girl's brother might have seen. I didn't think to find out if he, too, had been penetrated.

What nice social worker would dare to ask?

What male child, sunk in shame, would dare say "Yes?"

Then as now, CPS investigations into incest are defined as father-daughter, missionary position unless they definitely crossed the line into adultery; into "she wanted it." Isn't that what Tarantino said about Roman Polanski's 13 year-old rape victim? "She wanted it." But maybe that was before "Times Up" caught up with Tarantino.

But what of the sexual abuse of a boy? "Well then," they said, "He must have been a Sissy-boy all along. No real male would allow such goings on." As though male or female, gay or straight, adult or child, rape was something anyone "asked for."

As for the little girl's mother? "She should have known. She lived right there."

"How could I have let something like that happen?" the little girl's mother asked me. Sometimes she said she believed her husband. Sometimes she tried to convince the neighbors she had never seen anything. Sometimes she thought her daughter was the liar. Maybe her husband really was innocent?

Amid the chaos, she didn't divorce. She kept on working at the grocery store.

Perhaps that wife too heard the echoes: "No one in our family ever divorced."

"Just don't think about it. You'll drive yourself crazy."

And as for that little girl, the one who said, "Sometimes it felt good on my body, but it never felt good in my head?"

She was placed in the home of her maternal aunt, outcast, isolated and alone in a house just a few blocks away from her mother, father, and brother. The little girl was afraid to go back to school.

All summer, she looked out of windows, hung her head in shame. After all, it was all her fault, wasn't it? Hadn't her father warned her that if she ever told anyone their secret, mean social workers would come and spirit her away?

• • •

Undaunted by a justice system still mired in ancient assumptions, the court, the doctor, the aunt, and the little girl's Accidental Social Worker were all bent upon proving they were blameless "helpers." They weren't uncaring. They recognized her medical needs. Treating her for diabetes meant subjecting the little girl to insulin injections every day, "to save her life" the doctor said.

"Only a little poke."

"Now, be a Big Girl,"

The little girl objected to this new, ongoing violation of her person.

Had we all forgotten? For the little girl, insulin shots, just like #2 yellow pencils, her daddy's tongue, her daddy's penis, never "felt good in my head."

Insult to injury? No power to say "No" ever again?

"Necessary to keep her alive," the doctor said.

"Stop fussing," the nurse said. "This won't hurt very much."

Won't hurt very much?

Just what her father said before he penetrated her?

"This won't hurt very much," we said before we invaded her fragile boundaries in the name of "saving" her.

But the little girl cried, protested against the determined helpers denying her pain, invading her boundaries. Insulin needles, like her father's penis, said she was forever defenseless against violation. She learned the lesson "treated like a girl' was always meant to teach girls: Submission. Shame. Self-hate. Silence.

"Now be nice."

"A medical necessity," we said, "For her own good."

But denied the power to choose "Yes" or say "No," the body remembers. The little girl understood her lesson all too well.

Helpless to say, "No," one sunny day, despair set in.
She turned her face to the wall.

The little eight-year-old said "Yes" to death.

"Complications from childhood diabetes," the doctor
said.

Technically true.

My diagnosis differs. She was a child denied even the
protection of her own skin. Denied boundaries, her despair
was ignored. Pronounced "not hurt very much" by adults,
her terror spread. The #2 yellow pencils became needles.
When adult power and intrusion could be neither escaped,
denied nor any longer resisted, the little girl chose death,
the only power of choice left to her.

I knew even then: Death was her last stand, not only
against the Wolf but against the world that steadfastly
refused to hear.

"Too much information?"

"Too painful to read."

"Stop. Stop!" Even the Brave Little Green Fairy complained she didn't want to know. She said she had her own
troubles.

Even now, remembering that little eight-year-old
removes the safe distance between "just don't think about
it" and the enduring reality of despair made visible.

Alas, except for her too-soon death from "complications," the little girl's case was fairly typical, investigated
and reported and too soon "solved." Today, we still expect
nice little girls to point to dolls or say "down there."

We ask, "How did you hurt yourself?" We ask, "How
did you get yourself pregnant?" As though, in the age of
Zika virus and AIDS, we still believed in virgin birth. As
though a 13 year-old wanted rape. As though an incested
child could "just say no."

When mothers speak, when writers speculate, when
social workers remember incest, we all shift in our seats.

Meanwhile girls hurt "down there," turn their face to the wall, or numb-out, grow up and take their place as nice wives and mothers still stripped of the right to say "Yes" or "No" or take control of what happens to their own bodies.

Meanwhile, little boys, violated, raped, still say, "My stomach hurts."

When we all fall silent the Wolf cycles on.

Little boys are left to struggle on alone. Once grown, male survivors still struggle against the disempowering shame of being raped, of being 'unmanned,' of being told they "wanted it"

Suddenly, perhaps in the midst of a father's funeral, a man remembers and blames himself. Blames the little boy he used to be, blames the victim. Wonders, "Did I want it? Am I gay?" Perhaps he turns their homophobia on himself and pulls the trigger? Perhaps he is gay but never expected to grow up and choose a partner? He certainly never asked to be betrayed by the father he admired. What help is there for him?

Most men, even those forever struggling at the cross roads, do, somehow survive a rape that left them feeling deeply emasculated. Most become their own man. Most don't grow up to cycle on the path toward Black Tower. Most do not assume Paw-Paw-hood is manhood, whatever the Wolf may say. Most never commit suicide. Some of those who despair and do chose to trespass as adults, say, true or false, in their own defense, that they were molested in childhood. Often lost in the constant acrimony, is the fact the male rape victims often become stiff even while being raped very much against their will. But that is ignored, used against them. It just proves they "wanted it."

Most sexual assault victims, those who somehow over-come despair, whose capacity for empathy, for compas-sion remains—the somehow resilient, examine shrapnel wounds, choose to heal and make the choice to become honorable men and women. Most, even those biologically "attracted to children," discover courage and stop before they act. Most become adults determined to use their power as adults to protect the powerless, the vulnerable children entrusted to their care.

We seem to know so little about women who grow up to sexually abuse. I did once hear of a young boy sent to prison for life for murdering his mother. That young man said, "I know something about sexual abuse." But he dared go no further. He presented no defense. He refused to tell the judge even a puppy story.

But as an Accidental Social Worker, I still want to discover what makes the difference. What help is there for these children, these adults? How do I help myself? How intervene, journey along the 3rd path? Even if I could go back and magically find the little 5 year old who became my father, would there be help available to heal that wounded child and thus put paid to my family's tragic legacy?

• • •

The best reason to heal, to pick the scabs off shrapnel wounds, comes from another accidental survivor, from a little boy who grew up to be a man, a juvenile probation officer with courage to break the everlasting silence.

The man emails me to say:

"I've been trying to write this, but keep distracting myself. Do I have the correct email address? Should I heat some soup for lunch? Maybe I should mow the lawn first.

"Maybe I'm waiting for the 'If you think this is bad just wait and see what will happen if you tell,' the unknown terror of disclosure. After all, this and whatever else bad that eventually happens must be your fault. Accepting any other alternative means accepting that your father sees you as a thing to be used for his ends. Means accepting that no matter how hard you try, even succeeding, won't elevate your status to "loved."

"Means, accepting that those 'secrets' must be kept even from yourself. That you aren't good enough, man enough, to act independently without someone's direction. Your successes are accidental, unconscious. Owed to someone else. Left waiting, immobile and in fear of eventual failure.

"My whole life I've felt like my successes belonged to someone else. 'Act like a good father, and you'll eventually be seen as a good father. Act like a good partner and you'll eventually be seen as a good partner.' The list goes on and on of the 'good' things you can act like. Maybe you can't have a father, or mother (the hidden anger I feel towards her for only accepting the good & replying to the rest with 'you don't really feel that way' is almost as great as I feel towards my father. She wanted the secret kept.)

"Half of the time I don't know what the fuck I feel! It's hard to admit that I've spent most of my life trying to always act not like my father but like the man my father pretended to be in public. I don't know who I am. I do know who I'm pretending to be (I think), not that child who wasn't good enough to be loved by his father.

"I still keep the secrets, even from myself. I only feel really myself in my failures and in the desolation of that child whose father wasn't and whose mother wanted the secret kept but couldn't protect me or herself.

"I may have been good but I wasn't good enough to be rescued from the secrets. I've danced around this my whole damned life, walking on the edge of a stinking cesspool wondering if I've really crawled out or am just one more piece of crap destined to fall back in.

"The price I paid for survival has been not having access to all of me at once. Except in moments like this, I live in boxes.

"I know this email is chaotic. I didn't want my response to be what it 'should be.' If I'm going to pick at these damn scabs, I want it to be real blood that runs out otherwise what's the use? I'm tired of telling myself how I should feel and of being afraid of telling someone how I do feel for fear of being told I shouldn't feel that way. I'm angry. I'm relieved to 'tell' even this much and so, so scared."

End of story?

No.

Reading that man's story, looking in the face of my own resounding silence as a mother of abused children, I see that all of us, mothers, fathers, grown-up children, all of us, throw ourselves and our children away when, even as adults, we can't unhook from received belief, can't find the courage to speak out. But, if we don't share our experience how will we figure out what went wrong and discover different, better ways to proceed?

Lacking courage, we still adjudicate and imprison even impulsive sex curious children for exploring or for re-enacting harm done to them. Our continuing silence sends them cycling on the path to Black Tower: another label, another name affixed to the 900,000+ names affixed to the sex offender registry. Panicked, we re-enact the same old morality play complete with hanging tree, ignorant villagers and hate speech. The same old solution rendered "scientific" with the addition of computer registries and pseudoscientific labels?

Problem solved?

Hardly.

About five years ago, the Sex Offender Registries listed some 450,000 names. Now they list 900,000. One by one, a "forever victim" saved, a "forever monster" thrown on the garbage heap.

What shouts systemic failure more loudly than this mushrooming registry?

Revenge is not justice. Nor does it prevent the future.

• • •

Except for her early death, the eight-year-old little girl's story is the story of all the silenced, smothered little children who find the courage to "tell," yet are never listened to.

"Case closed."

"Next!"

As "helpers," we too insist upon Happily-Ever-After tales of successful helping.

Why "make ourselves unhappy?"

Why step outside the respectable box of our own construction?

Certainly, back then, I did not think outside the box. I obeyed convention. I did my Accidental Social Work one by one. Blinkered, I investigated reports of child sexual abuse in the little town to which Ben and I fled to await his arrest.

Today, I fear I always knew more about protecting other people's children than about protecting my own from a man strangely like my father. Maybe I, too, was too much like the man quoted above before he found the courage to speak up.

More likely, until I was forced to see, I was too much like that man's mother.

Maybe I too said, "Oh, you don't really believe that!" too many times. Maybe Benny and Carrie Marie, perhaps even Duncan hoped I would understand when they crept in to stand on my side of the bed once Ben was safely asleep.

Looking back, who can ever know? Unless someone tells? Unless someone breaks the 1st Commandment and someone else listens with their heart. Real blood flows when we unfreeze, when we pick scabs off remembrance. Unless we re-examine long-held beliefs, learn new, effective, ways to heal before it's too late, even our children's children won't escape the sex offender's legacy. Unless we find courage to speak up, say, "Me too," and examine our own silenced lives, we just mark time still believing we attracted them "past all endurance."

No one said it would be easy to take off our smiley face masks and "tell."

No one said telling it real was easy.

But then, the lonely life of a smiling pretender is no life at all.

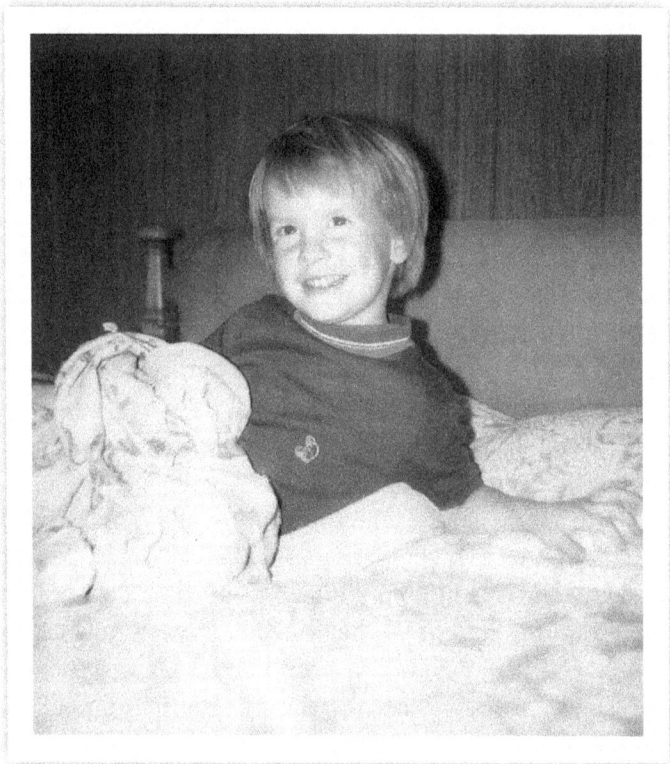

*Even a friendly, smiling, chatty little boy
knew something scary was going on.*

Chapter 29

As for Ben? He was arrested in front of our kids one lazy Saturday afternoon during the same hot summer the little girl turned her face to the wall and said "Yes," to death.

The local police took Ben to jail in handcuffs. Ben's only charge was a white-collar property crime: embezzling money. Ben was extradited back to stand trial.

Blindsided by Ben's arrest, I still rejected divorce. A good wife would keep our little family together. Doing CPS investigations, writing court reports, protecting other people's children—my job paid the rent. Bought groceries.

My only hope of keeping my job was to close off small-town curiosity, stifle loose talk. Risky business indeed but, as the Mackies well knew, veneer matters, appearance counts, smiling pretenders assimilate well.

Ben was an educated, white male with no previous convictions. His was a white-collar crime. After a few of hours of deliberation, the jury found Ben guilty but the judge only sentenced Ben to 364 days of work release, to be served in the county jail followed by a year of probation after his return home.

Ben wouldn't actually be serving prison time. We had dodged a bullet.

His less-than-one-year county jail sentence meant that, once off probation, Ben's record could be expunged. Once Ben's record was expunged, it would be as though Ben had never betrayed anyone, certainly not his children, or the children in the group home.

Stranger rape and armed robbery seem, in some ways, more honest. Each involves open violence. Crimes like fraudulent billing, embezzlement, date rape, and child sexual abuse are alike in that they are betrayals, crimes committed in silence by people we once trusted. As with child sexual abuse, such crimes are often committed by men whose crimes don't require violence simply because such men already occupy positions of power. They've already been granted trust and unquestioned authority in business, in politics and within their own families.

Middle class respectability provides cover for all sorts of secrets. In some cases, power itself renders the powerful too big to jail, frees them to call all their victims, "Liar. They wanted it. They asked for it." Of course they did.

• • •

My fear, as Ben's wife, was, should word of Ben's conviction get out, how in the world could I prevent the stigmatizing of my little family?" My family would suddenly be one of "those people," demoted, investigated and relegated to the fringes. We'd be one of the endangered less-than families nice social workers like me were hired to help.

Like Sara and Mama, like Elise and the "Perhaps Italian Lady," I was afraid the well-polished veneer would crack, and dangerous secrets pour out. What if I was fired from my job? What if I woke up to find my own children on someone's caseload? What if my children, too, went hungry?

After all, their father was now "one of them." How could even an Accidental Social Worker stand in line with other wives visiting their husbands in prison? How could I do that without being found out and fired?

"So, don't visit," the Green Fairy advised.

Easy-peasy. One problem solved. But what about all the others?

The Green Fairy shrugged.

Anyway, I thought, all I have to do is Pass for Normal, just keep my family above the invisible line where society turns a blind eye to the sins of the privileged; if I could just keep my family from falling below the line where the same behavior disgraces and prison becomes inevitable; if I could just hold it together until Ben got home and took the reins again. After all, Ben's conviction and sentence could be expunged. Wiped away. Dis-remembered. In the meantime, I just had to keep things quiet and look, well, Normal.

Easy-peasy? Well, maybe.

• • •

Driven by fear, I suddenly understood, firsthand, the purpose of all of Sara's well-crafted stories, stories I'd learned by heart in childhood. Sara's stories had been meant to silence questions, mute prejudice—to forget memories of Jewishness, homosexuality, suicide, alcoholism, family violence—for some, maybe even incest?

Dangerous Business solved with "Just don't think about it." Solved with "I can't believe you said that!" Silenced.

In times of trouble, the measure of a family's survival may depend upon a too-thin veneer, upon polishing conformity, fitting in, wearing the right dress, having the correct manners; being seen as "one of us."

But silence casts long shadows too.

Until Ben was convicted and jailed, I never consciously understood how a family's fear of being "profiled," cast out, stripped of privilege, labeled and stigmatized as one of "those people" could have so strongly influenced generations of "nice" women intent upon avoiding disaster. Women like Sara and my mother and now me, all bent on keeping a family's reputation above water, nice women all tasked with creating and maintaining a social safety net to cradle children, and family in the face of social sanction, implicit prejudice and the abiding fear of being forever cast out.

And if the bough breaks and the cradle falls? Mothers are to blame. Shamed, and lectured from the bench, rejected even by their own children when the magic of mother-love fails in its duty or prayer does not avert the fire storm.

Ben's conviction and sentencing meant he would be away for an entire year. How to explain a missing husband to neighbors and coworkers?

Duncan had seen his father arrested and cuffed. When I followed Ben down to the jail, Duncan was too afraid to go inside. Even a three year-old knew something scary was going on. What if the babysitter asked the kids where their father was?

I warned the older children not to say anything more to Duncan. Usually a smiling, chatty little boy, he couldn't be trusted not to answer his babysitter's too curious questions. What he didn't know, he couldn't tell. "And anyway," I said, "Duncan is too young to understand an explanation."

Fear, isolation and silence is an old pattern in families like ours. But isolating Duncan, creating him a little island set apart had consequences. It may be the best way to smother inconvenient truths, but after that, I think Duncan continued to feel excluded.

So why go to all this trouble? Why not just get a divorce and dump Ben?

Divorce seemed disloyal. A nice wife doesn't kick her husband when he's down. Plus, I still couldn't bear to believe Ben was guilty. If a man was guilty, then, by extension, so was his wife, so was his family.

Ben maintained his innocence. If Ben admitted guilt, it must follow that we were indeed "that sort of people." Most agree the wives and children, the mothers and the families thus labeled for whatever reason, deserve to be winnowed out, marginalized, and relegated to second-class citizenship. I didn't want my family to be classified as one of those people.

Oh, the arrogance of "better than." But then the Mackies, too, had good reason to hide dangerous secrets to protect family from pogroms, from prejudice, and from lynch mobs. Today what happens to families caught in the cross fire is called collateral damage.

I was too afraid to stop and think that all through.

I hoped against hope. I circled the wagons and fought off reality.

Spock's bible said, "Kids miss their father."

So I reassured my children Ben would be home soon.

I said, "I know you miss your father."

Benny and Carrie Marie just looked at me. Apparently not.

Years later, Benny said he felt relieved that Ben was gone. Benny said he wondered at the time why I thought he missed his father. Carrie Marie sighed, still too afraid to say. Even with Ben gone, she still believed Ben's threats. She still thought her silence guarded Benny's life, kept Duncan safe.

• • •

With Ben gone, Carrie Marie slept through the night. But she often flew into a rage. I put her anger down as a natural "stage" of child development. I arranged for the supervisor of the counseling department, located in an office adjacent to mine, to meet with Carrie Marie.

One day the counselor came to my office and asked, "Has Carrie Marie ever been molested?"

"Not to the best of my knowledge," I replied in my very best Accidental-Social-Worker legalese.

The therapist shrugged. She left it at that. Maybe she feared she too knew too much information. With Ben gone, maybe Carrie Marie had felt free to tell her therapist what had happened.

But no one listened, especially not me, the Accidental Social Worker going about investigating reports of child sexual abuse among "those people."

• • •

Soon after Carrie Marie met with the therapist, Ben finished his jail sentence. I drove up and brought him home. Our family was reunited, our marriage still nominally intact.

Once home, unemployed, waiting out his one-year probation, Ben laughed off the title "househusband" but he took immediate control. Ben rearranged all my kitchen cupboards, proclaiming them now more "efficient." Ben proclaimed himself the better cook, the better parent. Taking control awarded Ben untrammeled privacy to resume molesting Carrie Marie.

I imagined we were a modern couple, but Ben's methods were as old as the patriarchy, as sacrosanct as incest itself. Control, isolate, threaten, silence and repeat.

My role as Mother thus shouldered aside, I became the Accidental Breadwinner—the Good Provider Sara said I should marry.

Together we waited for Ben's twelve month probation to end.

Promoted to Supervisor of our field office, I was on call 24/7. Child protective services is an exacting profession. I wasn't a good mother, but I was a good social worker.

Work was my realm.

Home belonged to Ben. If the kids acted out, I followed Ben's rules. I put them in Ben-Spock time-out and told them to wait. Ben would come talk to them. Ben's Good Talking-to was apparently very similar to my father's Good Spanking –at least for Carrie Marie.

Is it any wonder Carrie Marie, and Benny too, assumed I already knew?

...

The Little Green Fairy complained that everything still felt weirdly out of balance. Never mind. I didn't want to admit I was still desperately unhappy, even with Ben's return. I did, once, insist that we all go to family therapy. "Just to ease the transition" of Ben's return, I said.

The whole family arrived at the appointed time, only to sit around tongue-tied, steadfastly silent, not once making eye contact with the family therapist I had dragged us all in to see.

The therapist, too, seemed eager to let us keep our secrets secret, to help us preserve our claim to not-know whatever "it" was.

Faced with our determined silence, the therapist didn't suggest individual appointments for anyone. If she glimpsed an elephant in the CPS supervisor's living room, she was professional enough to keep silent. If later called to testify in a messy child sexual abuse case, she could safely reply, "Not to the best of my knowledge."

We never went back. We all kept our Secrets secret.

At work I was promoted to Supervisor but "Go to your room. Wait for your father," was as close as I came to an equal partnership at home

Once Ben completed probation, and his conviction was expunged, what then?

Maybe another move, the tenth in fourteen years of wedded bliss, would be the fresh start I forever sought? Maybe, Limerick would magically appear over this next horizon? If we all just continued to maintain radio silence. If we tried, tried again? If, we somehow managed to leave all this behind?

Luckily for Ben, no investigator had accidentally opened The Director's lock box. Had a detective peeked inside, there might have been more, and different, charges filed. But Ben's lock box with evidence of Ben's risky business was still safely hidden in the top of a cupboard.

As we packed up again for our next move, Benny discovered the key and opened Ben's lock box. Benny recognized a young foster girl posed in the picture. Benny showed the evidence to no one. He relocked the box and said nothing.

Benny, too, was well-schooled in silence.

As for me, I thought maybe, just maybe, I'd finally get it right with this next move. Before the façade cracked, before all the water bugs in mourning started singing rounds of "I told you so," things might magically get better-than.

"Well . . . maybe." The Little Green Fairy sounded doubtful.

As for me? My life was not the one I thought I had chosen back when I said, "I do." No time to grieve over all that.

I could hear Sara, "No one in our family ever divorced."

Raised to be a nice wife, a Happily-Ever-After-Believer, I followed Sara's instructions, "Just don't think about it. Don't make yourself unhappy."

And the corollary to that? "You'll have only yourself to blame."

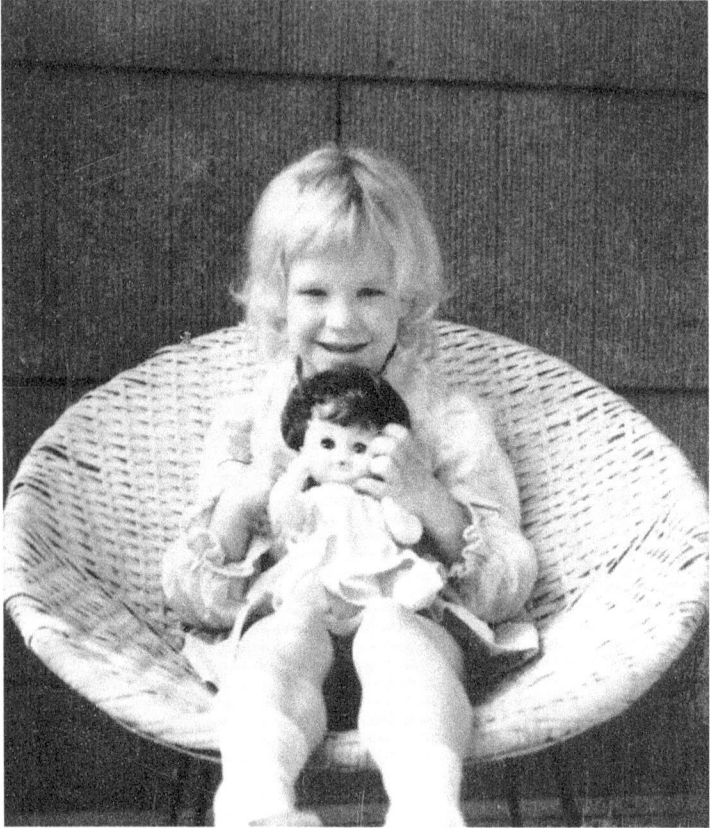

Carrie Marie's doll collection ballooned in the years between Ben's first business trips and when she moved into her "Big Girl" room.

Chapter 30

W*ith Ben's sentence served, and his white-collar crime expunged,* I sent out resumes, filled out applications, and was soon hired as a CPS supervisor in a distant state. Once again I packed up my dreams and set off in search of Limerick and the mythical American fresh start.

The problem? We took ourselves along.

I gave two weeks' notice. Ben made a trip to the new city in search of an apartment for the five of us. He came back with a proposal: "Why not rent a small apartment for us and then rent two studio apartments in the same complex, one for Benny and one for Carrie Marie?"

I wasn't going for it.

"Teenagers need their parents more than ever," I told Ben.

"They need their space," Ben-Spock insisted.

"But you can't just shove our kids out like that."

"Don't you want it to be just the two of us again?" he said. "Anyway, it's not like I wouldn't have a key. I'd go over and check on them."

"No."

What was Ben thinking?

"No, no and no."

Ben dropped the subject and went off promising to lease a three-bedroom condo.

I worked until Friday. Saturday we drove the moving truck to the next state. Sunday we unpacked the kitchen and set up the beds. Turned out, Carrie Marie's bedroom was isolated downstairs, a former TV room just off the kitchen; the little studio apartment of Ben's dreams. Our master bedroom was upstairs, as was Benny and Duncan's shared bedroom.

Monday I started my new job as CPS Supervisor in a much bigger city. The job was a complicated, demanding step up for me.

Ben said, "Why not convert the downstairs TV room into a Big-Girl room just for Carrie Marie. It'll help you make friends with her."

"Okay," I said, "But what do you think I've been trying to do all along?"

I told Carrie Marie, "Flip through your magazines, get ideas about what look you want for your bedroom. Next weekend, we'll go shopping together."

Carrie Marie actually smiled. "Okay."

"Don't forget you'll need shelves for your doll collection."

Carrie Marie's doll collection was huge. It had ballooned in the years between Ben's first business trip and her big girl room.

Carrie Marie's smile faded.

What did I say now? I turned and left, late for work.

This effort—like solving Carrie Marie's sleepwalking problem, like telling her to "do what Daddy says"—turned out to be just one more wounding exercise separating mother and daughter. What's more, the move further isolated Carrie Marie from Benny and Duncan. For his part, Ben gained the unfettered access necessary to act out his risky fantasies.

In the move I lost the feel of my own life. Living in darkness behind the imposter's mask had been a matter of survival since childhood, but the dead pool had grown as I grew. Water bugs crawled out of the unexamined silence.

With the added stress of another move and an even more stressful job, my life barely managed to sail on above the dead pool silence created. Darkness rose to flood stage; whirlpools tried to suck me under.

The Spiteful Little Green Fairy felt the undertow.

She lost faith in Mama's "Might as well laugh as cry."
She lost faith in Sara's Silence-as-Solution. The Little Green
Fairy made snarky comments.

She prepared for desperate times.

• • •

Once we settled into the condo, Ben got a job at
the western branch of a national stockbrokerage firm.
Thinking things were looking up at last, I emptied my
401K and bought Ben his stockbroker's license. It was in
the days of penny stocks and big gambles. Ben's local office
ignored the time difference between east and west. They
began trading with the opening bell of the New York Stock
Exchange.

Ben started work very early and came home early afternoons. No early riser, when Ben's alarm went off in the
morning, I clung to sleep.

"Don't get up," Ben said, "You need your sleep. I'll get
my own breakfast."

"What a good husband," I thought, before I closed my
eyes in order to catch yet another hour of not-knowing.

With the house to himself between 5 and 6 a.m., Ben
went straight to Carrie Marie's bedroom.

An hour later, my own alarm went off. Just in time for
me to get up, take a long, hot shower to wake myself up,
put on my social worker suit, and leave for work.

Just an Accidental Social Worker lost in a different
Limerick.

Time for Ben to drop the kids off at school.

Risky business, timed to the minute.

Unbelievable? Maybe you side with the DA who dismissed as "ridiculous!" the very idea of that other clockwork "arrangement" scheduled to take place right on the
dot while that other mother took her long hot bath after
work?

Still, as Benny and Carrie Marie got older, their age posed a growing danger to Ben. Benny, especially, focused on protecting Duncan, would have reported Ben had he walked in on him engaged in risky business.

Perhaps, in jail, Ben had heard of other men who took a child "mistress"—a teen they claimed "wanted it." Another child at fault, a child who tempted them "past all endurance?"

Maybe Carrie Marie's Big Girl room was just Ben's attempt to redefine the continuing rape of his daughter. Did it feel better to say "she wanted it" in a little "apartment" downstairs off the kitchen? Just another ignored case of "adultery" once teenage Carrie Marie turned eighteen?

Never incest? Always "consensual"?

Just like Paw-Paw with my own Aunt Carrie?

Just like that man my father pastored?

Ben's threats to kill Benny and Duncan had long held Carrie Marie captive, stripped her of the right to say, "No," forced her to say "Yes."

Carrie Marie didn't realize Ben was the one with the obsession, thus his over-riding need to control, to maintain access, to silence her and protect himself.

"I'll kill your brothers if you ever tell."

As for Ben, maybe Ben's obsessions, too, were also a young boy's shame run amuck? Just Ben re-enacting fantasies his wicked stepmother once reported? Ben was a strangely familiar Prince Charming who was him-self molested first as a child in a children's home, then unmanned, used and abused in detention. Told to "enlist or else," Ben's was a young boy's rage, resentment and trauma, another legacy of shame, blame and silence, not offered help but released upon still another generation.

Ben's bright blue eyes smiled across my grocery counter.

"Candy, little girl?"

Pocket lint.

Maybe Ben's fantasy was Paw-Paw's. Maybe Ben imagined Carrie Marie continuing to do for him in a studio apartment next door? For now, a separate room off the kitchen and an unfettered, well-scheduled hour every morning would have to do.

Déjà vu all over again?

Who knows? Who can ever really know unless we end the silence, compare stories, recognize patterns and find effective ways to break the legacy? Why do some merely change places with their abusers, effectively becoming Paw-Paw's in their own right, while others refuse but struggle in silence all their lives? Why do some demand better, while others settle for blaming themselves and applying the same formula again? Why do still others turn the tables on their abusers, change places in the same equation and in revenge, sell themselves but for a price? What makes the difference?

As for me, enmeshed in silence, I lived right there.

"If at first you don't succeed, blame yourself and try, try again."

Sara's catechism for Happily-Ever-After-Believers, learned by heart.

Once arrived in Limerick, water bugs in their thousands prepared to spread silent wings. Darkness, despair and depression grew. Below in the overflowing dead pool, not-knowing ballooned.

We moved into the condo. I blamed myself for past failures, vowed to try harder.

Carrie Marie's new bed was a convertible love seat. I helped Carrie Marie pick out her new bedspread. Then I nailed shelves on Carrier Marie's wall and arranged her doll collection. She must have felt just as arranged and nailed in as the dolls.

Mornings, right on schedule, I turned over, pulled up the covers and slept the extra hour.

"Such a good husband."

I left for work.

Ben stirred the pot. He added religion to mix. As director of the group homes, he'd always told people that saving kids was his "calling," a religion to him. Now Ben told me his calling was to help me by taking over parenting our kids, freeing me to save all the kids on CPS caseloads.

Ben said he carried the "burden of home" as a sacrifice to me. I was supposed to be grateful. Even then, Ben's reasoning seemed a little circular, a little self-serving, embarrassing even, but whatever. One more thing to not-think about.

Thus "freed" of the burden, I felt no gratitude. I felt isolated and lonely, sealed off in my compartment as surely as Carrie Marie was sealed off downstairs in her Big Girl room. I just didn't think about it. I made no unfortunate connections. I tried harder.

• • •

Counting myself a failed Mother, I focused on being a Good Provider.

My job as CPS supervisor was, indeed, extremely stressful—one that threatened to swallow my life whole while Ben, ensconced in the condo, went about indulging his obsession.

Ben's check came in when his ship came in. A stock broker, Ben periodically made a killing.

I said, "I want us to split the bills."

"But since you're paid every other Friday . . . and I can't always promise . . . How about I pay the car insurance? That comes due every six months," Ben said.

"Great," I said. "But you need to cover our monthly phone bill, pay doctor's bills and pick up the slack on some others. Okay?"

"Okay."

One day a police officer stopped me for a minor traffic violation.

I showed the officer my driver's license, then dug around in the glove box for proof of insurance.

"Ma'am, do you have another insurance card? This one expired six months ago."

"Oh?" Thankfully the officer just wrote out a ticket and said, "Show up in court with proof of current insurance."

At home, Ben shrugged. "I forgot."

"But you said . . ."

So much for sharing.

Ben's money was his play money, while mine, it seemed, was meant to pay bills, put bread on the table, and keep a roof over all our heads. My check was direct deposited every two weeks. With a steady income, I paid bills steadily. I juggled bills from paycheck to paycheck, always worried, always broke.

Ben, on the other hand, ran up bills for business suits and handmade leather shoes but was jealous when I bought the brand-name tennis shoes Duncan wanted. Ben said the thrift shop was the place to buy kids' clothes.

I was clearly not the mother Sara hoped I might be but I had, indeed, become the Good Provider Sara said I should marry.

Then something else went terribly wrong. About the same time I settled Carrie into her big girl room, Carrie Marie and Ben started having toe-to-toe screaming matches in the kitchen

The drill went like this: Accusing a protesting Carrie Marie of something, real or imagined, Ben raised his voice, pointed his finger. "Go to your room, young lady! Now!"

Maybe Ben wanted more than an hour in the morning?

Just like my father's Good Spankings, a time-out followed by a Good-Talking-To was still the Ben-Spock solution.

Ordered to her room, Carrie Marie waited alone, isolated and dreading the inevitable. Speaking for myself, as a child, the dread of what was to come was almost worse than the pain of a Good Spanking. Once Dad started in, at least the waiting was over. As for Carrie Marie, once

Ben determined she'd had time to "think about things," he went in, shut the door and "spoke to her."

Alone.

. . .

Meanwhile, the Good Provider focused on work and paying bills.

I did finally insist on opening my own, separate, checking account because I didn't want to bounce another check when Ben somehow forgot to tell me he'd made yet another cash withdrawal, forgot he'd paid his bar bill, forgot he'd wined and dined yet another client at my expense.

"Bounced checks look bad. We can't buy a house with bad credit."

Telling CPS colleagues, "My husband's a stockbroker" sounded respectable. I still entertained dreams of a normal life. I still dreamed of a snug little house nestled there on the corner of Limerick and . . . What were those cross streets? Well, whatever.

By then I knew I was forgetting more than just street names. I started forgetting ever more recent details. The flood of forgetting rushed in—and not just at home, where the persona of "Mother" had never been very shipshape anyway. Now the vortex of darkness started sucking important details out of the airtight compartment called Work. Forgetting undercut the persona of Competent Social Work Supervisor.

I felt myself being sucked under into growing darkness.

A strong backstroke wouldn't cut it this time.

Even the Little Green Fairy was caught in the vortex.

. . .

As always, I tried not to think about what was happening. Then, one day, coming back from court, I realized I could not remember whether the judge had just ordered me to return the kids in the backseat to their parents or take them back to the foster home.

I realized I could barely think at all.

I'd gotten by disremembering, compartmentalizing.

I knew to never to pay attention. But this?

This was different.

The damn broke. I was being sucked under, maybe for the last time?

Even a child's body left below in streaming darkness remembers secrets some are too afraid to tell. Forgotten memories bubbled up. Anger denied broke through the perimeter. Hordes of cockroaches scurried up through the widening black razor wire cracks in my universe. Wolf shadows on the wall and old, old scripts flashed on a screen, replaying long-ignored events.

Dead inside, I didn't laugh, I didn't cry. A dark pool of silent tears welled up.

At work, I looked, I questioned, and I investigated. Occasionally I even rescued a Paw-Paw's child. At home, I stood before the mirror and watched right become left and left right. I resolved to ignore the silent tears dripping off my chin.

What's the use?

Nothing will ever be Okay.

Never?

At home, life escaped me. I watched myself drowned. I felt nothing. I forgot to care. At work, I went into the restroom and brushed my fingertips across my face. Yes, those tears were real. I disconnected.

I turned away. I ignored the mirror. I ignored the tears.

"Just don't think about it" just stopped working.

The Spiteful Little Green Fairy got spiteful. She glared at me across black water. She refused to go under without a fight.

Swim as hard as I might, in the Black Hole of Forgetting, a hungry black fish, swimming just below memory's surface, captured knowing even before I myself knew, then took knowing down somewhere beyond remembrance.

Omnivorous unknowing swallowed up even simple, innocuous information.

Like, "Where are my car keys?"

Like, "Didn't I already turn here?"

Like, "Where am I?"

When did all of life drown along with the courage to see?

"I thought I was headed for the Court house."

"Did the Judge say 'yes' or 'no' an hour ago?"

Serious stuff indeed for a CPS Supervisor.

Seriously scary stuff even for a not-so-good mother.

It seems there actually is a limit to what the psyche can ingest and forget. A limit to what even a Spiteful Green Fairy, a long-suffering holdover from childhood, is willing to put up with before she too throws up her hands and back-strokes away.

Dark Matter rose up, full of water bugs, and drowned courage. Not-knowing wolfed down my whole life. I checked windows and doors. I recognized Wolf shadows on the wall.

To keep my job, to earn a paycheck, to be Sara's Good Provider, I had to function, if not at home, at least at work—but how could I function without memory of even life's simple things?

I was a terrified child.

Was this what happened to Mama the day she lay down on our scratchy maroon couch and forgot to get up?

. . .

I made a doctor's appointment.

"Doctor," I said, "I think I'm losing my mind."

"Really? When did this start?"

"I really don't remember."

The doctor didn't laugh.

The Green Fairy did an eye-roll.

The doctor sent me for psychological testing. After numerous tests, after answering a bunch of psychobabble questions, the doctor pronounced me psychologically normal. Meaning, I suppose, that I was not psychotic, schizophrenic, or even bipolar, not yet, and not yet floridly delusional either.

Good thing I didn't mention the Little Green Fairy.

The Green Fairy laughed, "Normal?"

"But," the doctor said, "You do have early-onset Alzheimer's."

What?

"Late thirties is a little early for early-onset Alzheimer's. But it's not unheard of," he said, smiling at me, displaying his best bedside manner. "Sorry to have to break the news to such a relatively young woman, but . . . You can expect to enjoy a few years of growing confusion before . . ."

Before what?

Before I stumbled off into the fog?

The Green Fairy stopped laughing. "Not funny."

Inside I was screaming "No!" just like the little guy screaming in Van Gogh's painting.

"Here, fill this prescription. It will help calm you down."

Next patient.

I stopped at reception, paid the bill, bought the pills, and stumbled back to work.

I had always been at least physically healthy. A little too imaginative according to Mama, I knew that, but intelligence, especially theorizing, intellectualizing, and labeling other people's problems, was an attribute upon which I prided my Social Worker self.

But this?

. . .

Returned to work, I couldn't work.

I took off early and headed home.

At home, my kids were laughing and joking; playing cards around the kitchen table. The sun streamed in on their happy faces; just a Happy-Family tableau. Duncan ran over and hugged me around the waist.

The sun spun in the sky. The moon went dark.

How could I allow my children to watch as I gradually disintegrated? Watch their mother stumble around becoming their burden?

No way.

Maybe all this wasn't really happening?

The Green Fairy demanded a second opinion.

My doctor referred me to a medical expert at a teaching hospital in another state. That day, I told Ben the awful news in private. I asked Ben to take me to see the second doctor. Surely all this was not true?

Otherwise, at Home and Work, as usual, I kept all my Secrets secret. Early-onset Alzheimer's isn't the sort of diagnosis a CPS supervisor bandies about at work. Anyway, there were bills to pay. I had to keep earning, keep my wits about me. I had to keep my Secrets secret as long as possible. Our health insurance was through my employer, not Ben's.

Ben agreed to drive me to the other state for the second opinion. But then, just days before the appointment, he backed out, "Can't do it. Too busy. Can't take time off."

I was stunned. I was afraid to drive on an unfamiliar freeway; afraid to drive around alone in a strange city. Not with early-onset Alzheimer's. I'd forget the doctor's address. I'd forget my way back home to our condo.

But I had to go. I had to know if the second doctor's expert opinion merely echoed the first.

So I asked Benny. I didn't tell him about the Alzheimer's; I simply asked if he would drive me out of state to see a doctor.

Benny said, "Yes."

A huge relief. Sort of.

But Fate wasn't done with me or with Carrie Marie either. Like a flock of black crows at dusk, consequences winged their way home, foretelling the end of time.

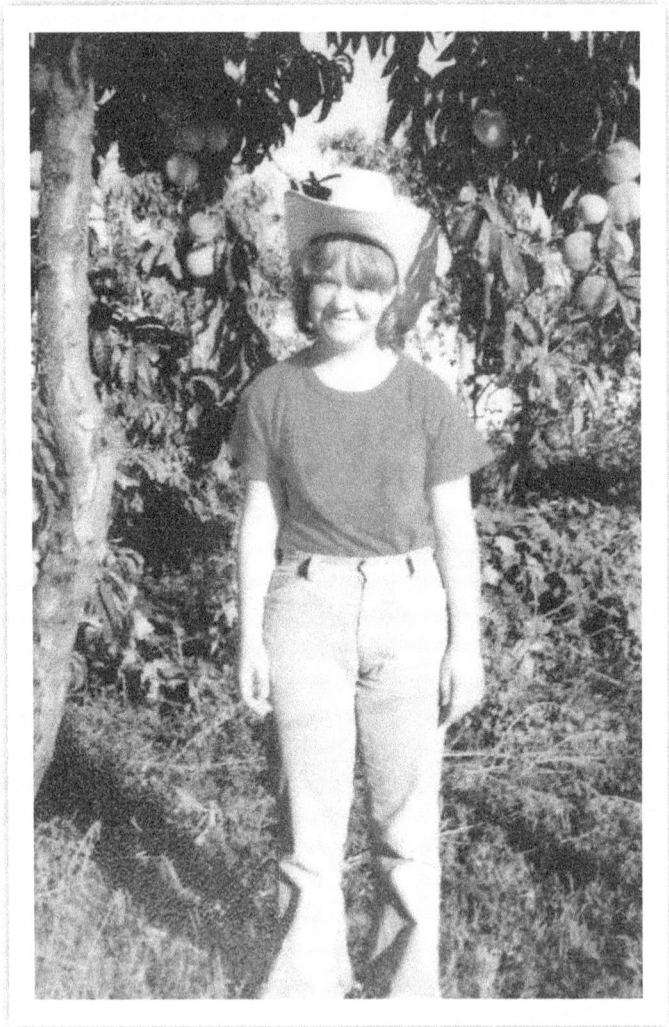

He offered to take her home so Carrie Marie put her purse in his jacket pocket and climbed onto to the back of his motorcycle but...

Chapter 31

The end of time arrived. A police officer brought Carrie Marie home one night just two days before Benny and I were set to drive off to see the second doctor.

Carrie Marie was silent.

"Your daughter," the officer said, "was raped by an acquaintance."

A motorcyclist had offered seventeen-year-old Carrie Marie a ride home.

She said, "Yes," tucked her purse in his coat pocket, and hopped onto the back of his motorcycle. The two roared off together.

Instead of delivering her home, the man took Carrie Marie to an empty lot on the edge of town.

Alone, out there in the weeds, Carrie Marie put up a good fight, but the man overpowered and raped her. Luckily a watchdog tethered in a neighboring yard alerted. The dog barked and barked and barked. He refused to stop until his owner turned on the yard lights and came out to investigate.

At the owner's approach, Carrie Marie's rapist roared off with Carrie Marie's purse still tucked in his pocket.

The homeowner found Carrie Marie bruised and bleeding and called 9-1-1.

At first Carrie Marie refused to say her name or tell where she lived. The officer said Carrie Marie either never knew or was afraid to remember the name of her rapist.

"But," the young officer said, "This guy knows where you live. He has her purse, her phone number. He could turn up at any time."

My skin crawled.

Lock all the windows. Bar the door. Stranger Danger. Wolf shadows.

"Call 9-1-1 if he makes contact. I'd like to get this guy."

But then what?

Carrie Marie refused to fill out a police report. She didn't want anyone, especially not a male doctor, checking out what she still referred to as "down there." Her shamed refusal meant no rape kit, and no sperm samples saved to test again when the new-fangled DNA testing became widespread.

It meant no testing for STDs; no rape crisis counseling. No nothing.

No morning-after pill even existed back then. Religion, then as now, proclaimed no woman had the right to choose. Even after Roe v. Wade re-affirmed a woman's long-lost right to "just say, no," absent the means to make "no" a reality, "No" still didn't really mean "No."

Based on the fact that Carrie Marie smiled and agreed to his offer of a ride, Carrie Marie likely would have been the one blamed. How dare a young girl accept a motorcycle ride? Accepting a "pickup" from some stranger?

Just more proof, had she been cross-examined in court, that Carrie Marie was to blame. She "asked for it." But in her favor? When attacked, Carrie Marie fought back.

Rape interruptus?

Carrie Marie's silence ensured no investigation. There would be no official pictures documenting the darkening bruises Carrie Marie suffered during the rape. Carrie Marie put up quite a fight, but afterward? She, too, was too well-schooled in shame and silence to speak up.

Ben must have been relieved. What if Carrie Marie started "telling" and didn't stop with the motorcyclist?

Luckily Carrie Marie wasn't pregnant. There'd be no need for her to carry her rapist's child for 9 months and give it away as had my Aunt Carrie. Absent the alert dog

and the intrepid homeowner, Carrie Marie's assault might
have had far different consequences.

Had she been murdered out there in the weeds and her
body disposed of, no one would have been the wiser. She'd
have been chalked up as just another rebellious seventeen-
year-old runaway. Maybe just another working girl, turned
out young?

And if not dead, maybe found eventually and sent to a
Group Home? Sent to some facility for incorrigible girls who
engaged in risky business. Her picture, too, perhaps savored
in some lock box filled with unmentionable souvenirs?

Instead, Carrie Marie's attacker had her address. Knew
her phone number.

I was terrified.

What if he did call her?

What if he was outside, watching? Right this minute?

Every time the phone rang, every time Carrie Marie left
the house or came home minutes late, I worried, checked
the locks, watched out the windows.

To make matters worse, Ben and Carrie Marie's toe-
to-toe screaming matches escalated. After all, Ben was the
one possessed of the long obsession. Like a jealous lover,
Ben accused Carrie Marie of engaging in "risky business."
She'd slipped beyond Ben's control. No more acquiescence.
Maybe Ben was suddenly afraid, not for Carrie Marie but
of her—afraid of all the other things she might tell the kind
police officer who still stopped by every so often.

In any case, Carrie Marie was clearly no longer safely
ensconced like clockwork in her big-girl bedroom, no longer sitting in time-out with her doll collection, dreading
Ben's Good-Talking-to.

• • •

Came time for my out-of-state doctor's appointment
and Ben changed his mind. "I'll drive you. No need for
Benny to take time off from school."

But by the time Ben changed his mind, my life, like Carrie Marie's, was shifting beyond Ben's control.

A door closed. A lock turned between man and wife.

I'd assumed married love, like trust, was reciprocal. I'd assumed that in desperate times my husband would come through for me much as I came through for Ben when he was arrested and jailed.

By the time Ben relented and decided to drive me to my doctor's appointment, our near twenty-year marriage was dead but not yet buried.

Final divorce proceedings took infinitely longer.

• • •

When Ben first heard news of my diagnosis, he wept copiously at what Ben seemed to feel was my impending abandonment of him. My Alzheimer's became Ben's poor-me puppy story, a tale he told to one and all around his office water cooler. Ben shared my private disaster over drinks in the bar while I still somehow hoped to keep the secret from my colleagues at work.

At home, as the hours and days passed, when Ben looked at me, there was a growing undercurrent of sexual excitement. Little by little it dawned on me: Ben was attracted by my approaching helplessness. He spoke of keeping me at home, of having me all to himself.

Behind Ben's words, his barely concealed fantasies waited to drag me under. Once Ben had me helpless and alone, I'd be at his mercy much like Carrie Marie. Ben could do as he pleased with a wife robbed of the ability to say "No."

The Little Green Fairy shivered.

Ben's clammy concern felt revolting.

The day Ben and I drove off to get a second opinion, I was already considering leaving Ben. What I didn't realize was that divorce from a man as obsessed as Ben, would be the most dangerous move of all.

• • •

After a full day of tests, some of which once again confirmed my mental health, the second doctor met with both Ben and me. The doctor talked past me to Ben. I'd been rendered invisible.

MIA in my own life.

The second doctor, as incompetent as the first, seconded his colleague's misdiagnosis: "Your wife has early-onset Alzheimer's," he told Ben, "If I'd been the first to make the diagnosis, I would have kept the information from your wife. Information like this is just too much for patients to handle, but"—he sighed—"the damage is done."

Ben took my diagnosis well.

But. . . No Butter mints for me?

Ben and I agreed to keep my diagnosis secret—well, as secret as Ben was capable of keeping his puppy stories.

Meanwhile, I waited. I kept on working.

In desperate times, Ben's invisible wife started making plans of her own.

• • •

Once Ben and I returned, I could see that, for Carrie Marie, no place felt safe.

I called Mama and told her about Carrie Marie's rape. I kept my Alzheimer's diagnosis secret.

Mama agreed: Carrie Marie should visit them for the summer. She'd be safe.

"How soon can I leave?" was all Carrie Marie said.

Sending Carrie Marie to Mama was one thing. But sending Carrie Marie to my father? How could I have forgotten?

Upon arrival, my father pronounced Carrie Marie ungovernable, promiscuous, out of control. Dad and Ben spent hours on the phone comparing tales of Carrie Marie's bad behavior. Ben told my father—in confidence, of course—that I had Alzheimer's. I couldn't be trusted to make decisions. Without telling me, the two decided Carrie Marie was unbalanced. They agreed she lied, a lot. Both said she was not to be trusted. They were afraid she might come unglued, might say something, expose unfortunate connections.

As far as they were concerned, Carrie Marie was The Problem.

Out of control, engaged in risky business, they agreed, Carrie Marie needed help.

Help, I'm sure, that didn't ask pointed questions; help that, of course, wouldn't endanger either of them.

They were right to worry.

As soon as she arrived, Carrie Marie reported Ben's sexual assault. She told everyone, except me, about the crimes Ben had regularly committed. She told both my parents and then my brother Bayard, who by then lived close by.

Dad called Ben. He reported that Carrie Marie was "saying things." Both agreed Carrie Marie was actually referring to her rapist-on-the-motorcycle, not to Ben.

Not family. Of course not. Not the rapist who appeared in her big girl room each morning like clockwork.

As for Mama, Bayard told me years later that she believed Carrie Marie.

Mama even went so far as to call Ben up and give him what-for over the phone—nicely of course, no swear words involved. But no one ever called me. No one called to tell me of the close-to-home crimes Carrie Marie was reporting.

Years later, when I heard the real story, I protested, "No one told me."

"Well," they said, "Well, you were always so supportive of Ben."

What did that mean?

Did they too decide I must have known all along? Did they all think I chose Ben instead of Carrie Marie?

One thing was certain, I had, indeed, succeeded at being a too-good wife; damned if I didn't follow Sara's pattern, damned when I did.

The old catch-22 cut-to-fit nice wives.

Ben told them all "the wife" was about to walk into the fog. Said I was too "not there" to include or even consult.

Maybe I would have failed Carrie Marie again. I don't think so, but . . .

As in the doctor's office, their decisions, taken in secret, denied me even opportunity to say "Yes" or "No." I might have taken Carrie Marie's side. I might have reported Ben.

Who knows at this remove? I hope so.

Certainly no one at Mama's house called the police. No one helped Carrie Marie make a police report. Once again, our family's well-schooled legacy closed over.

They labeled Carrie Marie promiscuous, crazy. Denied the dignity of recognition, the burden fell upon Carrie Marie. She was discredited—not because she wasn't believed but because she told. She broke the 1st Commandment. That was dangerous.

For that, she was sent away.

Not until my father told his visiting nurse the tale of witnessing incest in the living room when Carrie Marie was a toddler did anyone call the police. But that was much later. Much too late, really, to help Carrie Marie. The damage was done. Because by then she'd married her own strangely familiar Prince Charming.

• • •

Despair took over. My brother Bayard told me later, that one night, Carrie Marie came in past curfew. After a toe to toe battle with my father, Carrie Marie swallowed every dangerous prescription pill in my parent's medicine cabinet.

Despair sits at the secret heart of even an attempted suicide.

After Carrie Marie tried to kill herself, my father, who once failed to have Mama carted off to a mental hospital, got together with Ben and tried again.

Now self-styled as Carrie Marie's long-suffering father and grandfather, Ben and my Dad succeeded in having

seventeen-year-old Carrie Marie committed to a state mental hospital.

"For observation," they said.

"Carrie Marie is mentally unbalanced," they said. "In
need of psychotropic medication and professional help."
Sigmund Freud would, no doubt, have agreed.

Later, Ben used Carrie Marie's time in "observation"
against her.

"Further proof," Ben later said, "that Carrie Marie
is delusional, an inveterate liar. Everyone agrees the very
idea of suppressed memory surfacing later is just fictitious
psychobabble."

If pressed, Ben said he was so sorry his daughter was
an unbalanced young girl who, after being raped by a
stranger, made up stories of sexual abuse by her father in
childhood.

"False Memory Syndrome" is a pop psychology term
invented around that time by a couple whose own daughter accused her father of sexually abusing her all during
childhood. Ben, like my father, like Paw-Paw before him,
told puppy stories and garnered sympathy.

Paw-Paws must control the narrative at all costs.

Carrie Marie paid a terrible price.

Ben told listeners that Carrie Marie became unbalanced
because she'd secretly led a wild life. As a result of her wild
ways, Carrie had fallen victim to Stranger Danger, probably taken drugs, succumbed to date rape, and descended
into mental illness, permanently labeled "unreliable,"
never to be trusted again.

Between my father and hers, Carrie Marie was "scientifically" labeled as just one more promiscuous, uncontrol-
lable, mentally ill liar, a girl who engaged in risky business in
spite of her father's and grandfather's best efforts to save her.

They were teaching Carrie Marie what abuse is meant
to teach: No use to try. No use to tell. No power to say
"Yes" or "No." Once labeled, Carrie Marie was safely

fixed in place, like Freud's hysterical women a century before.

The truth, of course, was that Carrie Marie was telling too-dangerous tales. She talked. She'd managed to escape their control. Simple as that.

When Carrie Marie returned, tamed by her stint in Observation, Dad called me. "Elderly grandparents can't be expected to handle a girl with all Carrie Marie's problems," he said.

By then, I'd left Ben but I had no safe place to offer Carrie Marie.

Eventually, Carrie Marie went to live with a large family—a Mormon family that accepted her as one of their own, even when she refused to attend their church and persisted in small rebellions. They were good people. Carrie Marie was safe with them—safe perhaps for the first time, for perhaps the only time, in her too-short life.

After she left that foster mother's home, Carrie Marie came to live with me for a few years. She saw a therapist every week. Years too late, but it seemed to help. She worked to write down what she remembered and felt. No need for false memories; she had plenty of real memories of her own to decipher.

Carrie Marie did the work of rebuilding her life to the extent she could. The problem was that, even therapy didn't hold out hope for a different future. Instead of a paradigm shift, her therapy told her that if she tried, kept trying hard enough she too might learn to fit in and live Happily-Ever-After, happily married to a strangely familiar Prince Charming of her own.

No epiphany, no paradigm shift.

Just smile and remember not to think about what ever "it" was. Don't make yourself unhappy. Conform. It's Biblical.

Benny graduated but stayed, still trying to protect Duncan just as he and Carrie Marie had always tried to protect their little brother. (Both Benny and Duncan's faces are obscured to respect their privacy now that they are adults.)

Chapter 32

Once Carrie Marie flew off, I went back to work. Ben resumed his early-morning routine—but now, with Carrie Marie gone, he came back into our bedroom mornings. Like clockwork, before I even had the chance to wake up, Ben began what he referred to as "making love."

Perhaps Carrie Marie, too, had objected to the same sort of unsolicited early morning attention?

As for me, awake or asleep, Ben's nonconsensual sex made my skin crawl.

"Wake me up before you begin," I said. "I need to be awake, consenting, and participating when we have sex."

Ben didn't listen. Today, there are still husbands who think it's impossible for a husband to rape his own wife. "Well, if she's in her nighty, that's consent enough."

But marriage and a nighty not-with-standing, "Yes" means nothing absent the power or opportunity to say "No." No matter how often your rapist says, "But honey, I love you" afterward, the fact is "No" means "No."

I said. "No."

Ben didn't listen.

"No! No, a thousand, thousand times No!"

"I want a divorce."

Never mind Sara.

I found an apartment and prepared to leave.

"I will disappear Duncan if you file for divorce," Ben said. "Believe me, you will never see Duncan again."

I believed.

I didn't yet realize these were the same threats that Ben had used for so long to hold Benny and Carrie Marie captive.

"Do as Daddy says or else?"

"Or else," Ben said, "You'll never see Benny or Duncan again."

Afraid I would too-soon walk into the fog, I moved out anyway. But, due to Ben's threats, I put off filing for divorce. I left Duncan and Benny behind. Benny graduated but stayed, still trying to protect Duncan just as he and Carrie Marie had always tried to protect their little brother.

Trust broken, too late I escaped. How long before forgetting pulled me under? How long before I walked into the fog?

I got out, thinking I'd get a divorce before forgetting pulled me under, before I drowned in darkness, before isolation was complete.

• • •

I rented a two-bedroom across from Duncan's junior high school. I moved in and gave spare keys to Benny and Duncan thinking they could spend time with me before things went from bad to worse.

Ben came unglued. He left suicide notes for Duncan and Benny to find. He wept and told more poor-me puppy stories around the water cooler at work. He drank. He walked into traffic. He walked around the condo stark naked. He passed out on the couch and exposed himself. Duncan didn't dare bring his friends home.

There was more.

A friend at work said she and the other CPS investigators were getting weird sexual calls at night on their unlisted numbers. She'd recognized Ben's voice. I realized I'd left my on-call list of CPS workers' unlisted phone numbers in a nightstand at the condo.

I called Ben at work. "If your calls don't stop, I'll call the police."

"Don't you dare threaten me!" he shot back. "I'll send copies of the doctor's Alzheimer's diagnosis to your boss!" He laughed. "They'll fire you. Bitch!"

After that, the nocturnal calls to my coworkers stopped. But Ben's craziness didn't.

He knew I was on call. Knew I couldn't unplug my phone. I had to pick up.

Ben switched to making anonymous calls to me. He breathed, hissed, and screamed obscenities, then hung up and called back. Over and over. Again and again.

Ben stole the house keys I'd given to Benny and Duncan. He roamed my apartment, helped himself to what he wanted, stole my underwear, and left.

But never for good. And Ben always left behind some trace to say he'd been inside my house.

The traces said, "I can do more. Anytime I choose . . ."

I was terrified; another Wolf-shadow coming down the hall. Another "someone" standing watch; smiling, fantasizing, reaching out, touching me as I lay sleeping?

I stopped fearing rape. I expected Ben would murder me in my bed instead.

Just the thought triggered panic attacks.

Anxiety does nothing to cure Alzheimer's.

I was stuck and Ben knew it.

"Might as well laugh as cry," Mama always said.

I was afraid to divorce, afraid he'd kidnap and kill Duncan, afraid I'd be fired if my Alzheimer's diagnosis became known.

I was afraid that even in divorce court, with such a dangerous diagnosis, I, not Ben, would be the discredited parent. Ben was, after all, a stockbroker. I was a disintegrating wife.

Ben called my brother Bayard.

"Her Alzheimer's getting worse," Ben said. "She needs a husband's protection. She can't think straight. She got up and left me and both the boys. Isn't that proof enough? Call her and tell her she's got to come back."

To his credit, Bayard declined.

· · ·

I decided I needed a counselor to help me plan what future I had left. I called a therapist in the town where we lived.

Turned out, Ben was already her patient. Ben had explained everything. No Karen Horney, she offered couple's therapy—to help me reconcile with Ben, presumably, before I walked into the fog.

She said I needed Ben's care.

I refused her therapy, but finally agreed to meet Ben at a restaurant.

Over drinks, Ben said he'd take me back. No changes. No need for me to apologize. Just return. A helpless wife trapped at home, waiting for him to come in, like clockwork, each morning would be fine. He'd take up exactly where he left off.

Heck Fire!

If so, Ben said, all would be forgiven. Life could return to normal.

Whose life? What normal?

Sitting across from him, I felt the dangerous undertow of Ben's obsession.

The lady who thought she had Alzheimer's declined.

I think I actually said, "I'd rather die than get in bed with you ever again!"

The Little Green Fairy slammed and locked the door.

"Over my dead body!" she said.

I was afraid it might be.

Ben lashed out. "I'd never forgive you anyway! I don't want you back! Just remember, as your Alzheimer's progresses, you'll try to give it away on the street corner.

You'll get naked and climb on the back of a stranger's motorcycle."

"You're cut off," Ben stalked out without paying his bill.

What? No pocket lint for me?

Thank goodness for small favors.

Souvenirs continued to disappear into the thin night air. A Victorian wall clock brought back from England, and one of a pair of favorite shoes disappeared. I believed Ben when he said he would disappear Duncan too.

"You'll never see him again," Ben's hissing voice warned in dead of night. But then a happily married juvenile detective I worked with at CPS realized some of what was going on and took Ben aside. Over a drink, the detective clarified Ben's options for him.

After that, Ben calmed down a little. I decided to wait until Duncan was older before I actually got a divorce.

Physical escape would have to be enough for a while.

• • •

In the meantime, I thought, maybe, just maybe, a less stressful job would help, at least until I walked into the fog that one last time. By then it wouldn't matter. What was left of me would be some stranger's problem anyway.

I was hired to run a volunteer center. The courts sent us people mandated to do hours of community service.

Back then, laws against domestic violence were new. People who committed domestic violence went to jail for twenty-four hours. Period. If the violence was mutual, both partners went to jail.

A woman came in to the volunteer center, court ordered to do community service for striking her boyfriend. Striking back might have better described her situation, but her boyfriend was the one to call 9-1-1. He was the one who filed charges. She alone served time. Afterwards, she was court-ordered to do community service.

Fair's fair. Right? Women can't expect special treatment.

When I interviewed the woman, I saw she was broken inside. I offered her phone numbers; said I'd drive her to the local domestic violence shelter.

Too terrified to move, she cut her eyes toward the silent waiting room where her boyfriend sat leafing through a dog-eared issue of some Guns-and-Ammo magazine.

I tried again. "You'll be safe."

She didn't so much as blink.

The man in the waiting room cleared his throat.

She winced.

Defeated, I assigned her to do community service and sent her on her way.

By Monday, she was dead. Too terrified to accept help, she couldn't save herself. She was found bruised and beaten, shot, strangled and drowned in her own bath tub.

He scared the life out of her and then he killed the rest of her.

Like clockwork.

But then, there I was, a "professional" helpless to divorce. Cut to fit in childhood, it hadn't yet occurred to me that years of abuse bind us to our abusers. We give up belief in escape. Learned helplessness explains not only my own but Elise's and Mama's lost years, lost lives, and per- haps helps explain Carrie Marie's silenced life also.

Like a lot of other nice women, each of us had too-well learned the lessons abuse and domination teach. We find we must look in the mirror to know we are weeping, we must see our reflection to be sure we exist.

I forgot to listen to the Uppity Little Green Fairy.

I forgot there were shards to put together, conversa- tions to begin, truths to tell in hope of understanding and preventing the sex offender's legacy cycling on.

I didn't know what courage still had to teach me about letting go of fear and paying attention as life rushed ever onward.

I comfort my grief imagining Carrie Marie as a little girl
watched over by Mama and my darling Sara,
running along some sunny sea shore, laughing and playing
with all those who tried to believe they would find
sunshine somewhere someday.

PART VI: PETALS ON THE WIND

Chapter 33

Eventually, Ben moved on. He left Duncan behind. My divorce became final and Duncan came to live with me. Benny went to college, got a job, and was finally free to find a partner and choose his own life.

As for me, I eventually realized that if in all that time, I hadn't disappeared into Alzheimer's then I probably wouldn't.

Not for another forty years or so, anyway.

Yet, I know that if the second doctor with the second wrong opinion had had his way, kept more secrets from me, I might have gone on married to Ben, boxed up and labeled; still keeping secrets. With no real tomorrow, I might still be mired in learned helplessness. I might have ended up like Mama, trapped, trusting in an untrustworthy husband until I curled up and died.

Instead, free but not yet healed, our family scattered; each one still isolated, still burdened by silence and fear, we grew our separate ways, struggled to find our own tomorrows.

It was not until my father told his visiting nurse the tale of Carrie Marie's molestation, not until the nurse reported Carrie Marie's story to the authorities that the police finally called and asked Benny, Carrie Marie, and me about Ben's risky yesterdays.

Tasked with protecting children, the police investigator needed to make a decision as to whether minor children were currently in danger. The officer said Ben had gotten a job in social services. Ben had gained access to children so disabled they couldn't speak.

Without comparing notes, Benny and I made similar statements. Benny also mentioned the souvenirs of posed and smiling young girls he'd seen inside Ben's lockbox.

I have since asked around about Ben's adventures at the group homes. I was told by someone who should know that three years after the group homes closed, he spoke to a boy who reported that Ben also took advantage of him.

For my part, my own statement to the investigator reads, in part:

"I believe Ben must have molested Carrie Marie from the time he started taking Carrie Marie into the shower with him at Tinker AFB. I think Ben was molesting her all those years when I believed he was just being a good father getting up at night to check on her.

"Because Ben threatened to kidnap Duncan and made me afraid he would kill me when I left him, it rings true when Carrie Marie says the reason she was afraid to tell was because Ben said he would kill her brothers if she reported him.

"I think Ben kept on molesting Carrie Marie until she went to live with my parents."

• • •

I still remember how hard it was to finally break the silence and tell the investigator the truth about Carrie Marie, about myself and my marriage. Maybe that was the reason Mama never told even her sister Liza how she was treated.

For her part, when contacted by the police, Carrie Marie confirmed Ben's years of incest. Carrie Marie told the investigator from the sheriff's department she didn't want to dig back through remembered darkness, didn't want to speak out and disrupt the life she'd made. Carrie Marie refused to testify because, by then, she had married Kenneth, a man strangely like her father.

She told the investigator she had moved on. Married, she hoped for happy tomorrows. Carrie Marie and Kenneth attended church religiously, found marriage guidance in the Bible as interpreted by Kenneth. Their marriage was "Biblical." It met Kenneth's needs.

Kenneth said Carrie Marie would forever be his child bride.

Kenneth said, "No matter, Carrie Marie will always be my little girl." To please her husband, she watched cartoons and Disney movies, dressed like a ten year-old, never wrote a check, and never made a decision unaided by Kenneth.

Carrie Marie and Kenneth agreed, no children. Carrie Marie said all the medications prescribed for her ongoing depression would harm the fetus.

· · ·

One Christmas I called Carrie Marie. I asked what they wanted for Christmas. After consulting with Kenneth, Carrie Marie said they'd like a certain blue queen-size comforter set in the Sears catalog. I bought the set online and had it shipped to the state where Carrie Marie and Kenneth lived.

Later, when I visited, I looked in their bedroom. Carrie Marie's husband, Kenneth, slept under the blue quilt in the adult queen-size bed. Carrie Marie's bed was a little white, child's bed set against one wall of Kenneth's bedroom.

Marriage made their relationship legal. Grooming and Sara's schooling, handed down, made Carrie Marie just another nice girl in a long line of Happily-Ever-After-Believers.

In spite of refusing to testify, Carrie Marie did answer the investigator's questions. Her truth helped the investigator deny Ben access to fresh victims.

But for Carrie Marie, the damage was done. She was Kenneth's little girl, his child bride, for the rest of her life, proud to say, even as she lay helpless in hospice, dying of ovarian cancer, that their Happily-Ever-After marriage lasted nine years.

After the funeral, Kenneth moved on. He still calls Benny once in a while to revive memories of his forever-child bride, his faithful little Carrie Marie.

• • •

As for Ben? In our daughter's last days, he offered to let bygones be bygones. Ben sent word he'd come visit Carrie Marie in hospice "in spite of everything."

Carrie Marie said, "I don't care."

Ben never came.

The only amends I know Ben ever made to Benny happened once-upon-a-camping-trip when Benny was still living with Ben, still staying on trying to protect Duncan. Benny tells me Ben took him aside and told Benny he had been a bad father because, Ben said, he'd had a bad childhood.

Like Paw-Paw, like my father, Ben never chose change. None of the three ever sought therapy or found relief from harms inflicted during their childhoods. In Ben's case, neither a judge nor a jury ever rushed toward vengeance for anything more than a white collar crime.

Eventually, Ben gathered up his karma and passed on.

• • •

Today finds Duncan happily married with two nearly grown sons. I cherish hopes of great grandchildren growing up in safety.

As for me, I opened Pandora's Box, my father's unintended legacy. I read the letters, I looked at the sepia pictures, remembered stories and recognized the cycles of sexual abuse and began to write the truths I discovered there.

I hope to break the silence and join my tale with all the others so, together, we might discover how best to prevent this legacy of sexual abuse from cycling forth generation after generation.

Every child in my family was molested, terrorized, traumatized and silenced by an adult traumatized and shamed in their own childhood. Not all those whose tales

I've told here, grew up to cycle on and become a Paw-Paw in their own right. Most, even those still struggling to live their own silenced lives, chose to use their adult power, not to take advantage, but to protect. Yet until we speak out, listen to each other with our hearts, how will we know what might make the vital difference in the life of a child as near as tomorrow?

Could simple kindness be the difference? Empathy? What keeps alive the stubborn courage of a Little Green Fairie? Might early intervention, had it been available, have made a difference before the little boy who grew up to be my father died of shame and blame and chose Paw-Paw's path toward manhood?

How will we know, if we cling to shame, blame and silence and discover no new path? How will we ever know if we all agree to not think about it? Or think in old terms? Or imagine the longer and stronger the punishment, the more indelible the label, the safer we'll all be? Time's up to find answers and protect tomorrow's children.

...

As for me? Almost everyone I have loved has gone silent to their grave. I soothe my grief imagining Carrie Marie as that tiny girl running and playing along some sunny seashore, watched over by Mama and my darling Sara. I comfort myself imagining her running and playing with all the rest who tried to believe they would find sunshine somewhere, all those who waited, tried harder, prayed, chose not to think about it, tried to change.

Maybe if I can bear to look squarely at the truth of what was done, and what I failed to do, I'll discover reasons and remedies. Maybe, all our painfully true stories joined together, will stem the tide and gift the next generations with happier lives.

Maybe then my heart can let go of those I loved but lost.

Life steadily escapes me and my brothers, Bayard and Duncan. Life escapes in silence, too soon, too unexamined, too unlived. Soon there will be no one left to attest to Good Spankings or share our struggles once we too scatter like petals on the wind.

And with that, tales of the sex offender's legacy, the long-silenced tales of a son's life, a sex offender's wife, a daughter's death, a mother's voice are come to an end.

But wait, The Little Green Fairy, the Spirit of Courage in Childhood, reappears, and like all children, she begs for "just one more story, please, please, before we go."

"And make this story a happy one," She implores, "Give us reason to hope tomorrow won't just be a repeat of all our yesterdays, not only different-than but far better," she cries.

···

So here goes. The last and perhaps the best tale of all. A true story. Four years ago in a land as near to us as hope for a better tomorrow, a juvenile probation officer who had himself been molested as a child, asked a young boy in trouble for molesting his sister, "Why is it wrong to molest your sister?"

"Because it's illegal," the young boy said.

"Why is it wrong to molest your sister?" the probation officer asked again.

"Because incest causes deformed babies."

"Why is it wrong to molest your sister?"

"Because it gets me in trouble."

The probation officer decided to take another tack.

"Why is it wrong for me to just walk up and punch you in the face?"

"Because it's illegal."

"Why is it wrong for me to walk up and punch you in the face?"

"Because you would lose your job if someone found out."

"Why is it wrong for me to walk up and punch you in the face?"

"Because it would hurt me," the boy finally said.

"Okay," the probation officer said, then asked again, "Why is it wrong to molest your sister?"

A light came on.

"Because it hurts her."

And the boy began to cry.

A few weeks later, the probation officer got a call from the same boy,

"My parents just went away and left me alone with my little sister.

Please come help me."

The End

Some after thoughts on "Please come help me."

No one will reach out to help even a juvenile sex offender if he is indelibly labeled "forever evil" or if revenge, is our goal. But revenge is not justice. The specter of vengeance still shames, blames and silences lives. Old thinking denies help even to youngsters who say, "Please come help me."

As J. Wayne Bowers (Cure-Sort) makes clear:

Poor Advocacy Messaging Limits Progress

Pervert. Child molester. Monster. Sexually Violent Predator. Unredeemable. Sex Offender. These examples of negative terminology aimed at those with sex offenses, produced by law enforcement, legislatures, media and the public, continue to fuel hysteria when sex offense topics are mentioned. If a statement is repeated over and over constantly, there is a strong possibility the theme of that statement becomes believable.

If used constantly to refer to someone in a negative fashion, over and over, before long the impact of that phrase sticks. For the person in question, it gives a hopeless realization of how they are perceived and that can have damaging emotional impact for him/her and for the family. For the public, it has led to an attitude that anyone with a sex offense is forever dangerous and should stay locked up or under severe scrutiny – forever. These beliefs support heavy handed legislation and implementation by strong law and order advocates.

Use of such terms has been a strong strategy for decades by those promoting harsh laws related to persons who have a sex offense. Whether the material being stated is believed or understood by the speaker, the constant usage of wrong facts and incorrect studies has led to numerous lengthy sentences and the constant invention of more and more tracking laws said to "protect the public."

Advocates for those with sex offenses, and their families, have been beaten to the punch and constantly find themselves on the defensive. There has not been a strong narrative telling the extremely positive recidivism figures and confronting the horridly wrong information that has been bantered about since the 1980s, giving all levels of the court system and politics – not to say the media – a strong voice to be as punitive as possible on people they perceive to be unable to ever change their ways.

A case in point is the fact I constantly hear our own advocates saying "sex offender" in their conversation. Those we are now assisting, registrants, are no longer offending. Allowing that term to continue in the conversation just accentuates the harm. Granted, those other groups of people will continue to use the term but we advocates must get more savvy and selective in our communication if we hope to reach out and help. It is a tough topic to take on. Standing up for people who have committed crimes, especially those against children, takes a lot of courage. I rephrase the topic as helping to protect children by assisting those who once offended to have access to programs to help them change their thinking process.

• • •

If you think Silenced Lives, The Sex Offender's Legacy *was worth reading, please go to Amazon (or Kobo) and leave a review. Thank you so much, Janet Mackie*

About the author

Janet Mackie is a retired Child Protective Services Investigator and Supervisor. She spent the last ten years of her 40 year career working with young people at Job Corps. Until she inherited the dusty box of family letters, photos and memories that form the basis of her memoir *Silenced Lives, The Sex Offender's Legacy,* Janet Mackie had written only court reports, training manuals and poetry. Now, hooked on writing, she is working on a spec-script *Stone Killer Trilogy.* Janet Mackie is also busy writing *Tough Trip, How Sex-Curious Kids get Labeled and Locked up for Life.* The first book in this nonfiction series is expected to be out soon.

windharptree.jm@gmail.com

www.windharptree.net

@windharptree

www.facebook.com/windharptree

www.ingramcontent.com/pod-product-compliance
Lightning Source LLC
Chambersburg PA
CBHW031145270326
41931CB00006B/144